*3-1*

# The Black American and Education

**Earle H. West**
Howard University

**Charles E. Merrill Publishing Company**
*A Bell & Howell Company*
Columbus, Ohio

Published by
Charles E. Merrill Publishing Company
*A Bell & Howell Company*
Columbus, Ohio

International Standard Book Number: 0-675-09082-2

Library of Congress Catalog Card Number: 72-76947

1   2   3   4   5   6   7   8   9   10   —   76   75   74   73   72

Printed in the United States

# Preface

This collection of readings related to the history of Negro education
in the United States is designed to suggest the major issues, events,
and conditions from colonial times to the present. The materials
usually available to persons studying the development of education
in the United States make only brief mention, if any, of how that
development was related to the education of black Americans.
However, at this point in history it is clear that the issues involved
in the education of America's largest minority are not simply
expendable details relevant only to the narrow specialist, but that
they involve the fundamental ideals underlying education in a
democratic society. These readings, then, are designed primarily as a
supplementary source of material for thought and discussion by
those seeking an understanding of educational development in the
United States.

The history of black Americans has been variously conceived
as being that which has been done *to* Negroes, or done *for* Negroes,
or done *by* Negroes. While materials reflecting each of these
aspects are included here, there is perhaps a somewhat heavier
emphasis upon the ideas of Negroes themselves. The aim has been
to include materials which would be fairly representative of the
major issues, events, and conditions in the history of black education.
At the same time it is readily acknowledged that different choices
might accomplish the purpose equally well.

The readings have been arranged chronologically into three
chapters arbitrarily set off from each other by the Emancipation and
by World War I. Each chapter is introduced by a brief essay which
traces the main course of Negro education during that period and
indicates how the various readings fit into that history. Further
explanatory notes have been attached to individual documents

where it was felt they were needed. In some instances the document itself is of historical importance. In other instances the document is intended to suggest ideas, issues, or events which are important.

Grateful acknowledgement is made to the administration of Howard University for a grant which provided the time and resources for preparing these materials. Thanks are also due to librarians associated with the Moorland Room at Howard University, the Schomburg Collection of the New York Public Library, and the American Missionary Association Archives in New Orleans. Acknowledgement of publishers who graciously permitted use of their publications has been made in connection with each selection.

Earl H. West

April, 1972

# Contents

# 2    Emancipation to World War I    58

# 3    World War I to 1970    148

# The Black American and Education

# 1

# Before Emancipation

During the two-and-a-half centuries that the black man was in
America before emancipation, there was wide divergence both of
opinion and practice with respect to his education. The trends of the
pre-Civil War period, which would determine the course of Negro
education for another century, were well set. The precedent for
legal segregation had been set. While not unopposed, the idea of a
special kind of education for Negroes had strong support. The
philanthropic motive as the basis for its support was clearly at work.
While these trends could have led in various directions, the future
of Negro education was deeply influenced by the events of the
pre-Civil War period.[1]

    The vast majority of Negroes before 1863 were, of course, in
slavery; at first in both the North and the South; later in the South
alone. Early concern for educating slaves arose mainly from
Christian missionary motives. Godwyn's and Davies' sermons while
illustrating this motive, also exhibit an interesting intermingling of
economic motives which can provide grist for the cynic's mill.
There were, of course, many ministers who preached thus to
slaveowners and often conducted services and sunday school
classes for the slaves.

    By the third decade of the nineteenth century, the changing
nature of slavery, the rise of militant abolitionism, and the fear
of slave revolts brought about a determined repression of
education for slaves, as evidenced by documents sampling the
laws of South Carolina, Georgia, North Carolina, Virginia, and
the Cherokee nation. These laws were unevenly enforced but,

---

[1]The best treatment of Negro education before emancipation is Carter G.
Woodson, *Education of the Negro Prior to 1861* (Washington: Association for the
Study of Negro Life and History, 1919.)

even where rigid enforcement was attempted, slaves could not be entirely shut off from learning. Their own efforts continued in a determined fashion. Whites assisted in a variety of ways which will be illustrated in several of the following selections. Although accounts of many individual slaves attaining some degree of education are available, it must be understood that this entire class was an exception rather than the rule. Some slaves did learn various agricultural, mechanical, household and business skills. However, the dominant southern view, illustrated by an extract from George Fitzhugh, did not contemplate any significant education, in the literary sense, for the Negro.

With the decline of slavery in the North, attention turned to education for the free Negro. There was no question whether or not Negroes would seek education. Blacks embraced the American faith in education. Negro conventions and individual race leaders regularly exhorted parents and youths in their respective duties. Except for the underlying theme of racial struggle and elevation, these expressions by Negroes differed little from those of other Americans.

Blacks benefitted from the philanthropic efforts to provide educational opportunities both before and after the emergence of state school systems. Documents in this chapter will illustrate the philanthropic contributions of individuals like Anthony Benezet, and Thaddeus Kosciuszko. of organized groups such as Benjamin Franklin's proposed society, manumission and abolitionist societies, and the spontaneous efforts of sensitive individuals such as the Lane Seminary students. Self-help is illustrated by a Negro convention proposal, and by the constitution of the Phoenix society. In most northern communities, black children had access either to public schools or to private schools operated under one of the kinds of agencies previously mentioned. Education was much less available to the free Negro in the South. Despite the difficulties, there were well-educated Negroes, some having been sent abroad for their education. Before 1830, black apprentices benefitted from the usual requirement that all apprentices be taught to read and write. Some states, such as Maryland and North Carolina, repealed this provision when it applied to Negroes as tension mounted over slave revolts and abolition agitation. Further restrictive legislation made it impossible for a free black youth to return to his home state if he had been sent from that state to obtain an education. It has been estimated that in 1860, about four thousand Negroes were in school in the slave states and twenty-three thousand in the free states.

As public schools developed in the North, whites vacillated on the inclusion of Negroes. Some documents in this chapter will describe the changing practices in Boston and Worcester, Massachusetts. Probably the single most important legal development of the pre-Civil War period was the 1849 decision of the Massachusetts Supreme Court (*Boston v. Roberts*) which established the precedent for racial segregation in public schools. The decision of the court is presented, and is followed by selections from Charles Sumner, lawyer for the plaintiff, arguing the evils of racially segregated schools. The Roberts case was a part of a long fight by black leaders against segregated education in Boston. Indeed, Negro leaders were generally opposed to segregation as illustrated by the selections from Robert Purvis and Frederick Douglass, although some black families were willing to settle for segregated schools. Despite the relatively more liberal stance of northern opinion, the account of Prudence Crandall illustrates the bitterness and violence that Negro education sometimes encountered in the North.

Elementary education was available to the free Negro in the North, but most colleges practiced racial exclusion. The few exceptions like Oberlin and Antioch could hardly be expected to provide blacks with access to college on a scale even remotely approaching that available to whites. Then, too, there was always the problem of social isolation in those colleges which admitted Negro students. Documents in this section describe the beginning of the first two colleges established primarily for Negroes: Wilberforce in Ohio, and Lincoln in Pennsylvania.

Often overshadowing the issue of segregation was the question of what *kind* of education the black man should receive. This issue usually was argued in terms of racial strategy rather than strictly in terms of education. Long before Washington or DuBois appeared the issue had polarized around classical versus industrial education. The readings which follow in this chapter include statements presenting not only the stereotyped positions on the issue, but also perceptive critiques of education by David Walker and Martin Delany.

Emancipation came without a clear consensus among either Negroes or whites on the major educational issues. Perhaps the single exception lay in the determination of both slaves and free blacks to receive an education at nearly any cost. Whites in the South both proscribed and provided education for slaves and free Negroes. Blacks in the North both fought against and requested segregated schools. Blacks and whites alike advocated both classical and industrial education for Negroes as well as for whites. The war found perhaps ninety percent of all American Negroes illiterate. A handful had finished college, but the psychological effect of these few was significant in demonstrating what blacks could do. Thousands had received varying degrees of elementary and secondary education and as a result were living effective lives both in terms of general personal satisfaction and service on behalf of the race.

## A Plea for the Education of Slaves
*1680*[2]

I do here tender to the Public this Plea both for the Christianizing of our Negro's and other Heathen in those Plantations, and for settling (or rather reviving) of Religion amongst our own People there . . .

[W]hatsoever we enjoy, primarily is from God, our true Father, and Creator . . . . Now this being equally true, both of Slave and Lord; and God Almighty having this original Right and property in every Man . . . the Slaves Obligation and Right . . . to serve God, continues firm and inviolable, and no less unalterable than his Lords.

And questionless from our Negro's being slaves to argue their no Right to Religion, is more Oppressive and Injurious than that Force which first made them so: Because striking at their Souls, and subjecting them to Hell, as much (only for a longer time) as to their Tormenters here on Earth: And to have avoided which, it might have been wished, either that their Creation had failed, or not exceeded this fancied state and degree of Brutes. And this Injustice must upon all respects, be heightened by the consideration of those great Ends unto which all Momentany (sic) advantages ought to give way . . . And as a Crime of this nature marks the Oppressor with the blackest Guilt, so it cannot but render him Obnoxious to the severest Vengeance, that a provoked and just God can inflict upon him, both Body and Soul; and probably, no less in this Life, than certainly in the other.


## Objections to Christianizing Slaves Answered
*1681*[3]

Now for the Planter's late Objections against this Work, as I have heard them represented . . .

1.  They object their Negro's want of English; Whereas 'tis certain that there are some thousands of them, who understand English, no worse than our own People. Let them begin with those.

---

[2]Morgan Godwyn, *The Negro's and Indian's Advocate* (London: F.D., 1680), Preface, pp. 72, 80-81.

[3]Morgan Godwyn, *A Supplement To the Negro's and Indian's Advocate* (London: F.D., 1681). pp. 9, 10.

2.   That it would make them less governable; the contrary to which is experimentally known amongst their Neighbours, both French & Spaniards in those parts. Now 'twould be too great a blemish to the Reformation to suppose that Popery only makes its Converts better, but Protestancy worse; as this Allegation being admitted, it must be granted. And to prevent any fond conceit in them of Libertie, (an especial Branch of the same Article,) if there be any such danger, let two or three of each great Family be first baptised; whereby the rest seeing them continued as they were, that Opinion would soon vanish . . . .

3.   As for their pretended Aversion to Christianity, the contrary thereto is known of most of them. And tho it is to be confessed that some are more careless and indifferent (having been taught by the English to be needless for them) yet for the general they are observed to be rather ambitious of it. Nor, I dare affirm, can any single Instance of such aversion in any one of them, be produced.

4.   As to their, (alike pretended) Stupidity, there is a little truth therein: divers of them being known and confessed by their Owners, to be extraordinary Ingenious, and even to exceed many of the English. And for the rest, they are much the same with other People, destitute of the means of knowledge, and wanting Education.

5.   One thing more there remains to be added, of which, tho they may be most afraid, yet they carefully keep it to themselves, and that is the possibility of their Slaves Expectation, not of Freedom, but of more merciful Usage from them. (which is but reason they should have, whether made Christians or not;) As, That their frequent Emasculatings, Amputations of Leggs, cropping off of Ears (and of Heads too), scant Allowance for Food and Cloaths, and (often) no less working, than starving them to Death, and their unmerciful Correction of them, will not be so commendably practiced upon them, when (nor now by) Christians, as they are thought safe and allowable in their present State of Brutality and Gentilism. And this is the true meaning of their second Objection wherein they pretend it will make them less Governable.

## Condition of Slaves in Colonial Virginia
### *1724*[4]

The Negroes live in small Cottages called Quarters, in about six in a Gang, under the Direction of an Overseer or Bailiff. . . . Their Work

---

[4]Hugh Jones, *The Present State of Virginia* (London: J. Clarke, 1724), pp. 36-94.

is not very laborious; their greatest Hardship consisting in that they and their Posterity are not at their own Liberty or Disposal, but are the Property of their Owners; and when they are Free, they know not how to provide so well for themselves generally; neither did they live so plentifully nor so easily in their own Country, where they are made Slaves to one another, or taken Captive by their Enemies. . . .

Several of them are taught to be Sawyers, Carpenters, Smiths, Coopers, etc., and though for the most Part they be none of the aptest or nicest; yet they are by Nature cut out for hard Labour and Fatigue, and will perform tolerably well. . . .

[Virginians] . . . are not very easily persuaded to the Improvement of useful Inventions neither are they great Encouragers of Manufactures, because of the Trouble and certain Expence in Attempts of this kind, with uncertain Prospect of Gain; whereas by their staple Commodity, Tobacco, they are certain to get a plentiful provision. . . . Upon this account they think it Folly to take off their Hands (or Negroes) and employ their Care and Time about any thing, that may make them lessen their Crop of Tobacco.

As for baptizing Indians and Negroes, several of the People disapprove of it; because they say it often makes them proud, and not so good Servants. But these, and such Objections, are easily refuted, if the Persons be sensible, good, and understand English, and have been taught (or are willing to learn) the Principles of Christianity, and if they be kept to the Observance of it afterwards; for Christianity encourages and orders them to become more humble and better Servants, and not worse, than when they were Heathens.

. . . But as for the Children of Negroes and Indians, that are to live among Christians, undoubtedly they ought all to be baptized; since it is not out of the power of their Masters to take Care that they have a Christian Education, learn their Prayers and Catechism, and go to Church, and not accustom themselves to lie, swear and steal, tho such (as the poorest Sect in England) be not taught to read and write; which as yet has been found to be dangerous upon several political Accounts, especially Self-Preservation.

. . . Thus far as to the Education of the young Men in Virginia, and the Instruction most proper for the Indians; and as for the Negroes, each Owner ought to take Care that the Children born his Property, and all his intelligent adult Negroes be taught their Catechism and some short Prayers, be made to frequent the Church and be baptized, and hindered as much as may be from Swearing, Lying, Intemperance, Prophaneness, and Stealing and Cheating.

## South Carolina Prohibits Teaching Slaves
### 1740[5]

AND WHEREAS the having of Slaves taught to write, or suffering them to be employed in writing, may be attended with great Inconveniences; *be it therefore enacted* by the Authority aforesaid, That all and every Person and Persons whatsoever, who shall hereafter teach, or cause any Slave or Slaves to be taught to write, or shall use or employ any Slave as a Scribe in any Manner of Writing whatsoever, hereafter taught to write; every such Person and Persons shall, for every such Offence, forfeit the sum of *One Hundred Pounds* current Money.

## A Sermon to Masters
### 1757[6]

A creature formed for Immortality, and that must be happy or miserable through an everlasting Duration, is certainly a Being of vast Importance, however mean and insignificant he may be in other Respects. His Immortality gives him a kind of infinite value. Let him be white or black, bond or free, a Native or a Foreigner, it is of no Moment in this View: he is to live forever! to be forever happy, or forever miserable! . . .

In this View, the Crowds of neglected Negroe Slaves among us, have often appeared to me as Creatures of the utmost Importance. The same Immortality is entailed upon them, as upon us. They are Candidates for the same eternal State with us, and bound for the same Heaven or Hell. How awful and important a Trust, then, is the Care of a Soul! The Soul even of a poor Negroe Slave! . . . This solemn and important Trust, I must tell you, Brethren, is committed, not only to Parents, with regard to their Children, those dear other Selves; but to Masters, with regard to their Servants and Slaves, of whatever Country or Colour they are.

---

[5]Laws of South Carolina, 1740–42, page 23. Passed May 10, 1740. This is apparently the earliest law restricting the education of slaves, preceeding the majority of such laws by nearly a century.

[6]Samuel Davies, *The Duty of Christians to Propagate Their Religion Among Heathens* (London: J. Oliver, 1758), pp. 7-44.

. . . You are my Witnesses, that I have looked upon the poor Negroes as a part of my ministerial Charge; and used various Endeavors to bring them to the Faith and Practice of Christianity, not without promising appearances of Success, in sundry Instances. It affords me no small Pleasure to reflect, and I mention it with Gratitude to God and Man, that my Endeavors of this kind have, of late, met with no Opposition from the Masters, of whatever Denomination, in any one Instance that I can recollect. And it affords me a still greater Pleasure to reflect, that sundry of you not only consent that your Negroes should receive Instructions from me, but also zealously concur with me, and make conscience of your own Duty to them in this Respect. But alas! are there not some among you, and are there not Thousands in our Country, who must be conscious of their wilful Negligence? . . . Were your Negroes but so many Brutes, you might treat them as you do your Horses, fodder them, and make them work for you, without once endeavoring to make them Sharers with you in the glorious Privileges of Religion. . . .

. . . The Duty I am urging will appear, if you consider the happy Influence your religious Instructions might have upon your Negroes, even for your own Interest. Your own Interest inclines you to wish, they would become good Servants; faithful, honest, diligent and laborious. Now there is no Expedient in the World, that can so effectually render them such, as to make them real Christians.

. . . Some of you, perhaps, would object, "That your Negroes are such sullen perverse Creatures, or stupid Dunces, that it is impossible to teach them any thing that is good." This is undoubtedly the true Character of some of them, and it must afford a great deal of Grief to such of you, as are really concerned for their everlasting Happiness. . . . But I am apprehensive that objection, in many Cases, is but an idle Pretence. Your Negroes may be ignorant and stupid as to divine things, not for Want of Capacity, but for Want of Instruction; not through their Perverseness, but through your Negligence. From the many Trials I have made, I have Reason to conclude, that making Allowance for their low and barbarous Education, their imperfect Acquaintance with our Language, their having no Opportunity for intellectual Improvement, and the like, they are generally as capable of Instruction, as the White People. . . . But to be short—Be sure you make a Thorough Trial, before you start this Objection. Take all proper Means to teach them, before you conclude they are unteachable.

. . . Will any of you farther object, "That Christianizing the Negroes makes them proud and saucy, and tempts them to imagine themselves upon an Equality with white people?" But is this the native Tendency of real genuine Christianity? Is the true Christian Spirit Haughty and insolent? . . . A Man may be proud of his good Sense, Learning, Estate, or any real or imaginary Excellency. But will you hence infer, that you should Keep yourselves or your Children ignorant, illiterate, poor, and destitute of every good Quality, in order to keep you humble and pliant, and guard against Pride and Insolence?

Encourage your Negroes to learn to read, and give them all the Assistance in your Power. Encourage your Children to teach them: or let one of themselves be taught either at Home, or at School, and let him teach the rest.

## A Teacher Comments on the Ability of Negroes

*1760*[7]

I can with truth and sincerity declare, that I have found amongst the Negroes as great variety of talents, as among a like number of whites, and I am bold to assert, that the notion entertained by some, that the blacks are inferior in their capacities, is a vulgar prejudice, founded on the pride or ignorance of their lordly masters, who have kept their slaves at such a distance as to be unable to form a right judgment of them.

## Friend Anthony Benezet Provides for a School

*1784*[8]

Be it remembered That I, Anthony Benezet, a teacher of the Free School for the Black People in Philadelphia, being of a Sound and well disposed Mind and memory, do make this my last Will and Testament.

---

[7] Anthony Benezet as quoted in Roberts Vaux, *Memoirs of the Life of Anthony Benezet* (Philadelphia: James P. Parke, 1817), p. 22. In the absence of other ways to measure ability or achievement, there was much speculation as to the educability of the Negro. The only basis for reaching any conclusion before the rise of scientific measurement was provided by the subjective experiences of teachers such as Benezet.

[8] "The Will of Anthony Benezet," as quoted in George S. Brookes, *Friend Anthony Benezet* (Philadelphia: University of Pennsylvania Press, 1937), pp. 165, 166. This was a common form for educational philanthropy to take prior to the rise of great fortunes and the establishment of educational foundations nearly a century later.

First I nominate and appoint my dear Wife Joice and my Friends James Pemberton, John Field, Samuel Pleasants, Richard Wells, Henry Drinker, David Evans & James Cresson, Executors of this my last will, revoking all former Wills by me made. . . . And after the death of my Wife I give my above said House & Lot or Ground Rent proceeding from it and the rent and residue of My Estate which shall remain undisposed of after my Wife's decease, both real and personal to the overseers of the Public School of Philadelphia, founded by Charter, and to their successors forever in trust that they shall sell my House and Lot on perpetual ground Rent forever if the same be not already sold by my Executors as before mentioned. And that as speedily as may be they receive and take so much of my personal Estate as may be remaining and herewith purchase a yearly Ground Rent or Ground Rents, and with the income of such Ground Rent proceeding from the sale of my real Estate, hire and employ a religious minded person or persons to teach a number of Negroe, Mulatto, or Indian Children to read and write, Arithmetic, plain Accounts, Needlework &c. And it is my particular desire founded on the experience I have had in that service that in the choice of such a tutor special care may be had to prefer an industrious careful person of true piety, who may be or become suitably qualified, who would undertake the service from a principal of Charity to one more highly learned not equally so disposed. This I desire may be carefully attended to, sensible that from the number of pupils of all ages the irregularity of attendance their situation subject them to &c, will not admit of that particular inspection in their improvement usual in other schools but that the real well doing of the Scholars will very much depend upon the master making a special conscience of doing his duty; and shall likewise defray such other necessary expense as may occur in that service. And as the said remaining income of my Estate after my Wife's decease will not be sufficient to defray the whole expense necessary for the support of such a School, it is my request that the overseers of the said Public School shall join in the care and expense of such a School or Schools for the educating of Negroes, Mulattos & Indian Children with any Committee which may be appointed by the Monthly Meeting of Friends of Philadelphia or with any other body of benevolent persons who may join in raising Money and employing it for the education of such Children, my desire that as such a school is now set up it may be forever maintained in this City and I give to my kinsman, Joseph Marriott, School master in Burlington County, the sum of ten Pounds and I give unto my two Nieces Mary & Charity Pyrleus of Bethlehem to each of them the sum of ten Pounds. Dated in Philadelphia the third day of the fifth Month called May in the year one thousand seven hundred and eighty-four.

## Slave Urges Education
### 1787[9]

Those of you who can read, I must beg you to read the Bible, and whenever you can get time, study the Bible, and if you can get no other time, spare some of your time from sleep, and learn what the mind and will of God is. But what shall I say to them who cannot read? This lay with great weight on my mind, when I thought of writing to my poor brethren, but I hope that those who can read, will take pity on them and read what I have to say to them. In hopes of this, I beg of you to spare no pains in trying to learn to read. If you are once engaged, you may learn. Let all the time you can get be spent in trying to learn to read. Get those who can read, to learn you, but remember what you learn for, is to read the bible. It tells you what you must do to please God; it tells you how you may escape misery, and be happy forever. . . . Now, my dear friends, seeing the Bible is the word of God, and everything in it is true, and it reveals such awful and glorious things, what can be more important than that you should learn to read it; and when you have learned to read, that you should study it day and night. There are some things very encouraging in God's word, for such ignorant creatures as we are; for God hath not chosen the rich of this world.

## Benjamin Franklin's Proposal
## for Educating Negroes
### 1789[10]

The business relative to free blacks shall be transacted by a committee of twenty-four persons, annually elected by ballot, at the meeting of this Society, (The Society for promoting the Abolition of Slavery and the Relief of Free Blacks) in the month called April; and, in order to perform the different services with expedition, regularity, and energy, this

---

[9]Jupiter Hammon, *An Address to the Negroes of the State of New-York* (New York: Carrol and Patterson, 1787). Hammon, a slave of Joseph Lloyd, Long Island, New York, was a Baptist preacher and a poet. He was the first Negro to write and publish poetry in the United States. His appeal to fellow slaves illustrates again the dominant religious motive. Hammon, like Godwyn and Davies, appealed to self-interest beyond the purely religious motives. None of these men made such appeals cynically; rather they did so from the conviction that Christianity was true and would therefore be useful in the life of the believer.

[10]Jared Sparks, *Works of Benjamin Franklin,* Vol. II (Boston: Tappan and Whittemore, 1836), pp. 513, 514.

committee shall resolve itself into the following sub-committees, viz.

I.   A Committee of Inspection, who shall superintend the morals, general conduct, and ordinary situation of the free Negroes, and afford them advice and instruction, protection from wrongs, and other friendly offices.

II.   A Committee of Guardians, who shall place out children and young people with suitable persons, that they may (during a moderate time of apprenticeship or servitude) learn some trade or other business of subsistence. The committee may effect this partly by a persuasive influence on parents and the persons concerned, and partly by cooperating with the laws, which are, or may be, enacted for this and similar purposes. In forming contracts on these occasions, the committee shall secure to the Society, as far as may be practicable, the right of guardianship over the persons so bound.

III.   A Committee of Education, who shall superintend the school instruction of the children and youth of the free blacks. They may either influence them to attend regularly the schools already established in this city, or form others with this view; they shall, in either case, provide, that the pupils may receive such learning as is necessary for their future situation in life, and especially a deep impression of the most important and generally acknowledged moral and religious principles. They shall also procure and preserve a regular record of the marriages, births, and manumissions of all free blacks.

IV.   A Committee of Employ, who shall endeavour to procure constant employment for those free Negroes who are able to work; as the want of this would occasion poverty, idleness, and many vicious habits. This committee will, by sedulous inquiry, be enabled to find common labor for a great number; they will also provide, that such as indicate proper talents may learn various trades, which may be done by prevailing upon them to bind themselves for such a term of years as shall compensate their masters for the expense and trouble of instruction and maintenance. The committee may attempt the institution of some useful and simple manufactures, which require but little skill, and also may assist, in commencing business, such as appear to be qualified for it.

Whenever the committee of inspection shall find persons of any particular description requiring attention, they shall immediately direct them to the committee of whose care they are the proper objects.

In matters of a mixed nature, the committees shall confer, and, if necessary, act in concert. Affairs of great importance shall be referred to the whole committee.

The expense, incurred by the prosecution of this plan, shall be defrayed by a fund, to be formed by donations or subscriptions for these particular purposes, and to be kept separate from the other funds of this Society.

The committee shall make a report of their proceedings, and of the state of their stock, to the Society, at their quarterly meetings, in the months called April and October.

## Will of Thaddeus Kosciuszko
*1798*[11]

I, Thaddeus Kosciuszko, being just on my departure from America do hereby declare and direct that, should I make no other testamentary disposition of my property in the United States, I hereby authorize my friend, Thomas Jefferson, to employ the whole thereof in purchasing Negroes from among his own or any others, and giving them an education, in trades or otherwise, and in having them instructed, for their new condition, in the duties of morality which may make them good neighbors, good fathers or mothers, husbands or wives, and in their duties as citizens, teaching them to be defenders of their liberty and country, and of the good order of society, and in whatever may make them happy and useful, and I make the said Thomas Jefferson my executor of this. T. Kosciuszko. Fifth day of May, 1798.

## Education of a Slave
*1820*[12]

*An Act To Emancipate William, A Person of Color.*
  Sec. 1. *Be it enacted* by the Senate and House of Representatives

[11]The Will of Thaddeus Kosciuszko, Schomburg Collection, Harlem Branch of New York Public Library, New York. Kosciuszko was a Polish general and Revolutionary War hero. His own spelling of his name differs from the Americanized version. Although he emphasizes industrial education, yet there is nothing "special" for the Negro suggested here.

[12]Laws of Mississippi, 1820, Chapter XXV, Sec. 1 and 2, p. 38. William Johnson, the emancipated slave (and son of his owner), became a barber and real estate dealer in Natchez. His diary describes his efforts to teach his own children and one of his slaves. See William R. Hogan and Edwin A. Davis (eds.), *William Johnson's Natchez* (Baton Rouge: Louisiana State University Press, 1951), pp. 350, 369, 497, 700. This private enactment did not stand alone. The next act passed by the legislature provided for the "mulatto child" Eleanor, slave of Wilson B. Harper, in almost identical language.

of the state of Mississippi, in general assembly convened, that the mulatto boy named William, son of Amy, a free woman of color, and the slave of William Johnson of Adams County, be, and is hereby emancipated and set free from slavery . . . conditioned that the said boy William, shall never become a public charge, and that the said William Johnson shall educate and maintain said child, according to the provisions of the second section of this act.

*Sec. 2. And be it further enacted,* That the said William Johnson shall educate, or cause to be educated, and maintain or caused [sic] to be maintained, said child until he arrive at the age of twenty-one years.

## Boston Opens African Primary Schools
### *1822*[13]

In June, the people of color at the northerly part of the city presented a petition to the Board for a Primary School in that section, which the Standing Committee deemed it expedient to refer to the Grammar School Committee; "and the Secretary was directed to signify the willingness of the Primary Board to undertake the control of such African Primary Schools as the General School Committee may give them authority to institute in this City, with such expansion of powers as may thereby be deemed necessary. And they recommend a School in the North Section, and another in the West part of the City, to embrace the young Africans from four to seven years, and beyond that, if necessary, to qualify them to enter the regular African School in that quarter."

Upon the reception of this petition and recommendation, the Grammar Board appointed a sub-committee of their body, through whom a school was established for colored children at the North end. They also communicated a request and authority to the Standing Committee of the Primary Board to establish a Primary School for these children at the west part of the city. A sub-committee (Messrs. Benj. Guild and Moses Grant) was thereupon appointed to attend to the duty; and on the 7th of August, 1822, the first Primary School for colored children was opened in Belknap Street, in a room in the Rev. Mr. Paul's Church, at an annual rent of $72. At the commencement of this school, the number of scholars was 47 (19 girls and 28 boys), and it was placed under the charge of Miss Charlotte Foster (a young woman of color), whose

---

[13]Joseph M. Wightman (compiler), *Annals of The Boston Primary School Committee* (Boston: George C. Rand and Avery, 1860), pp. 68-70.

success was satisfactory to the Committee, and the school soon became a useful auxiliary to the Grammar School. The increase of pupils rendered a second school necessary, and it was established in December, 1822, in Southac Street, with only 6 pupils, which number, however, in a few weeks was increased to 33. Two Silver Medals were purchased, with the inscription "Reward of Merit" on one side, and "African Primary School, 1822," on the other. The Committee visited these schools weekly for some time after their establishment, and much credit is due to them for their faithful services, for the children were, generally, very poor and ignorant, many of them ten and twelve years old, without knowing a letter of the alphabet. In a school of 50 pupils, 42 were in the Alphabet class.

The City allowed $240 to each school, which included the salary of the teacher, rent of room, furniture, and fuel; but the condition of the children was such as to require charitable relief; and clothing, shoes and books were furnished by the liberality of the members of the Standing Committee, and particularly by the generous donation of $10 each quarter from the President of the Board (Hon. Thomas L. Winthrop), which continued until his resignation of the office.

## African Schools in Worcester, Massachusetts
### *1828*[14]

In 1828, in the hope of giving to colored children more successful instruction than they received, while attending with white children, and to promote their attendance at school, which it had been impossible to obtain, The African school was established for colored children exclusively. This was taught by some of the more competent and faithful female teachers, one of whom after long service here, was appointed teacher of the Female High School. It was legally and justly determined that these colored children had the right to be promoted to the Town Latin Grammar School and two or three on examination were found qualified and were promoted. In the Town school they were subjected to no intended humiliation, but they soon fell behind in scholarship and withdrew from school. . . .

---

[14]Stephen Salisbury to Henry Barnard, November 7, 1855. In the Henry Barnard Manuscripts, New York University.

. . . In the hope of improvement — which is much to be desired, the city school committee a year ago discontinued the African School with the intention of distributing the children according to locality. . . . I am also informed that the scattering of the colored children thru the schools is thought to have had a good effect on their attendance in the first year of the experiment. I enquired separately of the members of the board and cannot ascertain whether it is thought that these children learn as well or better than before. When the African school was discontinued, the number of scholars was very small.

In the present arrangement of the school, the youngest are called Primary, the next in advance Secondary; the next is the Grammar School, and the highest in rank is the Classical and English High School.

## School Advertisement
### 1829[15]

*African Free School.* Notice — Parents and Guardians of Coloured Children, are hereby informed, that a Male and Female School has long been established for coloured children, by the Manumission Society of this city — where the pupils receive such an education as is calculated to fit them for usefulness and respectability. The male school is situated in mulberry street, to which is attached a female school, and another female school in William street, near Duane-street; all under the management of experienced teachers. The boys are taught Reading, Writing, Arithmetic, Geography, and English Grammar — and the Girls, in addition to those branches, are taught Sewing, Marking, and Knitting, etc. . . . Pupils of 5 to fifteen years of age are admitten (sic) by the Teachers of the School, at the rate of twenty-five cents to one dollar per quarter according to the circumstances of the parents; and the children of such as cannot afford to pay anything are admitted free of expense, and enjoy the same advantages as those who pay.

Each School is visited weekly by a committee of the trustees, in addition to which a committee of Ladies pay regular visits to the Female schools, Care is taken to impart moral instruction, and such have been

---

[15]Advertisement in *The Rights of All*, Volume 1, No. 1 (May 29, 1829), p. 8. Aside from the racial designation, this New York school does not appear to have been different in curriculum and other arrangements from other schools of the time.

the happy effecti (sic) of the system pursued in these schools, that although several thousand have been taught in them since their establishment (now more than thirty years) there has never been an instance known to the trustees where a pupil having received a regular education has been convicted of any crime in our Courts of Justice.

## Editor Urges Education
### *1829*[16]

I ask why have we not a system of education established among us, connecting by one strong chain the common, the grammar, the collegiate and the professional school, where everything relating to a polished and useful education may be taught? . . . Why have we not mechanical institutions, where our children may obtain a thorough knowledge of all the useful arts — is it because we have not the means — NO — it is because we grasp after flowers and neglect solid and wholesome fruits!!! . . . Let our coloured population once become as learned, as refined, and as wealthy as other classes of community, and prejudice will hide her face.

## Georgia Prohibits Teaching Slaves
### *1829*[17]

*Sec. 10. And be it further enacted,* That if any slave, Negro, mustizzo, or free person of colour, or any other person, shall circulate, bring or cause to be circulated or brought into this state or aid or assist in any manner, or be instrumental in aiding or assisting in the circulation or

---

[16]*The Rights of All,* September 18, 1829. Editor Samuel Cornish was a black abolitionist. He established *Freedom's Journal* in 1827, the first Negro newspaper in the United States. In the quotation above, Cornish fully adopts the American faith in education and sees it as the solution to the Negro's problem. The assumption was that education would ameliorate those defects which cause prejudice. This has apparently been a major theme in Negro educational thought up to the mid-twentieth century.

[17]Georgia Laws, 1829, pp. 170, 171.

bringing into this state, or in any manner concerned in any printed or written pamphlet, paper or circular, for the purposes of exciting to insurrection, conspiracy or resistance among the slaves, Negroes, or free persons of colour, of this state, against their owners or the citizens of this state, the said person or persons offending against this section of this act, shall be punished with death.

*Sec. 11. And be it further enacted,* That if any slave, negro, or free person of colour or any white person shall teach any other slave, Negro or free person of colour, to read or write either written or printed characters, the said free person of colour, or slave, shall be punished by fine and whipping, or fine or whipping at the discretion of the court; and if a white person so offending, he, she or they shall be punished with fine, not exceeding five hundred dollars, and imprisonment, in the common jail at the discretion of the court before whom said offender is tried.

## North Carolina Forbids Teaching Slaves
*1830*[18]

Whereas the teaching of slaves to read and write has a tendency to excite dissatisfaction in their minds, and to produce insurrection and rebellion, to the manifest injury of the citizens of this State: Therefore,

*Be it enacted by the General Assembly of the State of North Carolina, and it is hereby enacted by the authority of the same,* That any free person, who shall hereafter teach or attempt to teach, any slave within this State to read or write, the use of figures, excepted, or shall give or sell to such slave or slaves any books or pamphlets, shall be liable to indictment in any court of record in this State having jurisdiction thereof; and upon conviction, shall, at the discretion of the court, if a white man or woman, be fined not less than one hundred dollars, nor more than two hundred dollars, or imprisoned; and if a free person of color, shall be fined, imprisoned, or whipped, at the discretion of the court, not exceeding thirtynine lashes, nor less than twenty lashes.

II. *Be it further enacted,* That the judges of the Superior Courts and the justices of the County Courts shall give this act in charge to the grand jurors of their respective counties.

---

[18]Laws of North Carolina, 1830–31, Chapter VI, p. 11.

## David Walker Appeals for Real Education
### *1830*[19]

An ignorant father, who knows no more than what nature has taught him, together with what little he acquires by the senses of hearing and seeing, finding his son able to write a neat hand, sets it down for granted that he has as good learning as any body; the young, ignorant gump, hearing his father or mother, who perhaps may be ten times more ignorant, in point of literature, than himself, extolling his learning, struts about, in the full assurance, that his attainments in literature are sufficient to take him through the world, when, in fact, he has scarcely any learning at all!!!!

I promiscuously fell in conversation once, with an elderly coloured man on the topics of education, and of the great prevalency of ignorance among us: Said he, "I know that our people are very ignorant, but my son has a good education: I spent a great deal of money on his education: he can write as well as any white man, and I assure you that no one can fool him," &c. Said I, what else can your son do, besides writing a good hand? Can he post a set of books in a mercantile manner? Can he write a neat piece of composition in prose or in verse? To these interogations he answered in the negative. Said I, did your son learn, while he was at school, the width and depth of English Grammar? To which he also replied in the negative, telling me his son did not learn those things. Your son, said I, then, has hardly any learning at all — he is almost as ignorant, and more so, than many of those who never went to school one day in all their lives. My friend got a little put out, and so walking off, said that his son could write as well as any white man. Most of the coloured people, when they speak of the education of one among us who can write a neat hand, and who perhaps knows nothing but to scribble and puff pretty fair on a small scrap of paper, immaterial whether his words are grammatical or spelt correctly, or not; if it only looks beautiful, they say he has as good an education as any white man — he can write as well as any white man, &c. The poor, ignorant creature, hearing this, he is ashamed, forever after, to let any person see him humbling himself to another for knowledge but going about trying to deceive those who are more ignorant than himself, he at last falls an ignorant victim to death in wretchedness. I pray that the Lord may undeceive my ignorant brethren, and permit them to throw away

---

[19]David Walker, *Walker's Appeal,* 3rd edition (Boston: David Walker, 1830), pp. 36-39. Walker, born a free Negro in North Carolina, moved to Boston where he supported himself by selling second-hand clothes. In 1829 he issued his first *Appeal* calling for Negroes to rise up and throw off slavery.

pretensions, and seek after the substance of learning. I would crawl on my hands and knees through mud and mire, to the feet of a learned man, where I would sit and humbly supplicate him to instill into me, that which neither devils nor tyrants could remove, only with my life—for colored people to acquire learning in this country, makes tyrants quake and tremble on their sandy foundation. Why, what is the matter? Why, they know that their infernal deeds of cruelty will be made known to the world. Do you suppose one man of good sense and learning would submit himself, his father, mother, wife and children, to be slaves to a wretched man like himself, who, instead of compensating him for his labours, chains, handcuffs and beats him and family almost to death, leaving life enough in them, however, to work for, and call him master? No! No! he would cut his devilish throat from ear to ear, and well do slave-holders know it. The bare name of educating the coloured people, scares our cruel oppressors almost to death. But if they do not have enough to be frightened for yet, it will be, because they can always keep us ignorant, and because God appreciates their cruelties, with which they have been for centuries murdering us. The whites shall have enough of the blacks, yet, as true as God sits on his throne in Heaven.

Some of our brethren are so very full of learning, that you cannot mention any thing to them which they do not know better than yourself!! — nothing is strange to them!! — they knew every thing years ago! — if any thing should be mentioned in company where they are, immaterial how important it is respecting us or the world, if they had not divulged it; they make light of it, and affect to have known it long before it was mentioned and try to make all in the room, or wherever you may be, believe that your conversation is nothing!! — not worth hearing! All this is the result of ignorance and ill-breeding; for a man of good-breeding, sense and penetration, if he had heard a subject told twenty times over, and should happen to be in company where one should commence telling it again, he would wait with patience on its narrator, and see if he would tell it as it was told in his presence before — paying the most strict attention to what is said, to see if any more light will be thrown on the subject: for all men are not gifted alike in telling, or even hearing the most simple narration. These ignorant, vicious, and wretched men, contribute almost as much injury to our body as tyrants themselves, by doing so much for the promotion of ignorance amongst us; for they making such pretensions to knowledge, such of our youth as are seeking after knowledge, and can get access to them, take them as criterions to go by, who will lead them into a channel, where, unless the Lord blesses them with the privilege of seeing their folly, they will be irretrievably lost forever, while in time!!!

I must close this article by relating the very heartrending fact, that I have examined school-boys and young men of colour in different parts of the country, in the most simple parts of Murray's English Grammar, and not more than one in thirty was able to give a correct answer to my interrogations. If any one contradicts me, let him step out of his door into the streets of Boston, New York, Philadelphia, or Baltimore, (no use to mention any other, for the Christians are too charitable further south or west!) — I say, let him who disputes me, step out of his door into the streets of either of those four cities, and promiscuously collect one hundred school-boys, or young men of colour, *who have been to school*, and who are considered by the coloured people to have received an excellent education, because perhaps, some of them can write a good hand, but who, notwithstanding their neat writing, may be almost as ignorant, in comparison, as a horse. — And, I say it, he will hardly find (in this enlightened day, and in the midst of this *charitable* people) five in one hundred, who, are able to correct the false grammar of their language. — The cause of this almost universal ignorance among us, I appeal to our schoolmasters to declare. Here is a fact, which I this very minute take from the mouth of a young coloured man, who has been to school in this state (Massachusetts) nearly nine years, and who knows grammar in this day, *nearly* as well as he did the day he first entered the school-house, under a white master. This young man says: "My master would never allow me to study grammar." I asked him, why? "The school committee," said he "forbid the coloured children learning grammar — they would not allow any but the white children to study grammar." It is a notorious fact, that the major part of the white Americans, have, ever since we have been among them, tried to keep us ignorant, and make us believe that God made us and our children to be slaves to them and theirs. *Oh! my God, have mercy on Christian Americans!!!*

## Education of a Slave

*1857*[20]

My mother, Keziah the cook, commonly called Aunt Kaisy, was possessed of an indomitable ambition, and had, by the hardest means, endeavored

---

[20]*Autobiography of a Female Slave*, (New York: Redfield, 1857), pp. 10, 11. Many of the published slave narratives include more or less brief passages describing educational efforts. It must be remembered that such was not the typical slave experience, and most slaves were illiterate.

to acquire the rudiments of an education; but all that she had succeeded in obtaining was a knowledge of the alphabet, and orthography in two syllables. Being very imitative, she eschewed the ordinary Negroes' pronunciation, and adopted the mode of speech used by the higher class of whites. She was very much delighted when Mrs. Woodbridge or Miss Betsy (as we called her) began to instruct me in the elements of the English language. I inherited my mother's thirst for knowledge; and by intense study, did all I could to spare Miss Betsy the usual drudgery of a teacher. The aptitude that I displayed, may be inferred from the fact that, in three months from the day she began teaching me the alphabet, I was reading, with some degree of fluency, in the "First Reader." I have often heard her relate this as quite a literary and educational marvel.

There were so many slaves upon the farm, particularly young ones, that I was regarded as a supernumerary; consequently, spared from nearly all the work. I sat in Miss Betsy's room, with book in hand, little heeding anything else; and, if ever I manifested the least indolence, my mother, with her mild ambition, was sure to rally me and even offer the tempting bribe of cakes and apples.

## Negroes Forbidden to Preach in North Carolina
### *1831*[21]

*Be it enacted by the General Assembly of the State of North Carolina, and it is hereby enacted by the authority of the same,* That it shall not be lawful under any pretence for any free Negro, slave, or free person of color to preach or exhort in public, or in any manner to officiate as a preacher or teacher in any prayer meeting or other association for worship where slaves of different families are collected together; and if any free Negro or free person of color shall be thereof duly convicted on indictment before any court having jurisdiction thereof, he shall for each offence receive not exceeding thirty-nine lashes on his bare back; and

---

[21]Laws of North Carolina, 1831-32, Chapter IV, p. 7. This law, incidentally, hindered the work of John Chavis, an outstanding Negro teacher and preacher. Chavis had been sent to Princeton by some white planters apparently to settle a dispute about the ability of Negroes to take a college education. He subsequently taught both white and Negro children in North Carolina from 1808 until restrictive legislation brought his work to a close. The best account of Chavis is in Edgar W. Knight, "Notes on John Chavis," *North Carolina Historical Review,* 7 (1930), pp. 326-45.

where any slave shall be guilty of a violation of this act, he shall on conviction before a single magistrate receive not exceeding thirty-nine lashes on his bare back.

# Prudence Crandall Jailed for Teaching Negroes
### *1833*[22]

Undismayed by the opposition of her neighbors and the violence of their threats, Miss Crandall received early in April fifteen or twenty colored young ladies and misses from Philadelphia, New York, Providence, and Boston. At once her persecutors commenced operations. All accommodations at the stores in Canterbury were denied her; so that she was obliged to send to neighboring villages for her needful supplies. She and her pupils were insulted whenever they appeared in the streets. The doors and door-steps of her house were besmeared, and her well was filled with filth. Had it not been for the assistance of her father and another Quaker friend who lived in the town, she might have been compelled to abandon "her castle" for the want of water and food. . . .

Foiled in their attempts to frighten away Miss Crandall's pupils by their proceedings under the provisions of the obsolete "Pauper and Vagrant Law," Mr. Judson and his fellow-persecutors urgently pressed upon the Legislature of Connecticut, then in session, a demand for the enactment of a law, by which they should be enabled to effect their purpose. To the lasting shame of the State, be it said, they succeeded. . . .

On the receipt of the tidings that the Legislature had passed the law, joy and exultation ran wild in Canterbury. The bells were rung and a cannon fired, until all the inhabitants for miles around were informed of the triumph. So soon as was practicable, on the 27th of June, Miss Candall was arrested by the sheriff of the county, or the constable of the town, and arraigned before Justices Adams and Bacon, two of the leaders of the conspiracy against her and her humane enterprise. . . .

The sun had descended nearly to the horizon; the shadows of night were beginning to fall around us. The sheriff could defer the dark deed no longer. With no little emotion, and with words of earnest deprecation,

---

[22]Samuel J. May, *Some Recollections Of Our Antislavery Conflict* (Boston: Fields, Osgood and Company, 1869), pp. 50-53, 56, 70, 71. Miss Crandall, a Quaker, lived in Canterbury, Connecticut, at the time of the events related by May. Upon admission of a Negro student to her girls' school, the white pupils withdrew. She then opened a school for Negro students with the results described here.

he gave that excellent, heroic, Christian young lady into the hands of the jailer, and she was led into the cell of Watkins. So soon as I had heard the bolts of her prison-door turned in the lock, and saw the key taken out, I bowed and said, "The deed is done, completely done. It cannot be recalled. It has passed into the history of our nation and our age." I went away with my steadfast friend, George W. Benson, assured that the legislators of the State had been guilty of a most unrighteous act; and that Miss Crandall's persecutors had also committed a great blunder; that they all would have much more a reason to be ashamed of her imprisonment than she or her friends could ever have.

Soon after their failure to get a decision from the Court of Errors, an attempt was made to set her house on fire. Fortunately the match was applied to combustibles tucked under a corner where the sills were somewhat decayed. They burnt like a slow match. Some time before daylight the inmates perceived the smell of fire, but not until nearly nine o'clock did any blaze appear. It was quickly quenched; and I was sent for to advise whether, if her enemies were so malignant as this attempt showed them to be, it was safe and right for her to expose her pupils' and her own life any longer to their wicked devices. It was concluded that she should hold on and bear yet a little longer. . . .

But a few nights afterwards it was made only too plain that the enemies of the school were bent upon its destruction. About twelve o'clock, on the night of the 9th of September, Miss Crandall's house was assulted by a number of persons with heavy clubs and iron bars; five window-sashes were demolished and ninety panes of glass dashed to pieces.

## Abolitionists Propose a Manual Labor School
### 1833[23]

To promote the virtuous and guarded education of the free Colored Youth in the United States; to form in them habits of industry, economy, and morality, as well as to extend to them the benefits of literature and science: — we, the subscribers, agree to pay to the Trustees, to be chosen

[23]Massachusetts Anti-Slavery Society, *First Annual Report of the Board of Managers* (Boston: Garrison and Knapp, 1833), back cover. Terms such as manual labor and industrial education were used without a clear delineation of meanings. Industrial education usually meant training in one or more trades. Manual labor referred to a combined work and study program designed primarily to reduce the cost of education and secondarily to provide a regime of physical experiences to offset the artificiality of wholly "book learning."

as hereinafter expressed, the sums affixed to our respective names, for the purpose of establishing a School in some part of New England, for the education of colored youth on the Manual Labor System, on the following terms:

ARTICLE I. Such part of the sums subscribed, as may be necessary, shall be invested in lands, buildings, and farming and mechanical stock and apparatus, and other things requisite for the establishment and support of the proposed institution, and shall remain forever a fund for the support of an institution for promoting an economical and judicious system of education for young persons of African descent, having especial reference to their qualifications to become extensively useful as teachers and examples and benefactors to their brethren.

ARTICLE II. The Trustees may invest such part of the funds as to them shall seem advisable in permanent stocks, the income to be appropriated to defray the expense of educating such pupils as may be otherwise unable to enjoy the benefits of the institution.

ARTICLE III. While virtue and piety are to be regarded as essential parts of the education to be given in the proposed institution, and while Christianity will form the basis of the system, young persons of all sects and denominations shall be equally admitted to the school, and shall enjoy equal rights and privileges therein; there shall be no infringement of the liberty of conscience in any manner whatever; and no measures shall ever be adopted tending to give any denomination the ascendancy in the government of the proposed seminary. In order to preserve these fundamental principles from violation, a majority of the Trustees shall never consist of persons of the same denomination of Christians. This article is to be unalterable.

ARTICLE IV. As soon as it shall be ascertained that ten thousand dollars or upwards have been subscribed, the President of the New-England Anti-Slavery Society shall call a meeting of the contributors, by giving notice in at least three newspapers published in Boston, and one or more in Providence, New-Haven, New-York, Philadelphia, and Washington, and by giving notice by mail to every person who may have subscribed to the amount of one hundred dollars or upwards to assemble in Boston at such time and place as he may designate, then and there, in conjunction with the Board of Managers of the New-England Anti-Slavery Society, to elect twenty Trustees, who, with their successors, shall have the perpetual government of the institution and management of its funds. If practicable, the Trustees thus chosen shall obtain an act of incorporation from the Legislature of the State in which the seminary may be situated, for the better security of the funds and interests of the institution and embracing the principles of these articles as far as possible. . . .

Boston, January 28, 1833.

## Education of a Male Slave
*1857*[24]

Col. Pocomoke was a Maryland gentleman of the old school; proud and haughty to his inferiors; bland and courteous to his equals. He was a large slaveholder, and owned several farms near "The Home Mansion." . . . The Colonel had a slave-boy of fine mind, for whom he conceived a great fancy. He sent him to the same school which I attended. The teacher, knowing the master's influence, and dreading his indignation, treated him kindly, and made no difference between him and the white boys. When the Colonel died, he willed him free, and to be sent to Pennsylvania. If a poor white man had sent the boy to school, he would have been driven home the first day he entered it by teacher and boys. The lesson we learn from this sketch is simply this, that the wealthy and influential men of the South can alter, abridge, or change any custom or prejudice at their pleasure.

## Constitution of the Phoenix Society
*1833*[25]

This Society shall be known by the name of the "Phoenix Society" of the City of New York, the object of which shall be to promote the improvement of the coloured people in Morals, Literature, and the Mechanic Arts. . . .

ARTICLE VIII. The funds raised after the necessary expenses of the Society are paid, shall be applied to the establishment and sustaining of a Manual Labour School, and for this object an effort shall be immediately made to raise at least Ten Thousand Dollars. . . .

---

[24]John Dixon Long, *Pictures of Slavery in Church and State* (Philadelphia: Published by the Author, 1857), pp. 177, 178. Long was born in New Town, Maryland, in 1817. His father was a slave holder and sea captain. Long became a minister, labored for a time in Maryland, then moved to Philadelphia where he became active in antislavery work.

[25]*Minutes and Proceedings of the Third Annual Convention for the Improvement of the Free People of Colour in These United States, held in Philadelphia, June 3-13, 1833* (New York: Published by order of the Convention, 1833), pp. 38-40. The Phoenix Society was one of the more influential of the many literary and educational societies organized by Negroes which paralleled the white lyceum organizations from which Negroes were excluded. Their promotional work in behalf of education was significant as well as their efforts in adult education.

This Society will aim to accomplish the following objects. To visit every family in the Ward, and make a register of every coloured person in it — Their name, sex, age, occupation, if they read, write, and cipher — to induce them, old and young, and of both sexes, to become members of this Society, and make quarterly payments according to their ability; — to get the children out to infant, Sabbath and week schools, and induce the adults also to attend school and church on the Sabbath, — to encourage the Females to form Dorcas Societies to help clothe the poor children of colour if they will attend school, the clothes to be loaned, and to be taken away from them if they neglect their schools; and to impress on their parents the importance of having the children punctual and regular in their attendance at school, — to establish circulating libraries formed in each ward for the use of people of colour on very moderate pay, — to establish mental feasts, and also lyceums for speaking and for lectures on the sciences, and to form moral societies, — to seek out young men of talents, and good moral character, that they may be assisted to obtain a liberal education, — to report to the Board all mechanics who are skilful and capable of conducting their trades, — to procure places at trades and with respectable farmers for lads of good moral character — giving a preference to those who have learned to read, write, and cipher, — and in every other way to endeavor to promote the happiness of the people of colour, by encouraging them to improve their minds, and to abstain from every vicious and demoralizing practice.

## African Free School, New York
### *1834*[26]

The next day Dr. Hosack — so well known to English travellers for his hospitality — took me with him in his carriage to the House of Refuge — an institution for the reception of juvenile offenders. Here we met Governor Marcy, who had come with a committee on an official visit to the establishment — one of the best, perhaps, of its kind, to be seen in any country. Comfort, cleanliness, and convenient arrangement were ob-

---

[26]E. S. Abdy, *Journal of a Residence and Tour in The United States Of North America,* Vol. I. (London: John Murray, 1835), pp. 4-10. This African Free School system described here by an English tourist was turned over to the New York Public School Society in 1834. Although the Negro schools remained separate, they probably received better supervision than they had under the Manumission Society.

servable throughout. I had, on a subsequent occasion, a better opportunity of viewing the institution. Having gone through the different portions of the building, we retired to the superintendent's room; where, as specimens of the literary proficiency made by the inmates, two papers, the one written by a boy, the other by a girl, were read to the company. They contained a sort of analysis of a lecture on anatomy, that had been delivered a short time before by a professional man to the children. Though neither of the writers was above fifteen years of age, both compositions exhibited a degree of correctness and reflection that would have done honor to persons of riper years and a happier lot. I could see, upon inspection, that the writing had not been corrected. It was painful to observe the studied manner in which the white and colored children were separated and distinguished from each other, as if moral improvement could be promoted in either by encouraging pride and inflicting humiliation. I should have made no remark on the subject, had not my attention been directed to it by one of the party. I observed that I could not see why the children of one common parent should meet with such different treatment. A contemptuous smile and a very silly assertion that Nature, by degrading the one race, had placed an insuperable barrier to a closer approximation with the other, were the only reply. I contented myself with remarking, that there was no color in the soul, and turned the conversation to some other topic. An Englishman may wish in vain that this feature in the national character were less frequently and less obtrusively thrust forward. The next day was that on which the governor was to inspect the schools, accompanied by some of the corporation. I took my seat in one of the carriages provided for the occasion, and the visitors proceeded to make their rounds. . . .

Eight or ten schools were visited during the course of the day; and at each of them, when the examination was over, an address was made to the children by the governor, one of the aldermen, or some other person. Satisfaction was expressed with the progress made and exhortation given for the future. The necessity of application to study and of strict obedience to their parents and teachers, preparatory to the due discharge of those social and political duties they would one day be called upon to perform, was particularly inculcated. They were told of the munificent provision made by the State for their education, and of the great interest felt for their welfare by its chief magistrate, in whom, and in many around them, they might see a living example of the successful career, by which patient and persevering industry might rise from obscurity to an honorable distinction. Attachment to the political system of their country was thus, at an early period of life, identified with the promotion of their own happiness, and national honor built upon personal improvement. This ceremony was omitted at the *African* schools, as they are called. In one of these I was struck, on our entrance, by the appearance of two boys, who had no signs of the Pariah caste about them. They were both of fair complexion with light, silky hair. I immediately pointed them out to one of the visitors, who was standing by me, and he looked as if he was shocked at the sacrilegious intermixture. Questions were eagerly put, and whispers passed mysteriously from one to another; when, at last, it was agreed that further inquiries should be made into the matter, and the incipient contamination be arrested, by removing the objects of their solicitude from the black sheep among whom they had been so improperly placed. The first Africo-American free school was established at New York in 1787, by the Manumission Society of the State. In 1790 the girls were taught needle-work by a female engaged for that purpose. In 1808 the school was incorporated, and the next year the Lancasterian system was introduced into it. There was not an instance, according to C. C. Andrews, who has published an account of the schools for colored children, of any pupil, instructed in this institution, having been, down to the year 1830, "convicted of crime in any of the courts of justice."

The Trustees of the Manumission Society, under whose care the "African" schools are placed by the commissioners of the school-fund — (some of them are Quakers), — have made a distinction between the white and black teachers, that is consistent neither with justice nor good policy. They give higher salaries to the former than to the latter, without reference to the qualifications of the master or the number of the scholars. A man of color, of the name of Hughes, receives but 500 dollars a year: while a white man, whose name it would be invidious to mention, as he is acknowledged to be inferior to the other in every respect, has 600, for performing the same duties in a school of the same class.

The city of New York paid, in the year 1832, the sum of 90,748 dollars, eighty-six cents, for the use of the public schools. As great remissness on the part of parents to have their children educated was experienced, an agent was appointed by the school society, with a salary of 800 dollars per annum, to visit the poor, for the purpose of removing whatever objections or obstacles might exist to the performance of this great parental duty: at the same time an ordinance of the corporation of the city excluded "from the participation of public charity, when it may be required, all out-door poor, whether emigrants or not, who, having children between the ages of five and twelve, neglect or refuse to send them to some one of the public schools."

In spite of what has been done in this and other States for popular education, a very large portion of the population is still deprived of its benefits. A writer in Niles's Register states, that there are nearly a million and a half of children in the United States destitute of the school instruction they require. Add to this amount the slaves and a great many of the free blacks, and the waste of human intellect is frightful indeed!

Having visited the schools, we proceeded to the City Orphan Asylum, a well-conducted establishment, containing about 140 objects of charity; boys and girls. The guardian had been, for twenty years, at the head of an "African" school. He assured me that he could not discover any difference of intellect in blacks and whites: — he thought that, with similar advantages, the former would be fully equal to the latter. This testimony is not to be hastily rejected, derived, as it is, from a man highly respected, of much experience in the tuition of both races, competent to form a sound opinion, and coming to a conclusion directly opposed to all that he had been taught and all he still hears.

## Lane Seminary Students Teach Freedmen
### 1834[27]

Lane Seminary
March 18, 1834

Dear Brother—You have seen by the Evangelist and Emancipator what we have done here on the subject of slavery. The preamble and constitution of our anti-slavery society will be published this week. I will send you one. The Lord has done great things for us here. Eight months ago there was not a single immediate abolitionist in this seminary. . . .

Some five or six more were absent from the institution. Every student in both departments, from slave states, has come out and taken right ground, with the exception of *one* — and he was absent from the institution until the debate was nearly completed, and refused to attend during the remainder of the debate.

But I must tell you something more. We believe that faith without *works* is dead. We have formed a large and efficient organization for elevating the colored people in Cincinnati — have established a Lyceum among them, and lecture three or four evenings a week, on grammar,

---

[27]Gilbert H. Barnes and Dwight L. Dumond, (ed.), *Letters of Theodore Dwight Weld, Angelina Grimké Weld and Sarah Grimké, 1822–1844*, Vol. I (New York: D. Appleton-Century, 1934), 132-34. Augustus Wattles was the first Lane student to interest himself in educating Negroes. When his school opened in March, 1834, some students had to be turned away even though it operated on shifts. Later women teachers were brought in for the girls and social clubs, temperance societies, an employment service and a freedom bureau were organized.

geography, arithmetic, natural philosophy, etc. Besides this, an evening free school, for teaching them to read, is in operation every week day evening; and we are about establishing one or two more. We are also getting up a library for circulation among those who can read, and are about establishing a reading room. In addition to this, two of our students, one theological and one literary, have felt so deeply their degradation, and have been so affected by the intense desire to acquire knowledge which they exhibit, that they have taken a dismission from the institution, and commenced a school among the blacks in the city. They expect to teach a year, and then take up their course in the seminary again, when others will no doubt be ready to take their places. The first went down and opened a school, and it was *filled* the first day, and that mainly with adults, and those nearly grown. For a number of days he rejected from ten to twenty daily, because he could not teach them. This induced the other dear brother to leave his studies and join him. Both are now incessantly occupied.

Besides these two day schools, and the evening school, and the Lyceum lectures, we have three large Sabbath schools and Bible classes among the colored people. By sections in rotation, and teaching the evening reading schools in the same way, we can perform an immense amount of labor among them, without interference with our studies.

In visiting among the blacks, and mingling with them, we have all felt the great importance of another species of Instrumentality in raising them, which was not within our reach. I mean a SELECT FEMALE SCHOOL. We know of no female, except Miss Crandall, who has resolution and self-denial enough to engage in the enterprize. But the Lord has provided Miss Lathrop, daughter of the late Mr. Charles Lathrop, of Norwich, Ct., and sister of the late Mrs. Winslow and the present Mrs. Hutchins, missionaries at Ceylon, and also of Mrs. Wm. A. Hallock, of your city — has had her heart moved by the Lord to enter upon the work. She has been teaching in a seminary near Cincinnati for a few months, but will relinquish that, and commence teaching the colored school in the city about the tenth of May next. She is admirably qualified in head and heart for the employment. We have hired a suitable building for the two male day schools for $140.

We can probably hire one for the female school for $70 or 80. Each school greatly needs fixtures and appendages, such as a Globe, Maps, and other simple apparatus. The students in this seminary have already subscribed nearly 500 dollars since January for Foreign Missions, Temperance, etc; and as we are Manual Labor Students, we have no means of aiding any object to much extent, the present year. We shall however be able, I hope, to sustain our two brethren who have given themselves to the work, with what they will receive from the colored people. Many of the people in Cincinnati call us fanatics, say the blacks can never be raised here, etc. And some of the most influential are striving to persuade Miss Lathrop from engaging in an effort to raise them. The colored people themselves will do all in their power to support the schools by contributing monthly, but that will not be a great deal.

## Slave Owner Provides for his Son
### *1834*[28]

In his last conversation had with Captain Quarles, just before he left Virginia for Ohio, Colonel Gooch had disclosed to him the earnest purpose of his friend to provide more thoroughly for the education of his three sons, by settling upon them a reasonable part of his estate; and by sending them to a free State, where he was assured they could gain public educational advantages, and secure such academic and collegiate opportunities as they might desire. Captain Quarles insisted that it was his desire, as it was his purpose, to have them so advanced and improved by study and learning, as to make them useful, influential members of society.

## Resolutions by Citizens of Southampton, Virginia
### *1838*[29]

RESOLVED, That it is the duty of the citizens of this county to give an energetic support to the magistrates and constables in the execution of

---

[28]John Mercer Langston, *From Virginia Plantation to the National Capitol* (Hartford: American Publishing Company, 1894), p. 40. Langston was the son of Captain Ralph Quarles and Lucy Langston whom Quarles had set free in 1806. Quarles died in 1834 and made Colonel Gooch guardian for his three sons. The above extract from Langston's autobiography refers to Gooch's disclosure to Langston of the educational provisions Quarles had made for his sons. Langston graduated from Oberlin in 1853.

[29]Manuscript in the Schomburg Collection, Harlem Branch of New York Public Library, New York. Southampton was the scene of Nat Turner's insurrection. Slaves who had learned to write could, and often did, provide "passes" for themselves and for others which would usually assure safety for a slave until he could reach free soil. For an example, see Frederick Douglass, *Narrative of the Life of Frederick Douglass* (Boston: Published at the Anti-Slavery Office, 1845), pp. 86, 87 of the Dolphin Books edition (1963).

the laws for the suppression of meetings of Negroes by day or by night and for the prevention of their having fire arms — and dogs.

RESOLVED, That the Education of persons of color is inexpedient and improper as it is calculated to cause them to be dissatisfied with their condition and furnishes the slave with the means of absconding from his master.     .

RESOLVED, That the foregoing resolutions be transmitted to our Delegates in General Assembly and to the Executive of the State, and that they be printed in the several newspapers in the State.

## Cherokees Prohibit Teaching Slaves
### *1841*[30]

*Be it enacted by the National Council,* That from and after the passage of this Act, it shall not be lawful for any person or persons whatever to teach any free Negro or Negroes *not of Cherokee blood* or any slave belonging to any citizen or citizens of the nation, to read or write.

## A Negro College: Pro and Con
### *1847*[31]

The Committee on Education reported, by Alexander Crummell, the expediency of the establishment of a college for colored young men. In this report was embodied a fund of argument illustrated with all that beauty of diction for which its talented author has long enjoyed a dis-

---

[30]Act of the Cherokee Nation, October 22, 1841, as quoted in William Goodell, *The American Slave Code* (New York: American and Foreign Anti-Slavery Society, 1853), pp. 418, 419. Negroes also owned slaves, and except in those purely *pro forma* instances where members of the family were "owned" there is no evidence that nonwhite owners were more lenient in providing educational opportunity than other owners.

[31]*The North Star* (December 3, 1847), Vol. 1, No. 1. The matter of such a college had been discussed since first proposed by Samuel Cornish twenty years earlier. The racial character of the school is the main issue in this selection, and Douglass opposed it as he opposed segregation everywhere. He later changed the views expressed here and urged establishment of a manual labor college as a temporary strategic adjustment in the face of discrimination. Crummell, a native of New York, was ordained to the Episcopal ministry in 1844.

tinguished reputation. It was ably supported by James McCune Smith, who brought in aid of it his extensive learning and tact in statistical expression. Their views were concurred in by a large party in the Convention, but more especially by the New York delegation. On the opposite side were arrayed talent, skill, and earnestness of argument, by Frederick Douglass, Thomas Van Rensallaer, Amos G. Beman, Charles Seth, H. H. Garnett, and others, who did not discover, at present, any necessity for a colored college. Among the reasons in favor was urged, that such an institution would excite, among the colored citizens, a more general desire for mental improvement; that the aspirants for learning would soon compose a class sufficient to fill it, as also to patronize those already existing; that a field would hereby be opened for the employment of those qualified for professorships in the various departments. It was also mentioned that one distinguished and wealthy individual had manifested a willingness to appropriate a large sum of money in aid of any tangible method of ameliorating the condition of colored Americans; and in the opinion of friends, the college was presumed to embody most of the features of an available plan. It was further urged that the colored youth, under care of colored teachers, associating with those of their own complexion and condition, would not feel depressed as likely to be in other institutions, surrounded by those whom he had always regarded as opposed to his equality, and, therefore, colored colleges were the most favourable to his mental growth.

In reply it was remarked that the establishment of a colored college was attempted many years ago, and could not succeed, being regarded by many as an extravagant and uncalled-for measure; that it was too late in the day for colored people themselves to found any exclusive institution; there are now colleges and academies where they can be admitted on equal terms with white students, and that, therefore, the necessity did not exist; and it was their glorious privilege to contend for *equality*, to secure every point gained, and still press on for more. The fear of colored children sinking under the weight of prejudice in a white institution, was not a conclusive argument against their exercising the right of entrance. The colored youth should be stimulated to establish such a character, in these seats of learning, by his energy in study, and deportment toward teachers and pupils, as to disarm opposition, show himself an equal, and, in spite of cold looks and repulsive treatment, hew out a path to eminence and respect, and, like the gem, which shines brighter by attrition, become himself among good scholars the very best. Perseverance will accomplish wonders. History is replete with examples, where young people have thus, by a harmonious association, converted enemies into good friends. Reference was made to Massachusetts and other States, where the doors of many institutions of learning are now thrown open, and the colored student was invited to participate freely with others.

Another argument, and one urged against every exclusive colored institution, was, that the *expense* and *trouble* necessary for their establishment, could be employed to a more practical and permanent advantage in securing access to those already organized. We should not entertain for a moment the idea of creating any more links of that prejudice which is now binding us to earth; but, as other Americans, push our way through the various avenues of improvement and elevation.

After an animated discussion, the question was taken by yeas and nays, and resulted in favor of the plan of a colored college, viz: — Yeas, 25; Nays, 17; and a committee of 25 was appointed to solicit funds in aid thereof.

# A Negro Convention on Education
## *1848*[32]

2. RESOLVED, That whatever is necessary for the elevation of one class is necessary for the elevation of another; the respectable industrial occupations, as mechanical trades, farming, or agriculture, mercantile and professional, business, wealth and education, being necessary for the elevation of the whites; therefore those attainments are necessary for the elevation of us.

3. RESOLVED, That we impressively recommend to our brethren throughout the country, the necessity of obtaining a knowledge of mechanical trade, farming, mercantile business, the learned professions, as well as the accumulation of wealth, — as the essential means of elevating us as a class.

4. RESOLVED, That the occupation of domestics and servants among our people is degrading us as a class, and we deem it our bounden duty to discountenance such pursuits, except where necessity compels the person to resort thereto as a means of livelihood.

5. RESOLVED, That as Education is necessary in all departments, we recommend to our people, as far as in their power lies, to give their children especially a business Education. . . .

16. RESOLVED, That we recommend to the colored people every where, to use every just effort in getting their children into schools, in common with others in their several locations.

---

[32]"Resolutions of the Cleveland Convention," *North Star* (September 29, 1848), Vol. 1, No. 40. Laudatory resolutions on education were typical of the conventions. The above resolutions are interesting in their rejection of any special kind of education for Negroes, and in the resulting breadth of education sought.

## South Carolina Judge Favors Teaching Slaves
*1848*[33]

SEC. 41.   By the Act of 1834, slaves are prohibited to be taught to read or write under a penalty (if a white person may offend) not exceeding $100 fine and six months imprisonment, if a "*free person of color,*" not exceeding 50 lashes and a fine of $50.

SEC. 42.   This Act grew out of a feverish state of excitement produced by the *impudent* meddling of persons out of the slave States, with their peculiar institutions. That has, however, subsided, and I trust we are now prepared to act the part of wise, humane and fearless masters, and that this law, and all of kindred character, will be repealed. When we reflect, *as Christians, how can we justify it, that a slave is not to be permitted to read the Bible?* It is in vain to say there is danger in it. The best slaves in the State, are those who can and do read the Scriptures. Again, who is it that teach your slaves to read? It generally is done by the children of the owners. Who would tolerate an indictment against his son or daughter for teaching a favorite slave to read? *Such laws look to me as rather cowardly.* It seems as if we were afraid of our slaves. Such a feeling is unworthy of a Carolina master.

## Douglass Opposes Separate Schools
*1849*[34]

It is very clear to us that the only way to remove prejudice, and to command the respect of our white fellow citizens, is to repudiate, in every form, the idea of our inferiority, by maintaining our right to civil, social, and political equality with them. If we are in doubt on this point, our despisers may well be resolved. If they can only say that the colored man himself is impressed with a sense of his unfitness for equal privileges, their own prejudices may be plausibly justified. For our own part, we are resolved to battle against all complexional distinctions among men. They are unnatural, and work naught but mischief and oppression in any com-

---

[33]John B. O'Neall, *The Negro Law of South Carolina* (Columbia: John G. Bowman, 1848), p. 23. O'Neall, a judge in South Carolina, made these comments in a paper read to the State Agriculture Society in 1848 and subsequently presented to the legislature.

[34]Frederick Douglass, "Colored Schools," *The North Star* (August 17, 1849), Vol. II, No. 34.

munity where they may exist; and nowhere may their injurious effects be seen more clearly than in the condition of our colored children. They find themselves excluded from white schools, and they learn that their complexion is the cause of their exclusion. The consequence is, they are induced to undervalue themselves, and to look upon white children as their oppressors. . . . There is no reason, nor can there be any reason, why a colored child should not be taught in the same schools with white children. . . . Both are in need of instruction, and both possess the capacity for it; and for one class to deny to the other any right of educational privilege, on complexional grounds, is an insult offered to . . . God. To elevate and improve the colored people, is but contributing to the general good of the whole community. . . . The only sources from which we have reason to expect opposition are from a few ignorant colored men themselves, and from that low, vulgar herd of whites. . . .

## Precedent for Segregation: Roberts vs. Boston
### *1849*[35]

The plaintiff, a colored child of five years of age, has commenced this action, by her father and next friend, against the city of Boston, upon the statute of 1845, c. 214, which provides, that any child unlawfully excluded from public school instruction, in this commonwealth, shall recover damages therefor, in an action against the city or town, by which such public school instruction is supported. The question therefore is, whether, upon the facts agreed, the plaintiff has been unlawfully excluded from such instruction.

By the agreed statement of facts, it appears, that the defendants support a class of schools called primary schools, to the number of about one hundred and sixty, designed for the instruction of children of both sexes, who are between the ages of four and seven years. Two of these schools are appropriated by the primary school committee, having charge of that class of schools, to the exclusive instruction of colored children, and the residue to the exclusive instruction of white children.

The plaintiff, by her father, took proper measures to obtain admission into one of these schools appropriated to white children, but pursuant

---

[35]*Roberts v. The City of Boston.* 5 Cushing 204-210. (Massachusetts, 1849). The effects of this case in Massachusetts were wiped out when the state legislature in 1855 passed a law forbidding racial distinctions. The ruling affected the nation, however, for it was cited in court decisions upholding segregation in other states and in 1896 by the United States Supreme Court in the Plessy v. Ferguson case, which established the "separate but equal" doctrine as constitutionally valid.

to the regulations of the committee, and in conformity therewith, she was not admitted. Either of the schools appropriated to colored children was open to her; the nearest of which was about a fifth of a mile or seventy rods more distant from her father's house than the nearest primary school. It further appears, by the facts agreed, that the committee having charge of that class of schools had, a short time previously to the plaintiff's application, adopted a resolution, upon a report of a committee, that in the opinion of that board, the continuance of the separate schools for colored children, and the regular attendance of all such children upon the schools, is not only legal and just, but is best adapted to promote the instruction of that class of the population.

The present case does not involve any question in regard to the legality of the Smith school, which is a school of another class, designed for colored children more advanced in age and proficiency; though much of the argument, affecting the legality of the separate primary schools, affects in like manner that school. But the question here is confined to the primary schools alone. The plaintiff had access to a school, set apart for colored children, as well conducted in all respects, and as well fitted, in point of capacity and qualification of the instructors, to advance the education of children under seven years old, as the other primary schools; the objection is, that the schools thus open to the plaintiff are exclusively appropriated to colored children, and are at a greater distance from her home. Under these circumstances, has the plaintiff been unlawfully excluded from public school instruction? Upon the best consideration we have been able to give the subject, the court are all of opinion that she has not.

It will be considered, that this is a question of power, or of the legal authority of the committee intrusted by the city with this department of public instruction; because, if they have the legal authority, the expediency of exercising it in any particular way is exclusively with them.

The great principle, advanced by the learned and eloquent advocate of the plaintiff, is, that by the constitution and laws of Massachusetts, all persons without distinction of age or sex, birth or color, origin or condition, are equal before the law. This, as a broad general principle, such as ought to appear in a declaration of rights, is perfectly sound; it is not only expressed in terms, but pervades and animates the whole spirit of our constitution of free government. But, when this great principle comes to be applied to the actual and various conditions of persons in society, it will not warrant the assertion, that men and women are legally clothed with the same civil and political powers, and that children and adults are legally to have the same functions and be subject to the same treatment; but only that the rights of all, as they are settled and regulated by law, are equally entitled to the paternal consideration and protection of the law, for their maintenance and security. What those rights are, to which individuals, in the infinite variety of circumstances by which they are surrounded in society, are entitled, must depend on laws adapted to their respective relations and conditions.

Conceding, therefore, in the fullest manner, that colored persons, the descendants of Africans, are entitled by law, in this commonwealth, to equal rights, constitutional and political, civil and social, the question then arises, whether the regulation in question, which provides separate schools for colored children, is a violation of any of these rights. . . .

The power of general superintendence vests a plenary authority in the committee to arrange, classify, and distribute pupils, in such a manner as they think best adapted to their general proficiency and welfare. If it is thought expedient to provide for very young children, it may be, that such schools may be kept exclusively by female teachers, quite adequate to their instruction, and yet whose services may be obtained at a cost much lower than that of more highly-qualified male instructors. So if they should judge it expedient to have a grade of schools for children from seven to ten, and another for those from ten to fourteen, it would seem to be within their authority to establish such schools. So to separate male and female pupils into different schools. It has been found necessary, that is to say, highly expedient, at times, to establish special schools for poor and neglected children, who have passed the age of seven, and have become too old to attend the primary school, and yet have not acquired the rudiments of learning, to enable them to enter the ordinary schools. If a class of youth, of one or both sexes, is found in that condition, and it is expedient to organize them into a separate school, to receive the special training, adapted to their condition, it seems to be within the power of the superintending committee, to provide for the organization of such special school.

A somewhat more specific rule, perhaps, on these subjects, might be beneficially provided by the legislature; but yet, it would probably be quite impracticable to make full and precise laws for this purpose, on account of the different condition of society in different towns. In towns of a large territory, over which the inhabitants are thinly settled, an arrangement or classification going far into detail, providing different schools for pupils of different ages, of each sex, and the like, would require the pupils to go such long distances from their homes to the schools, that it would be quite unreasonable. But in Boston, where more than one hundred thousand inhabitants live within a space so small, that it would be scarcely an inconvenience to require a boy of good health to traverse daily the whole extent of it, a system of distribution and classification may be adopted and carried into effect, which may be useful and beneficial in its influence on the character of the schools, and in its adaptation to the improvement and advancement of the great purpose of education, and at the same time practicable and reasonable in its operation.

In the absence of special legislation on this subject, the law has vested the power in the committee to regulate the system of distribution and classification; and when this power is reasonably exercised, without being abused or perverted by colorable pretences, the decision of the committee must be deemed conclusive. The committee, apparently upon great deliberation, have come to the conclusion, that the good of both classes of schools will be best promoted, by maintaining the separate primary schools for colored and for white children, and we can perceive no ground to doubt, that this is the honest result of their experience and judgment.

It is urged, that this maintenance of separate schools tends to deepen and perpetuate the odious distinction of caste, founded in a deep-rooted prejudice in public opinion. This prejudice, if it exists, is not created by law, and probably cannot be changed by law. Whether this distinction and prejudice, existing in the opinion and feelings of the community, would not be as effectually fostered by compelling colored and white children to associate together in the same schools, may well be doubted; at all events it is a fair and proper question for the committee to consider and decide upon, having in view the best interests of both classes of children placed under their superintendence, and we cannot say, that their decision upon it is not founded on just grounds of reason and experience, and in the results of a discriminating and honest judgment.

The increased distance, to which the plaintiff was obliged to go to school from her father's house, is not such, in our opinion, as to render the regulation in question unreasonable, still less illegal.

On the whole the court are of opinion, that upon the facts stated, the action cannot be maintained.


## Sumner's Argument Against Separate Schools
### *1849*[36]

IV.   The exclusion of colored children from the Public Schools, open to white children, is a source of practical inconvenience to them and their parents, to which white persons are not exposed, and is, therefore, a violation of Equality. The black and the white are not equal before the law. . . .

---

[36]Charles Sumner, *Argument Against the Constitutionality of Separate Colored Schools in the Case of Sarah C. Roberts v. The City of Boston* (Boston: B. F. Roberts, 1849), pp. 14-30.

V.   The separation of children in the Public Schools of Boston, on account of color or race, is in the nature of *Caste*, and is a violation of Equality. . . .

VI.   The Committee of Boston, charged with the superintendence of the Public Schools, have no *power* under the Constitution and laws of Massachusetts, to make any discrimination on account of color or race, among children in the Public Schools. . . .

It is clear that the Committee may classify scholars, according to their age and sex; for the obvious reasons that these distinctions are inoffensive, and especially recognized as *legal* in the law relating to schools. They may also classify scholars according to their moral and intellectual qualifications, because such a power is necessary to the government of schools. But the Committee cannot assume, *a priori*, and without individual examination, that an *entire race* possess certain moral or intellectual qualities, which shall render it proper to place them all in a class by themselves. Such an exercise of the discretion with which the Committee are intrusted, must be unreasonably, and therefore illegal. . . .

In determining that the Committee have no *power* to make a discrimination of color or race, we are strengthened by yet another consideration. If the power exists in the present case, it must exist in many others. It cannot be restrained to this alone. The Committee may distribute all the children into classes — merely according to their discretion. They may establish a separate school for the Irish or the Germans, where each may nurse an exclusive spirit of nationality alien to our institutions. They may separate Catholics from Protestants, or, pursuing their discretion still further, they may separate the different sects or Protestants, and establish one school for Unitarians, another for Presbyterians, another for Baptists, and another for Methodists. They may establish a separate school for the rich, that the delicate taste of this favored class may not be offended by the humble garments of the poor. They may exclude the children of mechanics from the Public Schools, and send them to separate schools by themselves. . . .

There are some other matters not strictly belonging to the juridical aspect of the case, and yet of importance to its clear comprehension, upon which I shall touch briefly before I close. . . .

Who can say, that this does not injure the blacks? Theirs, in its best estate, is an unhappy lot. Shut out by a still lingering prejudice from many social advantages, a despised class, they feel this proscription from the Public Schools as a peculiar brand. Beyond this, it deprives them of those healthful animating influences which would come from a participation in the studies of their white brethren. It adds to their discouragements. It widens their separation from the rest of the community, and postpones that great day of reconciliation which is sure to come.

The whole system of public schools suffers also. It is a narrow perception of their high aim which teaches that they are merely to furnish to all the scholars an equal amount in knowledge, and that, therefore, provided all be taught, it is of little consequence where, and in what company it be done. The law contemplates not only that they shall all be taught, but they shall be taught *all together*. They are not only to receive equal quantities of knowledge, but all are to receive it in the same way. All are to approach together the same common fountain; nor can there be any exclusive source for any individual or any class. The school is the little world in which the child is trained for the larger world of life. It must, therefore, cherish and develop the virtues and the sympathies which are employed in the larger world. And since, according to our institutions, all classes meet, without distinction of color, in the performance of civil duties, so should they all meet, without distinction of color, in the school, beginning there those relations of equality which our Constitution and laws promise to all.

## Ohio Supreme Court Upholds Segregation
*1850*[37]

In order to determine whether it was proper for the city council to give this sum the direction intended by law, whether they had the power to interfere with it, and to draw orders for it upon their treasurer, as liabilities might be incurred by the districts, it will be necessary to give some little attention to our school laws, and especially to the act of February 10th, 1849, "to authorize the establishment of separate schools for the education of colored children, and for other purposes." (47 Ohio L. 17.) . . .

Now suppose there had been no other provisions in this act, what would have been the consequence, so far as schools are concerned? Unquestionably, white and colored children must have been admitted into the same schools, and upon the same terms. There would have been no distinction on account of color. All would have an equal right of admission, and all must have been admitted, unless the law was palpably

---

[37] *The State, ex rel., etc. v. City of Cincinnati et al.* 19 Ohio 178 (December, 1850). It is interesting to note that in upholding the right of school authorities to make racial separations, the courts here and in the Roberts case imply the existence of cogent educational reasons for such separation. The reasons themselves, however, were not given.

violated and resisted. The eight hundred colored youth, and the thirty-three thousand white youth of Cincinnati would have been found in the same rooms, the same schools, under the same instructors, according to their locality in the different parts of the city.

In this state of case the colored youth of the city would have received precisely the same benefit from the school fund as is now claimed for them. By the general school laws, as they would have remained after this repealing clause, this right would have been secured to them.

But to avoid this difficulty of mingling in the same schools, youth of different colors, whites with blacks and mulattoes, the "board of trustees and visitors of common schools of the city of Cincinnati, on the 17th August, in the year 1849, passed a resolution that the city should be divided into two school districts, for the colored youth of said city, to be called the eastern and western districts."...

The whole subject of organizing and regulating schools is very properly left to the general assembly in the exercise of its legislative powers.

But although there is no such prohibitory clause, still it is insisted that this law, in the particular named, is in contravention of the spirit of the constitution. In my opinion, this is rather dangerous ground to tread upon in determining the constitutionality of a law. We may all agree as to the reading of the constitution, and generally as to its meaning, but when we come to talk of its spirit, it is a different matter. There is great danger that we shall conclude that spirit to be in accordance with our preconceived opinions or feelings of what it ought to be. . . .

As a matter of policy it is unquestionably better that the white and colored youth should be placed in separate schools, and that this school fund should be divided to them in proportion to their numbers.


## Martin Delany on Education
*1852*[38]


The branches of Education most desirable for the preparation of youth, for practical useful every-day life, are Arithmetic and good Penmanship, in order to be Accountants; and a good rudimental knowledge of Geography — which has ever been neglected, and under estimated — and of

[38]Martin R. Delany, *The Condition, Elevation, Emigration, and Destiny of the Colored People of the United States* (Philadelphia: Published by the Author, 1852), pp. 192-96. Delany was born in Charlestown, Virginia, in 1812. He attended Harvard Medical College, practiced medicine in Canada, and served as a major in the Union Army.

Political Economy; which without the knowledge of the first, no people can ever become adventurous — nor of the second, never will be an enterprising people. These are not abstruse sciences, or learning not easily acquired or understood; but simply common school primer learning, that everybody may get. . . . What did John Jacob Astor, Stephen Girard, or do the millionaires and the greater part of the merchant princes, and mariners, know about Latin and Greek, and the Classics? . . . What we most need then, is a good business practical Education; because, the Classical and Professional education of so many of your young men, before their parents are able to support them, and community ready to patronize them, only serves to lull their energy, and cripple the otherwise, praiseworthy efforts they would make in life. A Classical education, is only suited to the wealthy, or those who have a prospect of gaining livelihood by it. The writer does not wish to be understood as underrating a Classical and Professional education; this is not his intention; he fully appreciates them, having had some such advantages himself; but he desires to give a proper guide, and put a check to the extravagant idea that is fast obtaining among our people especially, that a Classical, or as it is termed, a "finished education," is necessary to prepare one for usefulness in life. Let us have an education, that shall practically develop our thinking faculties and manhood; and then and not until then, shall we be able to vie with our oppressors, go where we may. . . . Let our young women have an education; let their minds be well informed; well stored with useful information and practical proficiency, rather than the light superficial acquirements, popularly and fashionably called accomplishments. We desire accomplishments, but they must be useful. Our females must be qualified because they are to be the mothers of our children. . . .

## Negro Refuses to Pay School Tax
### *1853*[39]

Dear Sir: You called yesterday for the tax upon my property in this Township, which I shall pay, excepting the 'School Tax.' I object to the

---

[39]Letter from Robert Purvis to Joseph J. Butcher, November 4, 1853. In Carter G. Woodson (ed.), *The Mind of the Negro as Reflected in Letters Written During The Crisis, 1800-1860* (Washington, D.C.: The Association for the Study of Negro Life and History, 1926), pp. 178-79. Woodson cited his source as *Liberator,* December 16, 1853. Purvis, Philadelphia Negro leader, was born in Charleston, South Carolina. His white father provided for his education at Amherst College. He was active in the underground railroad, and other anti-slavery work, and was quite successful in business. The letter related to the school situation in Byberry, Pennsylvania, the township in which Purvis lived.

payment of this tax, on the ground that my rights as a citizen, and my feelings as a man and a parent, have been grossly outraged in depriving me . . . of the benefits of the school system which this tax was designed to sustain. I have borne this outrage ever since the innovation upon the usual practice of admitting *all* the children of the Township into the public schools, and at considerable expense, have been obliged to obtain the services of private teachers to instruct my children, while my school tax is greater, with a single exception, than any other citizen of the township. It is true, . . . I was informed by a *pious Quaker* director, with a sanctifying grace, imparting doubtless, an unctuous glow to his *saintly* prejudices, that a school in the village of Mechanicsville was appropriated for '*thine.*' The miserable shanty, with all its appurtenances, on the very line of the township, to which this *benighted* follower of George Fox alluded, is, as you know, the most flimsy and ridiculous sham which any tool of a skin-hating aristocracy could have resorted to, to cover or protect his servility. . . . I shall resist this tax, which, before the unjust exclusion, had always afforded me the highest gratification in paying. . . .

Yours, very respectfully,

Robert Purvis.

## Colored Convention Considers Educational Problems
### *1853*[40]

Two distinct, yet inseparable branches of education must be undergone by our youth ere they are fitted for the work of social elevation — that of the School-Room and that of the Fire-Side.

It is not our province to discuss either, briefly remarking upon each, so far only as they immediately bear upon our subject. In looking into the schoolroom, we can but approach this branch of education with some apprehensions since the methods for the most successful culture of our children, in the opinions of many leading minds amongst us, is materially different. The two more prominent may be briefly pointed out. The one holds that no special organization for the culture of colored youth at this time are necessary; that precisely the same species of learning imparted

---

[40]"Report of the Committee on Social Relations and Polity," *Proceedings of the Colored National Convention held in Rochester, July 6, 7, 8, 1853* (Rochester: Office of Frederick Douglass' Paper, 1853), pp. 22, 23.

to white youth will best serve for colored youth, that both schools and education, as at present constituted, especially for, and wholly directed by the whites, being so far superior; better training can be obtained therein than can be had in any that can be adapted to the especial wants of colored youth. On the other hand, it is held that colored youth is to be educated, so as to catch up in the great race we are running; and hence, schools must be adapted to so train him; not that he himself is so widely different from the white youth, but that the state of things which he finds around him, and which he must be qualified to change, is so widely different. The training, therefore, necessary to propel him, so that he can gain up with the whites, (as gain he must, or be utterly lost,) is to be obtained only in schools adapted to his wants; that neither schools nor educators for the whites, at present, are in full sympathy with him; and that he must either abandon his own state of things which he finds around him, and which he is pledged to change and better, or cease to receive culture from such sources, since their whole tendency is to change him, not his condition — to educate him out of his sympathies, not to quicken and warm his sympathies, for all that is of worth to him is his elevation, and the elevation of his people.

We are fully inclined to the latter opinion. We are more than persuaded in looking over the whole subject, that the force of circumstances compels the regulation of schools by us to supply a deficiency produced by our condition; that it should be our special aim, to so direct instructors, regulate books and libraries; in fine, the whole process of instruction to meet entirely our particular exigencies, continuing so long, only, as such exigencies exist.

Your Committee on Education will however place this subject fully before you.

But we go farther; we go beyond the school-room. We would approach the fire-side, and would remind you that something more definite must be done there, than has yet been accomplished. With all the precepts and examples of the whites before us, it is but too apparent that we have made too little progress in the fire-side culture of our youth; and it is equally apparent that this neglect enters too largely into all the ramifications of our social state, affecting its present and prospective advancement. With a badly fire-side trained youth, added to indifferent or objectionable school culture, such as has educated them out of their humanity, what progress, we ask, can a people expect to make, in a community like ours? From the fire-side we must receive and teach the great lessons of self-confidence, self-dependence, perseverance, energy, and continuity. Implements such as these are more precious than rubies. They will seek for us, and make us seek for, and engage in proper callings, such as tend to elevate. They will discourage in us all such as tend to humiliate, depress, and degrade. Employments have much more to do with the moulding and stamping the character of a people than we have yet calculated for. Implements such as we have just mentioned will enable us to carve out, unaided, our own road, and walk securely in it.

## Frederick Douglass Advises "Learn Trades or Starve"
### *1854*[41]

These are the obvious alternatives sternly presented to the free colored people of the United States. It is idle, yea even ruinous, to disguise the matter for a single hour longer; every day begins and ends with the impressive lesson that free Negroes must learn trades, or die.

The old avocations, by which colored men obtained a livelihood, are rapidly, unceasingly and inevitably passing into other hands; every hour sees the black man elbowed out of employment by some newly arrived emigrant, whose hunger and whose color are thought to give him a better title to the place; and so we believe it will continue to be until the last prop is levelled beneath us.

As a black man, we say if we cannot stand up, let us fall down. We desire to be a man among men while we do live; and when we cannot, we wish to die. It is evident, painfully evident to every reflecting mind, that the means of living, for colored men, are becoming more and more precarious and limited. Employments and callings, formerly monopolized by us, are so no longer.

White men are becoming house-servants, cooks and stewards on vessels — at hotels. — They are becoming porters, stevedores, wood-

---

[41]*Frederick Douglass' Paper* (March 4, 1853), "Learn Trades or Starve," Vol. VI, No. 11. Forty years before Samuel C. Armstrong and Booker T. Washington advocated industrial education for Southern Negroes, Frederick Douglass spoke out vigorously for this type of education. A widely hailed fad among white educators, industrial education was promoted by Douglass free from the charge of compromise on civil rights as was alleged with respect to Washington. Despite the importance to the Negro of entrance upon middle class trades, much more was involved than the availability of training for these trades. Douglass and other advocates of industrial education were slow to realize this and tended to assume that if the proper education could be obtained, the other parts of the system would somehow fall into place.

sawyers, hod-carriers, brick-makers, white-washers and barbers, so that the blacks can scarcely find the means of subsistence — a few years ago, and a *white* barber would have been a curiosity — now their poles stand on every street. Formerly blacks were almost the exclusive coachmen in wealthy families: this is so no longer; white men are now employed, and for aught we see, they fill their servile station with an obsequiousness as profound as that of the blacks. The readiness and ease with which they adapt themselves to these conditions ought not to be lost sight of by the colored people. The meaning is very important, and we should learn it. We are taught our insecurity by it. Without the means of living, life is a curse, and leaves us at the mercy of the oppressor to become his debased slaves. Now, colored men, what do you mean to do, for you must do something? The American Colonization Society tells you to go to Liberia. Mr. Bibbs tells you to go to Canada. Others tell you to go to school. We tell you to go to work; and to work you must go or die. Men are not valued in this country, or in any country, for what they *are*; they are valued for what they can *do*. It is in vain that we talk about being men, if we do not the work of men. We must become valuable to society in other departments of industry than those servile ones from which we are rapidly being excluded. We must show that we can *do* as well as *be*; and to this end we must learn trades. When we can build as well as live in houses; when we can *make* as well as *wear* shoes; when we can produce as well as consume wheat, corn and rye — then we shall become valuable to society. Society is a hard-hearted affair. — With it the helpless may expect no higher dignity than that of paupers. The individual must lay society under obligation to him, or society will honor him only as a stranger and sojourner. *How* shall this be done? In this manner: use every means, strain every nerve to master some important mechanical art. At present, the facilities for doing this are few — institutions of learning are more readily opened to you than the work-shop; but the Lord helps them who will help themselves, and we have no doubt that new facilities will be presented as we press forward.

If the alternative were presented to us of learning a trade or of getting an education, we would learn the trade, for the reason, that with the trade we could get the education, while with the education we could not get the trade. What we, as a people, need most, is the means for our own elevation. — An educated colored man, in the United States, unless he has within him the heart of a hero, and is willing to engage in a life-long battle for his rights, as a man, finds few inducements to remain in this country. He is isolated in the land of his birth — debarred by his color from congenial association with whites; he is equally cast out by the ignorance of the *blacks*. The remedy for this must comprehend the elevation of the masses; and this can only be done by putting the mechanic arts within the reach of colored men.

We have now stated pretty strongly the case of our colored countrymen; perhaps some will say, *too* strongly; but we know whereof we affirm.

In view of this state of things, we appeal to the abolitionists, What boss anti-slavery mechanic will take a black boy into his wheelwright's shop, his blacksmith's shop, his joiner's shop, his cabinet shop? Here is something *practical*; where are the whites and where are the blacks that will respond to it? Where are the anti-slavery milliners and seamstresses that will take colored girls and teach them trades, by which they can obtain an honorable living? The fact that we have made good cooks, good waiters, good barbers, and white-washers, induces the belief that we may excel in higher branches of industry. *One thing is certain: we must find new methods of obtaining a livelihood, for the old ones are failing us very fast.*

We, therefore, call upon the intelligent and thinking ones amongst us, to urge upon the colored people within their reach, in all seriousness, the duty and the necessity of giving their children useful and lucrative trades, by which they may commence the battle of life with weapons commensurate with the exigencies of the conflict.

## The Beginning of Wilberforce University
### *1853*[42]

In 1853 some of the ministers and members of the Methodist Episcopal Church saw and felt the necessity of a more liberal and concentrated effort to improve the condition and furnish the facilities of education to the thirty thousand colored people in Ohio and those of other free States. At the session of the Cincinnati Conference, held at Hillsboro, September 28th, 1853, on motion of Rev. A. Lowrey, it was ordered 'that a committee of seven be appointed by the President to inquire and report to the next Conference what can best be done to promote the welfare of the colored people among us.' . . .

---

[42]Daniel A. Payne, "The History of the Origin and Development of Wilberforce University," in David Smith, *Biography of Rev. David Smith* (Xenia, Ohio: Xenia Gazette Office, 1881), pp. 100, 101, 109. Both the Methodist Episcopal and the African Methodist Episcopal churches joined in the support of Wilberforce, whose students were largely children of Southern planters. After the war, the M.E. church withdrew, leaving the A.M.E. church in charge of the school.

A majority of the committee met on the call of the chairman, at the Methodist Book Concern, on the 9th of August, 1853, and on a full and free discussion, adopted the following brief outline of a plan which was judged best calculated to answer the end had in view, and which the chairman was requested to elaborate in a report to be presented to the Conference:

1.  *Resolved*, That it is of the greatest importance, both to the colored and white races in the free States, that all the colored people should receive at least a good common school education; and that for this purpose well-qualified teachers are indispensable.

2.  That the religious instruction of the colored people is necessary to their elevation as well as their salvation.

3.  That we recommend the establishment of a literary institution of a high order for the education of the colored people generally, and for the purpose of preparing teachers of all grades to labor in the work of educating the colored people in our country and elsewhere.

4.  That we recommend that an attempt be made, on the part of the Methodist Episcopal Church, to co-operate with the African Methodist Episcopal Church in promoting the intellectual and religious improvement of the colored people.

5.  That we recommend the appointment of a general agent to carry out the objects proposed in the foregoing resolutions, and to labor otherwise for the improvement of the people of color. . . .

On the 30th day of August, 1856, application was made in due form, to the authorities of Greene county, and State of Ohio, for the benefit of the general law of the State, passed April 9th, 1852; and every requisition of the law being complied with, the institution was organized and constituted a body corporate, under the name of The Wilberforce University.

## Sentence of Mrs. Douglass for Teaching Negroes
### *1853*[43]

JUDGE BAKER.    Upon an indictment found against you for assembling with Negroes to instruct them to read and write, and for associating with them in an unlawful assembly, you were found guilty, . . .

---

[43]"The Trial of Mrs. Margaret Douglass for Teaching Colored Children to Read, Norfolk, Virginia, 1853," in John D. Lawson, *American State Trials*, Vol. VII, (St. Louis: F. H. Thomas Law Book Company, 1917), pp. 56-60.

The law under which you have been tried and found guilty is not to be found among the original enactments of our Legislature. The first legislative provision upon this subject was introduced in the year 1831, immediately succeeding the bloody scenes of the memorable Southampton insurrection; and that law being found not sufficiently penal to check the wrongs complained of, was re-enacted with additional penalties in the year 1848, which last mentioned act, after several years' trial and experience, has been re-affirmed by adoption, and incorporated into our present code. After these several and repeated recognitions of the wisdom and propriety of the said act, it may well be said that bold and open opposition to it is a matter not to be slightly regarded, especially as we have reason to believe that every Southern slave state in our country, as a measure of self-preservation and protection, has deemed it wise and just to adopt laws with similar provisions. . . .

Teaching the Negroes to read and write is made penal by the laws of our State. The act imposes a fine not exceeding one hundred dollars, to be ascertained by the jury, and imprisonment not exceeding six months, to be fixed and ascertained by the Court. And now, since the jury in your case has in my opinion properly settled the question of guilt, it devolves on me, under the law, to ascertain and decide upon the quantum of imprisonment under the circumstances of your trial; and I exceedingly regret, that in being called on for the first time to act under the law in question, it becomes my duty to impose the required punishment upon a female, apparently of fair and respectable standing in the community. The only mitigating circumstance in your case, if in truth there be any, according to my best reason and understanding of it, is that to which I have just referred, namely, you being a female. Under the circumstances of this case, if you were of a different sex, I should regard the full punishment of six months' imprisonment as eminently just and proper. Had you taken the advice of your friends and of the Court, and had employed counsel to defend you, your case no doubt, would have been presented in a far more favorable light both to the Court and to the jury. The opinions you advanced, and the pertinacity and zeal you manifested in behalf of the Negroes, while they indicated perfect candor and sincerity on your part, satisfied the Court, and must have satisfied all who heard you, that the act complained of was the settled and deliberate purpose of your mind, regardless of consequences, however dangerous to our peace.

In conformity with these views, I am impelled by a feeling of common honesty, to say that this is not a case in which a mere formal judgment should be announced as the opinion of the Court. Something more substantial under the circumstances of this case, I think, is demanded and required. The discretionary power to imprison for the term of six months or less, in good sense and sound morality, does not authorize a mere minimum punishment, such as imprisonment for a day or week, in a case in which the question of guilt is free from doubt, and there are many facts and circumstances of aggravation. A judgment of that sort, therefore, in this case, would doubtless be regarded by all true advocates of justice and law as mere mockery. It would be no terror to those who acknowledge no rule of action but their own evil will and pleasure, but would rather invite to still bolder incendiary movements. For these reasons, as an example to all others in like cases disposed to offend, and in vindication of the policy and justness of our laws, which every individual should be taught to respect, the judgment of the Court is, in addition to the proper fine and costs, that you be imprisoned for the period of one month in the jail of this city.

## An Early College
### *1853*[44]

At a Stated Meeting of the Presbytery of NEW CASTLE, Held on the 5th of October, 1853, the following paper, after discussion, was adopted without a dissenting voice:

Considering the many Christian congregations of colored people in this country which are unable to secure educated ministers of their own color; considering the communities of such people in many parts who need educated men amongst them to fill the place of teachers and other responsible situations; considering the wants of Liberia, and the importance to its present and future welfare of having suitably qualified men to fill its offices and posts of authority, instruction and influence; considering the vast Missionary work yet to be done in Africa, and to be mainly done by persons of African descent; considering how extremely difficult it is for colored youth to obtain a liberal education in this land, arising from the want of schools for that purpose, and their exclusion from

---

[44]*Tenth Annual Catalogue of Lincoln University, Oxford, Pa., May, 1867*, pp. 20, 21. Ashmun Institute was the predecessor of Lincoln University. It was named for Jehudi Ashmun, founder of Liberia, and actually began instruction in January, 1857. One early advertisement of the school assured potential donors that the school would not interfere with the "civil or social condition" of its students!

all regular institutions of learning of a higher grade; considering the strong recommendation to that effect from our Board of Education, and its full endorsement by the General Assembly of our Church; and considering the favorable indications of Providence at this time apparently calling us to such a work:

This Presbytery, trusting in God, and, under Him, depending on the Christian liberality of the friends of the African race throughout our country, do determine as follows:

1.    There shall be established within our bounds, and under our supervision, an Institution, to be called the ASHMUN INSTITUTE, for the Scientific, Classical, and Theological education of colored youth of the male sex. . . .

## Views of a Southerner on Education and Society
### 1854[45]

We need never have white slaves in the South, because we have black ones. Our citizens, like those of Rome and Athens, are a privileged class. We should train and educate them to deserve the privileges and to perform the duties which society confers on them. Instead, by a law demagoguism depressing their self-respect by discourses on the equality of man, we had better excite their pride by reminding them that they do not fulfill the menial offices which white men do in other countries. . . .

The abolitionists taunt us with the ignorance of our poor white citizens. This is a stigma on the South that should be wiped out. Half of the people of the South, or nearly so, are blacks. We have only to educate the other half. . . .

We ought, like the Athenians, to be the best educated people in the world. When we employ all our whites in the mechanic arts, in commerce, in professions, &c., and confine the Negroes to farmwork, and coarse mechanical operations, we shall be in a fair way to attain this result. . . . Two causes are in active operation to fan and increase this hostility to the Negro race. The one, the neglect to educate and provide

---

[45]George Fitzhugh, *Sociology For The South* (Richmond: A. Morris, 1854), pp. 9, 144-48. Here Fitzhugh invokes Greek democracy as a social model and draws conclusions favoring the universal education of whites which the South did not practice, but forbidding the education of blacks which the South did practice.

means of employment for the poor whites in the South, who are thereby led to believe that the existence of Negroes amongst us is ruin to them. The other, the theory of the Types of Mankind, which cuts off the Negro from human brotherhood, and justifies the brutal and the miserly in treating him as a vicious brute. Educate all Southern whites, employ them, not as cooks, lacqueys, ploughmen, and menials, but as independent freemen should be employed, and let Negroes be strictly tied down to such callings as are unbecoming white men, and peace would be established between blacks and whites. The whites would find themselves elevated by the existence of Negroes amongst us. Like the Roman citizen, the Southern white man would become a noble and a privileged character, and he would then like Negroes and slavery, because his high position would be due to them. . . .

Educate the people, no matter what it may cost!

## Massachusetts Forbids Segregation
*1855*[46]

SECT. 9.   No person shall be excluded from a public school on account of the race, color, or religious opinions, of the applicant or scholar.

SECT. 10.   Every member of the school committee under whose directions a child is excluded from a public school, and every teacher of such school from which a child is excluded, shall, on application by the parent or guardian of such child, state in writing the grounds and reason of the exclusion.

---

[46]Massachusetts General Statutes, 1860, Chapter 41, Sections 9 and 10, page 229. The law was originally passed in 1855, and had the effect of reversing the Boston v. Roberts decision of the Massachusetts Supreme Court.

# 2

# Emancipation to World War I

The documents in this chapter will illustrate the events and issues affecting black education from emancipation through World War I. The hopes engendered by the coming of freedom were further enhanced by a period of intense educational effort by and for freedmen. So vigorous were these efforts, particularly before 1872, that observers occasionally remarked that Negro youths had better educational opportunities than white youths. These situations were temporary, and certainly did not reflect the place in society the white South intended for the freedman. By 1890, discriminatory educational provisions were added to the racial segregation which had been nearly universal in southern schools since the end of the Civil War. Although Rayford W. Logan has described the efforts to remand the blackman to a lowly place in American life as having reached "the nadir" at the turn of the century, the situation in education was worse by 1915 than it had been in 1900.[1] In 1915 the death of Booker T. Washington, who had dominated the scene for two decades, symbolized the end of both a theory of Negro education and an accommodating response to the discrimination of the period.

The Reconstruction Era (1865-1877), brought new forces to bear upon southern education in general and Negro education in particular. Hundreds of teachers, mainly "Yankee schoolmarms" supported by various northern churches and missonary societies, moved into the South to teach the freedmen. The first documents in this chapter will provide an insight into the motives and experiences of two of these teachers, one Negro and one white.[2]

---

[1]Rayford W. Logan, *The Negro in the United States* (Princeton: D. Van Nostrand Company, 1957), p. 55.

[2]The origins, motives, and experiences of the Northern teachers were carefully studied by Henry L. Swint in *The Northern Teacher in the South, 1862-1870* (Nashville: Vanderbilt University Press, 1941). Swint neglected the black teachers in this group, such as Robert Harris whose experiences are included in the readings of this section.

These documents suggest that while teachers often viewed education as auxiliary to more transcendent ends, they quickly become involved in somewhat more mundane problems.

The Union Army did much to educate freedmen.[3] Contrabands flocking to army lines were not only fed and clothed but also taught. Soldiers in Negro army units were encouraged to learn as a means of promotion, and one writer has estimated that 20,000 black soldiers thus received some education. Included in this section is a document by General N.P. Banks illustrating army activity in behalf of education. In 1865, the Bureau of Refugees, Freedmen and Abandoned Lands, popularly called the Freedmen's Bureau, was organized as an outgrowth of army activities. By a congressional act in 1866, it was authorized to work in education. Under General Oliver Otis Howard, the Bureau assisted in the establishment of over 4,000 schools. In the absence of effective state control, it provided a degree of coordination, and supervision, for what would otherwise have been a chaotic situation.[4]

The freedmen themselves constituted still another factor in the educational development of the South.[5] During the Reconstruction Era, at the state and national government levels, Negroes were in a position to influence educational law to an extent that has not been possible since then. Negro churches established schools. In hundreds of local communities, Negro citizens pooled their meager resources to furnish school buildings, pay teachers, and buy books and clothes.

A fifth force affecting the education of blacks during this period was the emergence of educational foundations, philanthropy in a new form. The first educational philanthropy with multimillion-dollar

---

[3]On the educational work of the army, see John W. Blassingame, "The Union Army as an Educational Institution for Negroes, 1862-1865," *Journal of Negro Education,* XXXIV (Spring, 1965), pp. 152-59. Also, Dudley T. Cornish, "The Union Army as a School for Negroes," *Journal of Negro History,* XXXVII (October, 1952), pp. 368-82.

[4]See George R. Bentley, *A History of the Freedmen's Bureau* (Philadelphia: University of Pennsylvania Press, 1955). Doctoral dissertations have been done on the work of the Bureau in various states, including South Carolina (Martin L. Abbott), Virginia (William T. Alderson), Tennessee (Paul D. Phillips), and Louisiana (Howard A. White).

[5]The educational leadership of Negroes is briefly treated in such general works as W.E.B. DuBois, *Black Reconstruction in America, 1860-1880* (Cleveland: World Publishing Co., 1964, but first published in 1935), and John H. Franklin, *Reconstruction After the Civil War* (Chicago: University of Chicago Press, 1961). See also R.R. Wright, Jr., *Self-Help in Negro Education* (Cheyney, Pa.: Committee of Twelve, n.d.) and W.E.B. DuBois, *Some Efforts of the American Negroes for Their Own Betterment* (Atlanta: Atlanta University Press, 1898). Studies of Negro leadership in individual states include those by Alrutheus A. Taylor (Virginia, South Carolina, Tennessee), Vernon L. Wharton (Mississippi), Joel Williamson (South Carolina), Joe M. Richardson (Florida), and Alan Conway (Georgia).

resources, interested in an entire region of the country, and without sectarian religious objectives was the Peabody Education Fund founded in 1867. This fund influenced other philanthropists, leading to the establishment of the John F. Slater Fund (industrial education and teacher preparation) in 1882, the General Education Board (industrial education and school supervision) in 1903, the Anna T. Jeanes Fund (black rural schools) in 1909, and the Julius Rosenwald Fund (Negro school buildings) in 1911.[6]

Following the Compromise of 1877 and the election of Rutherford B. Hayes as President, there emerged the concept of a "new South" which northern leaders felt should be allowed to solve its own problems without external interference. The views of southern white leaders ranged from the bitter racism of South Carolina's Tillman and Mississippi's Vardaman, to the liberalism of George W. Cable. Perhaps more nearly typical of the dominant position were the moderate views expressed by William H. Ruffner, the father of Virginia's public school system. For the South, the major issues of this period were school segregation, and the kind of education needed by the Negro. While these issues had been extensively discussed in the North before Emancipation, they were new to the South. Here, the context in which the issues were debated was different, since the battle to establish state public school systems was only now being fought out, and the socio-economic basis for race relations differed from that in the North.

Several documents in this section illustrate the spectrum of opinion regarding racial segregation in schools. Most of the constitutions written during the Reconstruction Era, said nothing about segregation. Although the constitutions of South Carolina and Louisiana required public schools to admit all pupils alike, neither of these states nor any other southern states had racially integrated schools. Slowly, what began as a custom was written into law, as will be illustrated by the document from West Virginia. Outside the South, the issue of school segregation was still unsettled. Extracts from an Ohio court case and from Wyoming's optional segregation law indicate strong support for the Boston v. Roberts doctrine. At the national level, congressional debates on civil rights bills and on federal aid to education provided an open forum for arguments for and against school segregation. Benjamin F. Butler's speech in which he with-

---

[6]An old but still good treatment of the foundations can be found in Ullin W. Leavell, *Philanthropy in Negro Education* (Nashville: George Peabody College for Teachers, 1930).

drew his civil rights bill indicates that the provision for mixed schools had been the target of much pressure. An example of arguments brought to bear upon Butler is found in Barnas Sears' statement concerning the anticipated effect of mixed schools upon southern education. Butler withdrew his bill after a visit by Sears who, as general agent for the Peabody Education Fund, was using Fund money to stimulate state systems of public education throughout the South.

Despite the general acceptance of segregated schools, there are documents indicating that the idea was not unopposed. Negroes (included in this chapter are John Mercer Langston, John R. Lynch, and Richard H. Cain) and northern liberals were vigorous in their opposition, although their arguments were somewhat weakened by the fact that some of their constituents either preferred or were willing to accept segregated schools.

National acquiescence in the implicit racism of segregation is further illustrated by a selection from the New York court case, King v. Gallagher. This selection is interesting not only for its almost exact replication of the Boston v. Roberts rationale, but also for its clear invitation to bring instances of inequality into court. Further illustrations of national acquiescence are provided by the extract from New York school law of 1894, and by the Plessy v. Ferguson decision of the U.S. Supreme Court in 1896. Thus, the "separate but equal" doctrine became firmly welded to American educational practice.

Although school segregation had been widely practiced in the North, and uniformly practiced in the South, its intimate connection with inferior educational provisions did not become marked until after 1890. Legislatures of the Reconstruction Era treated the two emerging school systems equally. Democratic Redeemers who came into power with promises to treat all alike (see extract on page 91), seemingly were sincere in their efforts to do so until policies of financial retrenchment, a severe economic recession, the rapidly growing school population, and latent racism rendered equal treatment, in their eyes, no longer possible.[7] During the 1890's, many southern states passed laws which disfranchised Negro citizens, and gave local school boards the right to divide state education funds

---

[7] On the matter of emerging educational discrimination, see Horace M. Bond, *The Education of the Negro in the American Social Order* (New York: Octagon Books, Inc., 1966), pp. 203ff. See also Louis R. Harlan, *Separate and Unequal* (New York: Atheneum, 1968), *passim*, and Irving Gershenberg, "The Negro and the Development of White Public Education in the South: Alabama, 1880-1930," *Journal of Negro Education*, XXXIX (Winter, 1970), pp. 50-59.

according to their best judgment. Despite the loss of political power, not all Negroes were passive in the face of this blatant discrimination.

Not only was the idea of equality not given serious consideration between 1890 and World War I, but inequality actually received indirect sanction from the U.S. Supreme Court. The extract from Cumming v. County Board of Education (Georgia, 1899), indicates that at a time when the high school was emerging as part of the American common school system, Negroes might with impunity be denied access to secondary education.

With the question of integration or segregation "settled," interest was again centered on what kind of education was best. Debate on this issue reached a peak of intensity prior to World War I, and polarized around Booker T. Washington and W.E.B. DuBois. Washington's views usually are associated with industrial education leading toward life on the farm or in a trade. DuBois' views usually are associated with liberal, higher education for a "talented tenth" who would enter the professions and assume race leadership. Both men, however, favored higher education as well as industrial education. Both men were concerned with race advancement through education, and with producing leaders for the race. The differences between the two men were not so much differences in educational emphasis, as differences in the broad racial strategy of militancy versus accommodation. There were also elements of political rivalry. Washington was generally supported by northern philanthropy and southern whites. Black editors, educators and other leaders were divided in loyalty between DuBois and Washington and selections from both sides are included. The selections included in this chapter deal with the *kind* of education needed by the Negro and should be read with the understanding that differences over educational issues were only one facet of the total picture.

Although the DuBois-Washington controversy was most directly concerned with race strategy and advancement, it was not totally unrelated to curriculum issues in American education. Some DuBois partisans advocated "classical" education, although DuBois himself favored reducing the study of Latin and Greek and expanding the study of social sciences. At the same time, there were elements in the educational thought of Washington which showed strong kinship to the Progressive movement and its emphasis on the concrete as opposed to the abstract and on the real problems of living rather than problems of the remote past or future. A community service role for schools was a significant element in the thought of both men.

The documents in this chapter are intended to provide insight into the views of Negroes (militant and accommodationist) and whites (northern and southern, moderate and radical) on the major issues in black education between emancipation and World War I. They also indicate the general conditions of Negro education within this period. While Negro education had received general approval and had been the object of intense efforts on a national scope, the early interest it had aroused had died and been replaced by an implicit agreement that it would be left in the hands of southern whites. Racial segregation in schools was apparently accepted. The educational provisions for the two races were far apart in quality. Those individuals favoring industrial rather than academic or professional education for Negroes seemed to be in ascendence. The voice of the black man, divided by differing convictions, diminished by exclusion from political life, and muted by the psychology of accommodationism, could hardly utter an effective nay to all that was happening.

## Application to Teach in the South
### 1864[1]

Dear Sir:

Desirous of assisting in the noble work of elevating and evangelizing our oppressed and long abused race, and of promoting the interests of Christ's spiritual Kingdom on Earth, I make this application to you for an appointment as a Teacher of the Freedmen of the South. I am nearly 25 years of age, in general good health, and of strong powers of endurance. A Plasterer by trade, but during the past year engaged in Rail-Roading. I am unmarried but have the care of a small family, consisting of a widowed mother and a younger brother and Sister who are dependent

---

[1]Robert Harris to Rev. George Whipple, August 26, 1864, in the American Missionary Association Archives, Amistad Research Center, New Orleans, Louisiana. Negro teachers were a small minority in the first waves of teachers, but by World War I they comprised practically the entire teaching force at all levels. The development of teachers was one of the major accomplishments of Negro education during this period. It appears that more of the graduates of the industrial schools and land grant colleges became teachers than went into trades or farming.

on me for support. I respectfully ask you to be as liberal as you can afford in the matter of salary. I wish to engage for Six months, and at first should prefer to be associated with, or located near my brother W. D. Harris, who is now at Portsmouth, Va.

I have had no experience in Teaching except in privately teaching slaves, in the South, where I lived in my youth.

If any more information is needed please advise me.
and oblige,

Your Hum. Servt.

Robert Harris
162 Ohio St.
Cleveland, Ohio

## Negro Missionary Teacher Reports from the South
*1864[2]*

Upon my arrival here, according to your instructions, I reported myself to Prof. Woodberry, requesting him to assign me a field of labor.

Owing to the large number of ladies who accompanied me, he could not locate me immediately but required my assistance in locating the lady teachers, all of whom were to be attended to first. In conjunction with Bro. Bell, I have been engaged in fitting up the various schoolhouses, arranging the schools, and assisting the ladies in canvassing the town and "gathering in" the children who were not attending school. We have met with much success, but find hundreds who are unable to attend from the lack of necessary clothing and shoes. We have, as yet, no adequate means of supplying these demands. . . .

I have assisted in organizing and teaching a night school which is largely attended, and growing in interest.

I am also teaching in the Sunday Schools, both forenoon and afternoon and attend a Bible Class in the evening.

I have had ample opportunities for visiting the various Hospitals for sick and wounded soldiers located in this place. The soldiers manifest much pleasure at our visits and desire us to come frequently.

[2]Robert Harris to George Whipple, November 29 and December 29, 1864. ALS in the American Missionary Association Archives, Amistad Research Center, New Orleans, Louisiana.

I have spent much time visiting among the poor and destitute Freedmen, which has only increased my desire to labor among them, relieving their wants, and teaching them the way of Salvation.

I am now to take charge of a school on the "Providence Farm" about four miles from Norfolk. There is a large field for labor and I pray God that I may be successful in my undertakings.

There is a fine prospect for a large and interesting school as soon as the schoolhouse is properly fitted up. . . .

December 29

I have the honor to report that I am teaching a school at "Providence Church" about four miles South-East of Norfolk. There is no thick settlement, but the colored people live on various farms in the neighborhood at considerable distances from each other. Most of the people are refugees, who fled from their masters on the advance of the Union Armies. They are squatted on different farms, some occupying cabins of their own construction, others living in the negro cabins attached to the Farm houses. The latter are occupied by the Gov't. Superintendents who employ the colored men to raise the crops. The Gov't. furnishes them with rations and pays them wages also. As most of them have large families their pay is inadequate for their wants. They are very poor and need much assistance. They are like children just beginning to walk, and must be assisted until they can walk alone. If the Gov't. pursues a liberal policy towards them they will soon be self-sustaining.

They have never had a school here and regard it a great privilege to be allowed to learn.

They entreat us to continue the school until they are able to sustain it themselves, which they are confident of being able to do, at no very distant day. Owing to their extreme poverty and the lack of accommodations in their houses I have been unable to obtain a boarding house near my school. During the past month I have boarded at the Mission House in Portsmouth, walking out to my school in the morning and returning at night. . . .

I have not been able to visit much among the people in the neighborhood of my school but those I have visited manifest a hearty appreciation of our efforts in their behalf and promise to do everything they can by way of sympathy and cooperation in our work.

One of the men said to me, "The Lord sent you to this place, brother, just the same as he sent Massa Lincoln to *his* place."

Our school is held in the Colored Methodist Church. It was built before the war, but has been sadly abused by the Rebel soldiers. The floor, seats, window sash, and nearly everything combustible were torn up and burned by them, and at one time it was used as a stable for their horses. The Church members intend to refit it as soon as they are able, but they are very poor and get along slowly. They raised enough money to buy the sash and glass, and last week I had them put in. The pupils at first sat on logs but the Gov't. has now furnished us with benches and I hope soon to get some desks, blackboard, and what is most needed of all a good floor. The present floor consists of rough boards, laid down loosely and is but little better than no floor at all. Although in very bad order at present I hope to have it comfortably fitted up "in course of time."

Meanwhile I shall go on trusting in God and hoping for the best.

## Cooperation of Planters Required
*1864*[3]

HEADQUARTERS DEPARTMENT OF THE GULF
New Orleans, June 27, 1864

*To the Provost Marshal of _____ Parish:*

SIR — Representations are made to me that planters, or other persons resident in your parish who are requested to board teachers, unnecessarily decline this accommodation. Where circumstances make it greatly inconvenient, I would not press such request upon any family, but I desire you to notify all persons interested, that it is indispensible to the cultivation of the soil, that schools for colored children shall be maintained. The policy of the Government demands this, and nothing will be allowed to interfere with its success. If persons resist them they will be removed. Unless laborers are assured that the education of their children will be provided for, they become discontented, and will be allowed to remove to parishes where such provisions are made. It is for this reason that I desire you to notify all parties that whenever provision for teachers is

---

[3]Circular in *Report of the Board of Education for Freedmen, Department of the Gulf, for the Year 1864* (New Orleans: Office of the True Delta, 1865), Appendix D. Northern white missionary teachers frequently complained that they were excluded from southern white society and thus had difficulty finding living accommodations. Union army officials aided them even to the point of physical protection when necessary.

required by the Board of Education, it must be accorded, with respectful and courteous reception.

> I have the honor to be,
> With much respect,
> Your obedient servant,
> N. P. BANKS,
> Major General Commanding

# Fisk School Opens
## *1866*[4]

In January, 1866, the Fisk School was established by the American Missionary Association and the Western Freedmen's Aid Commission, for the education of the colored children of Nashville and vicinity, and during the various sessions thus far there has been an average monthly attendance of about eight hundred. During this time the city authorities had no schools established for colored children, and the Fisk School was conducted as one of the great public schools of Nashville. As such it has been remarkably successful.

We have learned with pleasure, through the published reports of the action of the School Board of the city, that two large free schools for colored children are to be opened in September, and that experienced Superintendents have already been appointed. We gladly welcome this action, and cheerfully modify the organization of our work to suit the new order of things.

The Fisk School will accordingly be opened in September as an *Academy and Normal School.*

A systematic and thorough course of study will be established, and the organization and discipline will be modeled after the best institutions of a similar character in the North.

Professor John Ogden will continue in charge as Principal, and will be assisted by a corps of accomplished teachers.

Possessing extensive buildings, well furnished school rooms, and beautiful grounds, and having secured the services of the same teachers

---

[4]"The Fisk School," circular in the American Missionary Association Archives, 1866, Amistad Research Center, New Orleans, Louisiana.

that have made it thus far such a wonderful success, we confidently expect to make this institution meet fully the wants of all who are seeking higher and better advantages than public schools can give. The academic department will be so arranged as to be preparatory for the normal or training school department, and thus especial attention will be given to the work of preparation for teaching.

We offer the advantages of this school to those from all parts of the State, as well as those in Nashville, who are seeking the advantages of a thorough education.

The School year will be divided into three terms and the tuition will be three dollars a term, or one dollar per month, payable in advance.

Those who wish to enter the school next September can give in their names at the office in the school buildings.

We expect to furnish the best facilities for those who attend, and shall limit the number of pupils received if necessary. In behalf of the Societies,

E. M. Cravath, Sec'y.

# The Proper Work of Missionary Teachers
*1866*[5]

Reubin Tomlinson, Esq.
State Superintendent of Education

Dear Sir:

You ask for the name of our informant, in respect to affairs on James Island. I reply, but in strict confidence, that our information was received not from Military Officers, nor from the Webbs, but from one of our most successful teachers, late of your city. It was reported that the ladies conducted the school, mostly, while the young men were devoting their time to other matters. And Miss Parsons, one of the teachers on the Island says, "Mr. Bigelow has some knowledge of medicine and is much with the sick. Mr. Andrews walks daily through the sun to camps one and two miles away, gathering in each place a crowd of eager learners." Now

---

[5]James J. Woolsey to Reubin Tomlinson, April 14, 1866. In Education 1866-77, Free School — Letters, South Carolina Archives Department, Columbia, South Carolina.

we send teachers, not doctors. And Mr. Andrews gathering crowds, at different places, seemed to indicate anything rather than the strict regulations of the school room. The lady teacher from Charleston, was very positive that, the time of the gentlemen was not properly devoted. We wish to know what is truth.

Yours truly,

James J. Woolsey
National Freedmen's Relief Association
New York

# Educational Work of the Freedmen's Bureau
### 1866[6]

SEC. 12.  *And be it further enacted,* That the commissioner shall have power to seize, hold, use, lease, or sell all buildings and tenements, and any lands appertaining to the same, or otherwise, formerly held under color of title by the late so-called confederate states, and not heretofore disposed of by the United States, and any buildings or lands held in trust for the same by any person or persons, and to use the same or appropriate the proceeds derived therefrom to the education of the freed people; and whenever the bureau shall cease to exist, such of said so-called confederate states as shall have made provision for the education of their citizens without distinction of color shall receive the sum remaining unexpended of such sales or rentals, which shall be distributed among said states for educational purposes in proportion to their population.

SEC. 13.  *And be it further enacted,* That the commissioner of this bureau shall at all times co-operate with private benevolent associations of citizens in aid of freedmen, and with agents and teachers, duly accredited and appointed by them, and shall hire or provide by lease buildings for purposes of education whenever such associations shall, without cost to the government, provide suitable teachers and means of instruction; and he shall furnish such protection as may be required for the safe conduct of such schools. . . .

---

[6]U.S. Statutes at Large, Vol. XIV, Chapter CC, p. 176. The act establishing the Bureau of Refugees, Freedmen, and Abandoned Lands did not mention educational functions.

# A Virginia Educator Speaks on Negro Education
## *1867[7]*

2.    I remark that the education of the colored people should be special and peculiar in its character; at least, in the fifteen ex-slave States. By special and peculiar, I do not mean that it should be substantially different from that given to the whites, but that there should be an adaptation in the selection and arrangement of studies and in the methods of instruction to the peculiar character and wants of the people to be educated. They have interesting race-peculiarities which ought to be specially cultivated, and so they have peculiar deficiencies and weaknesses which ought specially to be looked after. The histories of the white and colored races up to a recent period have been so very, very different, and even now their general opportunities and their daily lives are so different, that a moment's reflection ought to convince any one that special treatment is a necessity for bringing the colored people up to the general average. There is not one of you that speaks to a freedman, or addresses a colored audience, that does not practically recognize these principles. And there is not a church or missionary organization that does not recognize them in its plans. This is reason enough, if there were no other, why the races should be taught in separate schools. If the colored children were allowed to go to the white schools they would not have as suitable instruction as in good Schools of their own.

Besides this, I might dwell upon the value of separate schools in cultivating that pride of race, which as I have already said, promotes self-respect, purity of morals and intellectual advancement — a pride which cures the spirit of slavish imitation, which inspires a spirit of independence, and of faith in the ability of the race to create an honorable future for itself. . . .

But it may be asked if this separate education of the colored people is not calculated to unfit them for American citizenship. I think that if the hotch-potch now constituting the nation does not endanger its well being, there need be no fear of allowing the negro presence something distinctive. Have not the Jews in their history demonstrated the harmlessness of race-segregation as well as its power? . . .

3.    It seems plain that the preachers and teachers of the colored race should be raised up from and among its own people. Reasons for this have already been hinted at. And it may be added that there is a sym-

---

[7]W. H. Ruffner, *The Proper Educational Policy For The Colored People* (n.p.: n.p., 1867), pp. 2-4. Pamphlet in The William A. Graham Papers, Southern Historical Collection, Chapel Hill, North Carolina.

pathetic action and reaction between teacher and taught, which is itself an educational power whose highest manifestations can exist only among members of the same race. The late history of missions has demonstrated this fact wonderfully.

These colored teachers should in the first instance, be trained by the best *white* instructors so as to give them the full benefit of the superior civilization. If you want an illustration of just how this ought to be done observe the working of Hampton Normal Institute!

4.    There should of course be institutions like Howard University, where the picked men of the colored race may receive a liberal training. But there cannot be many such institutions wanting for some time to come, because the natural demand of superior education must be small, and it should not be unnaturally stimulated. Apart from the want of preparatory education, there is the more serious lack of that *property basis* on which the cultured vocations must rest. Colored lawyers and doctors, for example, cannot depend on white patronage, and there are very few places where their own people can support them sufficiently to enable them to take rank with those whites who have all the wealth and culture of the white race to build upon. And so with engineering, high grade teaching, mercantile and manufacturing agencies, and everything else that represents wealth and high position.

Hence it would really be unkind in the friends of the colored race to educate a large class in a style that would fit them only for occupations in which but a very small number could hope to succeed.

It is a proverb in social science that the two great sources of power are *knowledge* and *property*. Knowledge must have property as its instrument, and property must have knowledge as its guide. On the basis of these fundamental ideas, I would frame an educational policy for the colored people. We cannot give them property, but we can give them knowledge, and give it in such a form that it will create property; and that too is just what this Hampton school is doing today.

The special object of the colored race at this time should be to *accumulate property*. And this object should pervade every part of its education — for just here we antagonize the master temptation of the race, and of all freedmen. They should be taught that politics and processions, trinkets, hotels, bar-rooms, theatres, railcars, and all that, are of less importance, than *homes of their own*.

As a rule, all must begin with wages and handicraft of some sort; and this is a good way to start life. If the worker is intelligent, honest and skillful, he is sure of a good place and good wages; and may soon begin to save a little every month. Presently, there will be a little capital for investment in trade, tools, or realty. And from such beginnings often grow competence, and even wealth by middle life.

## Zeal for Learning among Freedmen
*1868*[8]

Dear Brethren and Sisters;

It is Christmas day here in Batesville the great holiday of the year for both white and black or rather, the beginning of a series of holidays which lasts until after New Years. I do not teach today as I could not with impunity deprive any Southern person white or black of their Christmas. So I amuse myself by listening to the firing of cannon and guns and of watching the bright faces of the children as they display to one another their Christmas gifts.

Since I last wrote I have commenced my school and have now been teaching just four weeks. Everything was finally arranged so that on Monday Nov. 30th I opened school with twenty-five scholars. Since then the number has been steadily increasing and now it numbers forty-two with a prospect of large additions after their great holiday Christmas week is past.

From all the accounts of Freedmen's schools which I had heard and read previous to coming here I expected to find them anxious to learn but after all, I confess I was unprepared for the amount of zeal manifested by most of them for an education. I can say as one did of old, "The half had not been told me." I am surprised each day by some new proof of their anxiety to learn.

Nearly all ages, colors, conditions and capacities are represented in my school. Ages ranging from five to sixty-five; Colors from jet-black with tight curling hair to pale brunette with waving brown hair.

Some, a few of them could read quite readily in a second reader and many more knew the alphabet and were trying patiently to spell out short easy words, while by far the greater number could not distinguish a letter. I have had as many as nineteen in my alphabet class at one time but it is now reduced to four.

---

[8]Pamelia A. Hand to the Church at _____, Batesville, Arkansas, December 25, 1868, in American Missionary Association Archives, Amistad Research Center, New Orleans, Louisiana. The omission of a church name as addressee is due to the fact that the letter was intended as a circular letter to be forwarded by the Association to several churches which contributed to Miss Hand's work.

One old woman over sixty after spending three weeks on the alphabet and finally conquering it, said she wanted to learn to spell Jesus first before spelling short easy words for said she, "Pears like I can learn the rest easier if I get that blessed name learned first." So now she looks through the Bible for that name and has learned to distinguish it at sight from other words. The older members of the school are as quiet and orderly as I could desire but the children are not so very different from other children. They love mischief and play and the prevailing vice among them is deceit. But education has all the charm of novelty to them and they learn with astonishing rapidity. They come to school as well provided with books as children usually do.

The Sabbath School has increased in numbers very much since I came and now scarcely a scholar comes who cannot repeat at least one Bible verse correctly. Some little S. S. papers that were donated for me to bring please them wonderfully and they are sure to contrive some way to learn their contents. Thus far I have been unmolested in my work here by enemies and have received the cordial co-operation of my friends — the union people here. I feel that I have abundant reason to "thank God and take courage." I feel that I need as much as ever God's blessing on my labors and to this end I ask the prayers of Christians in my behalf. Also letters from pastor or people would be gratefully received.

Your Sister in Christ

Pamelia A. Hand.

# Rules of Fisk University
## *1868*[9]

In order to aid students in the proper division of their time, and the right employment of their energies, the following *Rules and Regulations* have been adopted. All students, therefore, on entering the Institution, are expected to acquaint themselves with them.

I.   To attend promptly and cheerfully all the prescribed exercises of the Institution, unless for good and sufficient reasons excused.

II.   To observe neatness and order, both in person and in the arrangement of books, desks and other furniture, in and about their private rooms, the school-room, and on the grounds.

---

[9]Rules and Regulations of the Fisk University, April 4, 1868. Circular in the American Missionary Association Archives, Amistad Research Center, New Orleans, Louisiana.

III.    To rise promptly at the ringing of the *first bell*; and to observe quiet and good order in their private rooms, in the schoolrooms and on the school-grounds during hours of study.

IV.    To retire at or before ten o'clock at night; and to see that all lights in their rooms are extinguished, and fires properly secured *before* retiring.

V.    Students boarding on the grounds will not leave them on any occasion without the knowledge and consent of the Principal, or some authorized person.

VI.    They are expected to attend Chapel service every morning, Wednesday afternoon lecture and regular services on the Sabbath at the Chapel of the University.

VII.    Students are not allowed to visit each other's rooms during hours of study, or after nine o'clock at night, nor to be absent from their rooms after that time.

VIII.    Ladies and Gentlemen are not allowed to visit each other, strangers or friends, under any circumstances, at their private rooms. All interviews must be public and in presence of a Teacher.

IX.    The use of ardent spirits, tobacco in any form, and all games of chance are strictly forbidden, at all times and in all places, while connected with the Institution.

X.    Students are expected to abstain at all times and in all places, from profane, indecent or indecorous language or allusions, to be kind, courteous and polite to one another and to strangers, and respectful and obedient to instructors.

XI.    To prevent losses and needless expenditures, all Students boarding on the grounds, on entering the Institution, are required to deposit all their money with the Treasurer who will give them a receipt, and to draw upon him as they may have need.


# Self-Help in Education
## *1868–72*


The colored people of this place own a large piece of land . . . and are doing everything in their power to collect money enough to erect a building to be used as a church and school house; but most of them are poor and it takes a great while to get a little money together.[10]

---

[10]H.C. Bullart to E.P. Smith, Raymond, Mississippi, January 23, 1868. ALS in American Missionary Association Archives, Amistad Research Center, New Orleans, Louisiana.

I am sure, if the story of the erection of all these school-houses, the payment of tuition, the purchase of books, and the exertions made to clothe children for attendance, could all be told, it would be found that out of their deep poverty these people have done well and even nobly.[11]

They have built houses when necessary, and spared their children from the duties of the field when it was well known that it would diminish their means of subsistence, and increase their personal labor.[12]

Slavery entailed not only ignorance but self-distrust. It broke a man's confidence in his own abilities. And the only way to restore this confidence is to put the man in the harness, start him in the right direction, and thus demonstrate that he is equal to the load. When new schools have been organized, people have been called together and a board of trustees has been chosen of the most intelligent men among them who shall have entire management of the school. . . . This system has been adopted to give the freedmen confidence and accustom them to manage their schools and do it properly.[13]

## Segregation Required in West Virginia
### *1870*[14]

White and colored persons shall not be taught in the same school; but to afford to colored children, as far as practicable, the benefits of a free school education, it shall be the duty of the trustees of every school district to establish therein one or more primary schools for colored persons between the ages of six and twenty-one years whenever the number of such persons residing therein, and between the ages as aforesaid, exceeds fifteen, according to the enumeration made for school purposes.

---

[11]The full story of black self-help in education is untold. The details lie buried in brief scattered references such as the four given here. Superintendent John Kimball as quoted in J.W. Alvord, *Seventh Semi-Annual Report on Schools for Freedmen* (Washington: Government Printing Office, 1870), p. 13.

[12]*Annual Report of the Superintendent of Public Instruction of the State of Mississippi for the Year Ending December 31, 1872*, p. 151.

[13]Superintendent T.K. Noble as quoted in J.W. Alvord, *Sixth Semi-Annual Report on Schools for Freedmen* (Washington: Government Printing Office, 1868), p. 51.

[14]West Virginia Code, 1870, Chapter 45, Section 19, p. 294.

# Ohio Court Upholds School Segregation
## *1871*[15]

The plaintiff is a colored citizen having three children, and resides in school subdistrict number nine in the township of Norwich, Franklin county, Ohio. . . .

The township board of education has formed a joint district, within the limits of the two districts, for the education of colored children, as provided by law. They have erected a school house, and established a school in the joint district for the education of colored children, which school affords to such children all the advantages and privileges of a common school, equal to those of the school for white children, in subdistrict number nine. . . .

During all the time the plaintiff insisted on having his children instructed in subdistrict number nine, in the school established for white children, an equally good school was open for them in the joint district established for colored children, as provided by law, where they could enjoy the full advantages and privileges of a public common school. . . .

It is quite apparent from this state of the case, that the proceeding is brought, not because the children of the plaintiff are excluded from the public schools, but to test the right of those having charge of them to make a classification of scholars on the basis of color. This is the principal question in the case, and we propose to consider it without reference to the question made as to the proper parties to the proceeding, for, in the view we take of the case, this becomes unnecessary. . . .

We have seen that the law, in the case before us, works no substantial inequality of school privileges between the children of both classes in the locality of the parties. Under the lawful regulation of equal educational privileges, the children of each class are required to attend the school provided for them, and to which they are assigned by those having the lawful official control of all. The plaintiff, then, cannot claim that his privileges are abridged on the ground of inequality of school advantages for his children. Nor can he dictate where his children shall be instructed, or what teacher shall perform that office, without obtaining privileges not enjoyed by white citizens. Equality of rights does not involve the necessity of educating white and colored persons in the same school, any more than it does that of educating children of both sexes in the

---

[15]The State ex rel. Garnes v. McCann, et al., 21 Ohio 198 (December, 1871).

same school, or that different grades of scholars must be kept in the same school. Any classification which preserves substantially equal school advantages is not prohibited by either the state or federal constitution, nor would it contravene the provisions of either. There is, then, no ground upon which the plaintiff can claim that his rights under the fourteenth amendment have been infringed.


## Integration in South Carolina
### *1873*[16]


Prof. N. F. Walker
Supt. of the South Carolina Institution for the
Education of the Deaf and Dumb, and the Blind
Cedar Springs, S. C.

Dear Sir:

I wish in behalf of the Board of Commissioners of the Deaf and Dumb, and the Blind, to state that the following points relative to the admission of Colored pupils into the Institutions now under your supervision, will be strictly and rigidly insisted upon:

1. Colored pupils must not only be admitted into the Institution, on application, but an earnest and faithful effort must be made to induce such pupils to apply for admission.
2. Such pupils, when admitted, must be domiciled in the same buildings, must eat at the same table, must be taught in the same class rooms, and by the same teachers, and must receive the same attention, care, and consideration as white pupils.

Respectfully,

J. K. Jillson
Sec., Board of Commissioners
Deaf and Dumb, and the Blind.

---

[16]Superintendent of Education Letterbook #13, 1873, pp. 164, 165, South Carolina Archives Department, Columbia, South Carolina. This represents an attempt to enforce South Carolina school law which required that public schools be open to all citizens. No significant racial mixing occurred in the day schools; the above special school closed as a result of Jillson's order. Similar results occurred in Louisiana, the only other Southern state with a school law requiring public schools to make no racial distinction.

## Optional Segregation in Wyoming
*1873*[17]

Where there are fifteen or more colored children within any school district, the board of directors thereof, with the approval of the county superintendent of schools, may provide a separate school for the instruction of such colored children.

## Kentucky Provides for Negro Schools
*1874*[18]

Be it enacted by the General Assembly of the Commonwealth of Kentucky:

1.   That there shall be a uniform system of common schools for the education of the colored children of this commonwealth.
2.   That the school fund for this purpose shall be known as the colored school fund, and shall consist of the following provisions, viz:

1.   The present annual revenue tax of twenty-five cents, and twenty cents in addition, on each one hundred dollars in value of the taxable property owned or held by colored persons, which tax shall be devoted to no other purpose whatever.
2.   A capitation tax of one dollar on each male colored person above the age of twenty-one years.
3.   All taxes levied and collected on dogs owned or kept by colored persons.
4.   All State taxes on deeds, suits, or on any license, collected from colored persons.

---

[17]Compiled Laws of Wyoming, 1876, Chapter 103, Section 34, p. 532. Approved December 12, 1873.

[18]Kentucky Laws, 1873-74, Chapter 521, pp. 63-66. Kentucky first passed a law in 1866 setting aside taxes paid by Negroes for the support of separate Negro schools. Laws of this kind were much discussed but seldom enacted. Except for the added ingredient of racial prejudice, they reflected an attitude much like that of northern opponents of public schools in the 1830's and 1840's who felt it illegal to take one man's money to educate another man's children. Laws permitting local school authorities to apportion the state education fund as they pleased were passed in the 1890's and achieved the same results.

5.    All the fines, penalties, and forfeitures imposed upon and collected from colored persons due to the State, except the amount thereof allowed by law to attorneys for the Commonwealth.

6.    All sums of money hereafter received by this Commonwealth under or by virtue of an act of the Congress of the United States distributing public lands, or the proceeds of the sales thereof: *Provided,* the pro rata share to each colored pupil child shall not exceed, in any one year, the apportionment made to each white pupil child of this Commonwealth.

7.    All sums arising from any donation, gift, grant, or device, by any person whatsoever, wherein the intent is expressed that the same is designed to aid in the education of the colored children of this Commonwealth, or of any county or school district therein. . . .

14.    That applicants to teach the schools provided for in this act shall obtain certificates in the same manner as now provided by law for applicants to teach white schools, except that the examination may not be extended beyond spelling, reading, writing, and common arithmetic; . . .

18.    No school-house erected for a colored school shall be located nearer than one mile of a school-house erected for white children, except in cities and towns, where it shall not be nearer than six hundred feet.

## Effect of Mixed Schools Debate on Southern Education
### *1874*[19]

To form a correct general estimate of the state of education in the South, it will be necessary to keep steadily in view the fact that, while popular sentiment is, on the whole, favorable to public schools, the preponderance is so slight that it would require but a little change to turn the scale. Only about one third of the population are decidedly friendly to free schools; about one third are, at heart, as decidedly opposed to

---

[19][Barnas Sears], "Education," *Atlantic Monthly,* XXXIV (September, 1874), pp. 381, 382. Sears was General Agent of the Peabody Education Fund from 1867 to 1880. Authorship is established by Barnas Sears to Robert C. Winthrop, September 17, 1874, in The J.L.M. Curry Papers, Library of Congress.

them. The remaining third are indifferent or passive, and will be influenced and governed by the dominant party. The first class are now in the ascendency. They owe their success not so much to their numbers as to their enterprising character. They are the more hopeful, energetic, and progressive portion of the community. The consciousness that they have the civilized world with its philosophy and literature on their side, increases their natural courage and enables them to inspire hope in others. . . .

At no time since the war has the party of progress been in so critical a condition as it has been since the agitation of the question of "mixed schools" in Congress. Even the shadow of coming events has had a disastrous influence. In two or three States contracts with mechanics for school-houses, and with teachers for opening schools, were immediately suspended; and the highest and best school officers of the State, seeing that their fondest expectations were likely to be blasted, were looking around for other more hopeful spheres of labor. Already an amount of mischief has been done which it will take years to repair. Confidence has been shaken; and men who stood firm before have become despondent, and are retiring from the field.

Upon no part of the community would the threatened calamity fall so heavily as upon the colored people. Others can without any personal sacrifice return to the old system of private schools. Having none but their own children to provide for, they would be relieved of the great expense of maintaining schools for the blacks. These, on the other hand, would in most places be left completely destitute of schools. Southern charity will be dried up if the Negro is made the instrument of breaking up the existing systems of public instruction. Northern contributions have nearly ceased long ago. Religious societies which have founded theological schools will have enough to do to educate ministers, without undertaking to educate the immense body of the colored people. The latter have neither the funds nor the intelligence necessary to carry on the work successfully. Nothing but public schools maintained, organized, and controlled by the State can meet their wants.

Let us look at this question in the light of their interest simply. What advantages of education have they now in fact, or in law? The same that white people have. If there is, in certain localities, any difference, it is purely accidental and temporary; and is quite as often to the prejudice of the white children as of the colored. The laws in all the States require the same provision to be made for both. Nor can any distinction be safely made in administering them. The colored people are of sufficient importance in every State to make it unsafe for men in authority to abuse their power. From the very nature of the case, the State governments must, in the end, adopt and carry out the same rule for both races. This grand provision for the education of the whole colored population, chiefly at the expense of others, is secure as long as the present school systems shall be preserved. But let them be disturbed by any unhappy excitement, and the disaffected will seize upon the opportunity to abolish the public schools and to return to their favorite plan of private schools, each man paying what he pleases for the education of his children. The colored children will, of course, be left to grow up as ignorant as the brutes. We will not speak of the political bearings of the subject, except to say that any measure, no matter how plausible in theory, which shall in fact take the light of knowledge from the Negroes of the South, will come with an ill grace from those who have given them the boon of liberty.

## Civil Rights Bill Withdrawn
### *1874*[20]

MR. BUTLER, of Massachusetts . . .

. . . But there are reasons why I think this question of mixed schools should be very carefully considered. The Negroes, children as well as parents, have never, till the last few years, had any opportunity for education. It is to them the greatest boon on earth. It is to them the manna from heaven. They seek it as eagerly as did the Israelites seek the good gift of God which fed them from the clouds. Therefore, in Negro schools which I established as military commander during the war I found that while I had plenty of schoolboys with "shining morning faces," there were none "creeping unwillingly to school." They sprang to the school as to a feast; their advancement and acquirements were wonderful. And I shall move to recommit this bill, among other reasons, because I want time to consider whether upon the whole it is just to the Negro children to put them into mixed schools, where, being in the same classes with the white children, they may be kept back by their white confreres, and not get on in learning as fast as they otherwise would.

[20]*Congressional Record*, 43rd Congress, 1st Session, Vol. II, Part I, 1874, pp. 456, 457. The mixed schools provision of Butler's civil rights bill was the target of much opposition. Withdrawal of the bill was due in part at least to Barnas Sears, General Agent of the Peabody Education Fund, whose views were presented in the preceeding selection.

I do not think there will be any difference in the races in the next generation. There may be unwilling colored school-boys then as there are unwilling white school-boys now in my own State. I do not mean that white boys in Kentucky are different from white boys in Massachusetts. In Massachusetts we have truant-commissioners, who go round to see that our children go to school, because the schools are an everyday task to them — but for the colored child there is no need of any commissioner, and for this generation there never will be. And, therefore, I am quite content to consider this question in the light of what on the whole is best for the white and the colored child before the matter is again before the House. . . .

## Opposition to Mixed Schools Answered
### 1874[21]

The special committee of the trustees of the Peabody School Fund are of opinion that the Civil Rights Bill would destroy the public-school system in the Southern States. Senator SCHURZ has expressed the same opinion in a speech in St. Louis. It is, in fact, the only serious argument that has been urged against the bill. The plea is that the white citizens of the Southern States will not consent to mixed schools, and that wherever they control legislation they will lay no tax for the support of schools, or if they can not do that, they will refuse to allow their children to attend. . . . Moreover, it is asserted by the opponents of the bill that equal rights do not demand mixed schools, but only schools of equal excellence. This last suggestion is puerile. Every man of common-sense knows that in a community where color prejudice is so strong as to abandon the whole school system rather than to provide for schools in common, schools of equal excellence are simply impossible. . . .

But while the Peabody committee and others make the assertion, what is the fact? Has the experiment been tried? and how did it work? MR. THOMAS W. CONWAY, Superintendent of Education in Louisiana from 1868 to 1872, has answered this question. The Louisiana constitution of 1868 required that the public schools should be opened to black and white alike. The usual clamor was raised. The ruin of the

---

[21]"Theory and Practice," *Harper's Weekly*, XVIII, 933 (November 14, 1874), p. 930.

school system was foretold as it is now. The opposition was rancorous and intense. . . . At first some of the white children were kept away by their parents, for there was no antagonism among the children themselves; but very soon they returned, and "the year actually closed with a larger number of white pupils in the schools than ever before." . . .

All this seems to us to be very much more to the point than speculations at a distance upon the force or the probable consequences of a prejudice. That the prejudice exists, like the prejudice against the Irish, against Hebrews, against Roman Catholics, is very true; but if Congress, because of prejudice, should deliberately sanction the doctrine that there might be caste and classes among the citizens of the United States, the government would have ceased to be one of equal laws. . . .

## Racial Segregation and the Common School Idea
### *1874*[22]

A common school should be one to which all citizens send their children, not by favor, but by right. It is established and supported by the Government; its criterion is a public foundation; and one citizen has as rightful claim upon its privileges and advantages as any other . . . Schools which tend to separate the children of the country in their feelings, aspirations and purposes, which foster and perpetuate sentiments of caste, hatred, and ill-will, which breed a sense of degradation on the one part and of superiority on the other, which beget clannish notions rather than teach and impress an omnipresent and living principle and faith that we are all Americans, in no wise realize our ideal of common schools, while they are contrary to the spirit of our laws and institutions.

Two separate school systems, tolerating discriminations in favor of one class against another, inflating on the one part, degrading on the other; two separate school systems, I say, tolerating such state of feeling and sentiment on the part of the classes instructed respectively in accor-

---

[22]John Mercer Langston, "Equality Before the Law," in Carter G. Woodson, *Negro Orators and Their Orations* (Washington: Associated Publishers, 1925), p. 446. The speech was delivered at Oberlin, Ohio, May 17, 1874. Note that whereas most polemic material on segregation stressed the effect upon blacks, Langston gave attention to its effect upon whites as well. This strand of thought has continued in the literature, although always in a minor key.

dance therewith, cannot educate these classes to live harmoniously together, meeting the responsibilities and discharging the duties imposed by a common government in the interest of a common country.

The object of the common school is two-fold. In the first place it should bring to every pupil, especially the poor child, a reasonable degree of elementary education. In the second place, it should furnish a common education, one similar and equal to all pupils attending it. Thus furnished, our sons enter upon business or professional walks with an equal start in life. Such education the Government owes to all classes of the people.


## Argument in Favor of Mixed Schools
### *1874*[23]


The public school is an epitome of life, and in it children are taught, so that they understand those relations and conditions of life which, if not acquired in childhood and youth, are not likely afterward to be gained. To say, as is the construction placed upon so much of this bill as I propose to strike out, that equal facilities shall be given in different schools, is to rob your system of public instruction of that quality by which our people, without regard to race or color, shall be assimilated in ideas, personal, political, and public, so that when they arrive at the period of manhood they shall act together upon public questions with ideas formed under the same influences and directed to the same general results; and therefore, I say, if it were possible, as in the large cities it is possible, to establish separate schools for black children and for white children, it is in the highest degree inexpedient to either establish or tolerate such schools.

The theory of human equality cannot be taught in families, taking into account the different conditions of the different members and the families composing human society; but in the public school, where children of all classes and conditions are brought together, this doctrine of human equality can be taught, and it is the chief means of securing the perpetuity of republican institutions. And inasmuch as we have in this country four million colored people, I assume that it is a public duty

---

[23]Speech of George Boutwell of Massachusetts. *Congressional Record*, Forty-third Congress, First Session, Vol. II, Part I, May 21, 1874, p. 4116.

that they and the white people of the country, with whom they are to be associated in political and public affairs, shall be assimilated and made one in the fundamental idea of human equality. Therefore, where it would be possible to establish distinct schools, I am against it as a matter of public policy.

But throughout the larger part of the South it is not possible to establish separate schools for black children and for white children, that will furnish means of education suited to the wants of either class; and therefore in all that region of the country it is a necessity that the schools shall be mixed, in order that they shall be of sufficient size to make them useful in the highest degree; and it is also important that they should be mixed schools in order that, when the prejudice which now pervades portions of our people shall be rooted out by the power of general taxation, they will be able to accumulate in every district those educational forces by which the public schools shall be made useful to the highest degree for which there is capacity in the public will with the power of general taxation.

## Self-Help in North Carolina
### *1875*[24]

Sir, I write you for information about Peabody Schools. The colored people here have organized themselves as an educational Association to receive some of the funds from Peabody. They have agreed to pay $5.00 apiece for that purpose. The School commenced Sept. 1, 1875, and is to continue 10 months as the law directs in that case, but there seems to be a dispute as to who is eligible to attend school. There are about 15 or 20 grown persons who want to be seated as Scholars. They claim that there is no restriction in regards to Adults, and furthermore, they say that they haven't any children to send. Therefore they think that they are entitled to the benefits of their money.

---

[24]J. S. Murphy to S. D. Pool, September 28, 1875, in North Carolina Department of Archives and History, Raleigh. The Peabody Education Fund, in order to stimulate establishment of public schools, offered to provide about one-fourth of the expense of a school if local citizens would raise the remainder. The strategy of the Fund was to develop an acceptance of the idea of free schools and a willingness to be taxed for their support. Both Negro and white schools were aided.

Please inform me forthwith whether they can be entitled to the benefits of their money or not, in such schools.

By so doing you will confer a favor.

I am Sin. Your Obt. Servt.

J. S. Murphy

## Negro Congressman Urges Mixed Schools
*1875*[25]

If it were true that the passage of this bill with the school clause in it would tolerate the existence of none but a system of mixed free schools, then I would question very seriously the propriety of retaining such a clause; but such is not the case . . . It simply confers upon all citizens . . . the right . . . to send their children to any public free school that is supported in whole or in part by taxation, the exercise of the right to remain a matter of option as it now is — nothing compulsory about it.

My opinion is that the passage of this bill . . . will bring about mixed schools practically only in localities where one or the other of the two races are large in numbers, and that localities where both races are large in numbers separate schools and separate institutions of learning will continue to exist, for a number of years at least.

It is just as wrong and just as contrary to republicanism to provide by law for the education of children who may be identified with a certain race in separate schools to themselves, as to provide by law for the education of children who may be identified with a certain religious denomination in separate schools to themselves.

The colored people in asking the passage of this bill just as it passed the Senate do not thereby admit that their children can be better educated in white than in colored schools; nor that white teachers because they are white are better qualified to teach than colored ones. . . . Let us confer upon all citizens, then, the rights to which they are entitled under the Constitutions; and then if they choose to have their children educated in separate schools, as they do in my own state, then both races will be

---

[25]John R. Lynch, speech on the Civil Rights Bill of 1875, *Congressional Record*, Vol. III, Part II, Forty-third Congress, Second Session, pp. 943-47. Lynch was a representative from Mississippi from 1873-1883.

satisfied, because they will know that the separation is their own voluntary act and not legislative compulsion.

## Negro Congressman Equivocates on Mixed Schools
### *1875*[26]

MR. WHITE.    I now yield five minutes to the gentleman from South Carolina.

MR. CAIN.    Mr. Speaker, in the discussion of this question of the civil-rights bill, it has become a question of interest to the country how the colored people feel on the question of the schools. I believe, sir, that there is no part of this bill so important as the school clause. The education of the masses is to my mind of vital moment to the welfare, the peace, the safety, and the good government of the Republic. Every enlightened nation regards the development of the minds of the masses as of vital importance. How are you going to elevate this large mass of people? What is the means to be employed? Is it not the development of their minds, the molding and fashioning of their intellects, lifting them up from intellectual degradation by information, by instruction? I know of no other means so well adapted to the development of a nation as education.

Especially is this true in the Southern States of this Union, where the great cry against the colored people is their ignorance. Admit it, sir, and it is a lamentable fact that the past laws and customs and habits and interests of the Southern States have prevented the colored people from attaining that education which otherwise they would gladly have attained. I was a part and parcel of the system of slavery to prevent education; for the moment you remove ignorance and develop the minds of those who are enslaved the less likely they are to remain contentedly in servitude. For this reason it was the policy of the South to keep in ignorance that part of the community that they controlled for their benefit as their slaves. Now that there is a change throughout the land, now that these

---

[26]*Congressional Record*, Forty-third Congress, Second Session, 1875, Vol. III, Part II, pp. 981, 982. Richard H. Cain represented South Carolina in the House of Representatives from 1873-1879. Although he had a role in forming South Carolina's school law which required public schools to be open to all citizens without racial distinction, the equivocation found in this speech made it possible for opponents of mixed schools to say that Negroes themselves preferred segregation.

millions formerly enslaved are free, it is essential to the welfare of the nation that they should be educated.

But the question arises in the discussion of this bill, how and where are you to do this work? As a republican, and for the sake of the welfare of the republican party, I am willing, if we cannot rally our friends to those higher conceptions entertained by Mr. Summer — if we cannot bring up the republican party to that high standard with regard to the rights of man as seen by those who laid the foundation of this Government — then I am willing to agree to a compromise. If the school clause is objectionable to our friends, and they think they cannot sustain it, then let it be struck out entirely. We want no invidious discrimination in the laws of this country. Either give us that provision in its entirety or else leave it out altogether, and thus settle the question.

I believe the time is coming when the good sense of the people of this country, democrats as well as republicans, will recognize the necessity of educating the masses. The more the people are educated the better citizens they make. If you would have peace, if you would have quiet, if you would have good will, educate the masses of the community. Objection is made to the ignorance of the colored people, and the State of South Carolina is cited as an illustration of that ignorance operating in legislation. Why, sir, if it be true that the legislators of South Carolina are to some extent ignorant, I answer that it is not their fault; the blame lies at somebody else's door.

Now, sir, let the democracy, instead of reproaching us with our ignorance, establish schools; let them guarantee to us schoolhouses in all the hamlets of the country; let them not burn them down, but build them up; let them not hang the teachers, but encourage and protect them; and then we shall have a great change in this country.

Sir, we must be educated. It is education that makes a people great. We are a part and parcel of this great nation, and are called upon to assume the responsibility of citizenship. We must have the appliances that make other people great. We must have the schoolhouses and every appliance of education. If your objection is to guaranteeing to us in the civil-rights bill an equal enjoyment of school privileges, then I say surround us with all the other appliances; say nothing of the school-house if you choose, but enforce our rights under the law of the country, and we shall be enabled to exercise every other privilege in the community.

MR. GUNKEL.    Let me ask the gentleman from South Carolina whether the colored people of the South want mixed schools.

MR. CAIN.    So far as my experience is concerned I do not believe they do. In South Carolina, where we control the whole school system, we have not a mixed school except the State College. In localities where whites are in the majority, they have two white trustees and one colored.

MR. COBB, of Kansas. I desire to ask the gentleman what in his opinion will be the effect of the passage of the Senate civil-rights bill so far as regards the public-school system of the South.

MR. CAIN. I believe that if the Congress of the United States will pass it and make it obligatory upon all the people to obey it and compel them to obey it, there will be no trouble at all.

MR. KELLOGG. Would the gentleman prefer to retain the provision in regard to schools which I have moved to strike out in the House bill, or would he rather have that provision struck out according to my amendment.

MR. CAIN. I agree to accept it.

MR. KELLOGG. I offered it in the interest of your people as well as ours.

MR. HYNES. Let me ask the gentleman a question, whether from his knowledge of the white and black people of the South does he not believe in every State controlled by the democratic party they would not abolish the school system rather than permit mixed schools? In other words, Mr. Speaker —

MR. COX. Let me answer.

MR. HYNES. I did not understand my friend to my left was from South Carolina. I ask my friend from South Carolina whether he does not believe that the prejudice against mixed schools in the South is not stronger in the minds of the white people there than their love for the public school system?

MR. CAIN. I do not know; I cannot judge of the democracy.

MR. WHITE. I have allowed the gentleman to run beyond the time given to him, and I must now take the floor.

MR. KELLOGG. O, let him go on without interruption.

MR. WHITE. It cannot be done, as I will have no time left to myself.

MR. CAIN. One word in conclusion. I think I have answered all questions put to me. But I say this, if we pass this bill, make it satisfactory. I know we are in the minority in this country — I speak of course of the colored people. We are willing to accept anything which is deemed necessary to the welfare of the country. Spare us our liberties; give us peace! give us a chance to live; give us an honest chance in the face of life; place no obstruction in our way; oppress us not; give us an equal chance, and we ask no more of the American people.

## Democratic Political Promises
*1876*[27]


. . . I will guarantee to colored people as well as white that the right
of person and property will be better protected all over the country than
it has for the last four years. My friends, if we are elected we mean to
take our places and serve faithfully the whole people, irrespective of
color, and as near as we know, we mean to do what is just and fair to all.
We mean to try to give you better levees and better schools, and better
prosperity and a happier country.


## Methods of Instruction, Wilberforce University
*1876*[28]


In the Classical and Mathematical Department, are the same as generally
obtained in American colleges.

In the Normal, we have the methods of Oswego. In the practicing
schools of the Normal Department there is nothing peculiar but our
manner of teaching Orthography and Orthoepy; here we employ analysis,
that is to say, immediately after a pupil has spelled a word, he is required
to tell how many letters, how many vowels, and how many consonants it
contains, then to give the quality and quantity of every vowel, and to
distinguish the characteristics of the sub-vocals and the aspirates.

We deem this the best method of teaching the art of spelling, because
it is the most thorough; and also because, when the principle is continually
applied and the habit is formed, in subsequent life the individual will be
satisfied with nothing short of a thorough knowledge of *any object* which
he may take to scrutinize; or any subject he may begin to investigate.

---

[27]"Notes for a speech to Colored and White in favor of Democratic Candidates,"
in Albert A. Batchelor Papers, Sept.-Oct., 1876, Department of Archives and Manuscripts, Louisiana State University. Apparently the kind of assurance found in this
campaign promise was fairly typical of the appeal made by the native Democratic
Redeemers as they sought the Negro vote to aid them in ending Republican rule.
Democrats returned to power and Reconstruction ended in Louisiana in 1877.

[28]David Smith, *Biography of Rev. David Smith* (Xenia, Ohio: Xenia Gazette
Office, 1881), pp. 120-21.

In our Theological Department, we employ both the inductive and deductive methods, allowing the largest liberty of investigation and of expression; excepting that which borders upon impiety and blasphemy. Our aim is to make Christian scholars, not mere book-worms, but workers, *educated workers* with God for man — to effect which we employ not the Classics and Mathematics only, but Science and Philosophy; also, the former for their discriminating, polishing and cultivating influences, the latter for the quickness and exactness which they impart to the cognitive faculty, and the seed thoughts which they never fail to sow in the mind. And yet we hold that the Classics and Mathematics, as Science and Philosophy, can and must be consecrated to human well-being by the teachings, the sentiments, and the spirit of Jesus.

## Racist Argues Against Public Education
### *1876*[29]

Further, I must premise that I am the friend of the Negro, but a friend to him in his proper place of subordination; a far better friend than those who inflate him with ideas of his importance, which will only lead him to his ruin. Born and bred on a plantation of Negroes, the owner of slaves until robbed of by property under the forms of law, I have always entertained the most kindly feelings towards them, which I still cherish whenever in their speech and conduct they acknowledge their true position, a thing — so strong in them is the instinct of inferiority — they never fail to do, except in the very few cases in which their brains have been addled by the miserable teachings of a fanatical philanthropy. Having observed all my life I well understand the peculiar qualities of the race, and they are exactly such as fit them for menial offices and subordinate positions, and of necessity disqualify them for the higher walks of life, and particularly for the great functions of citizenship. . . .

The public school system recognizes the doctrine of Negro equality, and professes to prepare him for the highest functions of life, the duties

---

[29]Civis [Bennett Puryear], *The Public School In Its Relations To The Negro* (Richmond: Clemmitt and Jones, Steam Printers, 1877), pp. 4, 16, 17, 19, 25, 26. Reprinted from *The Southern Planter and Farmer*.

of political sovereignty. If he is, by congenital inferiority, not competent to such functions, the attempt to prepare him for them is a manifest absurdity. If he is competent to such functions, then inferiority does not belong to his race. Having shown, in former articles before referred to, that the public school, even without reference to the question of races, is utterly indefensible, both as a matter of morals and of policy, I oppose it in its application to the Negro race: —

1.   Because it is an assertion, in the most dangerous form, of the hideous doctrine of Negro equality. How this blasphemous heresy seeks the amalgamation of the races as its culmination, was clearly shown in our last article. I cannot dwell on this topic; it is too revolting, it is too disgusting for contemplation.

2.   I oppose it because its policy is cruelty in the extreme to the Negro himself. It instills into his mind that he is competent to shine in the higher walks of life, prompts him to despise those menial pursuits to which his race has been doomed, and invites him to enter into competition with the white man for those tempting prizes that can be won only by a quicker and profounder sagacity, by a greater energy and self-denial, and a higher order of administrative talent than the Negro has ever displayed. . . .

3.   I oppose the public school, because it brings paralysis to our industrial pursuits. We are poor to the point of derision; yet exhaustless wealth lies hidden in our soil. Broad acres of deep alluvium, which would yield to honest toil some sixty and some an hundred fold, lie untilled, and only serve to poison the atmosphere with mephitic exhalations. The utilization of our natural resources is our only pathway to prosperity. The great need of this Commonwealth is labor — labor that can be relied on and controlled. Work, work, work is our salvation. And yet, instead of encouraging labor, our legislation puts it as much as possible under ban. . . .

That individual Negroes may be stimulated by the system into a mechanical familiarity with the elements of education, so-called, no more settles the question of the capacity of the race than the fructification of a tropical plant in a hot-house proves that it can stand the rigors of our climate and may be made to entrench itself permanently and profitably in our soil. But if the Negro, moved by his own instincts, stimulated by his own aspirations, make good, in his own way, by his own strength, and at his own expense, his fitness for citizenship, then the question is put beyond cavil, and the doctrine of Negro equality is settled affirmatively and forever. If, under the circumstances indicated, he should fail, however, to make good his claim, then it would as clearly appear that he is congenitally an inferior, and that his proper position is menial and subordinate. We are guilty, then, of the supreme folly, of the outrageous wickedness of expending annually vast sums of money, extorted by unjust taxation from a disheartened and poverty-stricken people, upon the pretended education of Negroes, with the view of settling the question of their fitness for citizenship, while this very expenditure in their behalf renders a correct solution of the problem an utter impossibility. On the other hand, without the expenditure of a single dollar, the question would settle itself naturally, and so settled, would lead us to the only safe and wise conclusions.

## North Carolina Negroes Urge Education
### *1877*[30]

RESOLVED that wealth, equally with an education, is an indispensable requisite to our elevation to a place of equality with our more favored white fellow-citizens, and inasmuch as the only path to wealth lies along the line of persevering labor and close (not penurious) economy, we earnestly urge it upon the colored people to be industrious and economical, and to accumulate property; and we earnestly exhort our young men, after obtaining an education, to turn their attention not in the direction of school teaching, the ministry, law and medicine alone, but to agriculture and the mechanical trade as well, through the intelligent and successful pursuit of which they may be able to achieve a competency in life and contribute to the aggregate wealth of their race. . . .

RESOLVED that it is the sense of this Convention that the General Assembly of North Carolina should enact a law compelling all citizens of the state to send their children between the ages of 6 and 21 years to the public school during the school months of the year for a period of 3 years at least.

---

[30]*Proceedings of the State Convention of Colored Citizens held in the City of Raleigh, North Carolina, October 18 and 19, 1877* (Raleigh: Edwards, Broughton and Company, 1877), pp. 6, 9.

# Purpose of the Slater Fund
## *1882*[31]

GENTLEMEN: It has pleased God to grant me prosperity in my business, and to put it into my power to apply to charitable uses a sum of money so considerable as to require the counsel of wise men for the administration of it.

It is my desire at this time to appropriate to such uses the sum of one million of dollars ($1,000,000); . . . and I intend that the corporation, as soon as formed, shall receive this sum in trust to apply the income of it according to the instructions contained in this letter.

The general object which I desire to have exclusively pursued, is the uplifting of the lately emancipated population of the Southern States, and their posterity, by conferring on them the blessings of Christian education. The disabilities formerly suffered by these people, and their singular patience and fidelity in the great crisis of the nation, establish a just claim on the sympathy and good will of humane and patriotic men. I cannot but feel the compassion that is due in view of their prevailing ignorance, which exists by no fault of their own.

But it is not only for their own sake, but also for the safety of our common country, in which they have been invested with equal political rights, that I am desirous to aid in providing them with the means of such education as shall tend to make them good men and good citizens — education in which the instruction of the mind in the common branches of secular learning shall be associated with training in just notions of duty toward God and man, in the light of the Holy Scriptures.

The means to be used in the prosecution of the general object above described, I leave to the discretion of the corporation; only indicating, as lines of operation adapted to the present condition of things, the training of teachers from among the people requiring to be taught, if, in the opinion of the corporation, by such limited selection the purposes of the trust can be best accomplished; and the encouragement of such institutions as are most effectually useful in promoting this training of teachers. . . .

---

[31]John F. Slater to Trustees, March 4, 1882, in Trustees of the John F. Slater Fund, *Documents Relating To The Origin and Work Of The Slater Trustees* (Baltimore: Published by the Trustees, 1894), pp. 7-10. The trustees were: Rutherford B. Hayes, Morrison R. Waite, William E. Dodge, Phillips Brooks, Daniel Coit Gilman, John A. Stewart, Alfred H. Colquitt, Morris K. Jesup, James P. Boyce, William A. Slater.

I purposely leave to the corporation the largest liberty of making such changes in the methods of applying the income of the Fund as shall seem from time to time best adapted to accomplish the general object herein defined. But being warned by the history of such endowments that they sometimes tend to discourage rather than promote effort and self-reliance on the part of beneficiaries; or to inure to the advancement of learning instead of the dissemination of it; or to become a convenience to the rich instead of a help to those who need help; I solemnly charge my Trustees to use their best wisdom in preventing any such defeat of the spirit of this trust; so that my gift may continue to future generations to be a blessing to the poor. . . .

## New York Court Upholds School Segregation
### 1883[32]

The question broadly stated presented by this appeal is whether the school authorities of that city have the right to classify the pupils in such schools in the administration of their authority to regulate the methods of education pursued therein, or whether the provisions of the Constitution of the United States require that each person attending such school, shall, without regard to sex, color or age, be awarded upon demand the same privileges in the same places and under the same circumstances as those enjoyed by any other scholar therein. . . .

It would seem to follow, as the necessary result of the appellant's contention, that the action of the legislatures of the various States providing schools, asylums, hospitals and benevolent institutions for the exclusive benefit of the colored as well as other races, must be deemed to be infractions of constitutional provisions and unlawful exercise, of legislative power. The literal application of its provisions as interpreted by him would prevent any classification of citizens for any purpose whatever under the laws of the State, and subvert all such associations as are limited in their enjoyment to classes distinguished either by sex, race, nationality or creed. If the argument should be followed out to its legitimate conclusion, it would also forbid all classification of the pupils in public schools founded upon distinctions of sex, nationality or race, and

---

[32]People ex rel. King v. Gallagher, 93 New York Reports 438 (October, 1883). The case arose in school district No. 5 of Brooklyn, New York. The decision contains an extensive review of supporting precedents.

which, it must be conceded, are essential to the most advantageous admin-istration of educational facilities in such schools. Seeing the force of these contentions the appellant concedes that discrimination may be exercised by the school authorities with respect to age, sex, intellectual acquire-ments and territorial location, but he claims that this cannot, under the Constitution, be extended to distinctions founded upon difference in color or race. We think the concession fatal to his argument. . . .

If it could be shown that the accommodations afforded to one race were inferior to those enjoyed by another, some advance might be made in the argument, but until that is established, no basis is laid for a claim that the privileges of the respective races are not equal. Institutions of this kind are founded every day in the different States under the law for the exclusive benefit of particular races and classes of citizens, and are gen-erally regarded as favors to the races designated instead of marks of inferiority. . . .

It is undoubtedly true that in many localities in this State the school authorities have not availed themselves of their authority to cause separate places of education to be established for the respective races. And in those places the joint education of the races has been carried on. This fact seems to show that this question may safely and fairly be left to their discretion, and in time, where that course may be deemed best, it will be voluntarily adopted by such authorities.

## Second Morrill Act Forbids Discrimination
### 1890[33]

*Be it enacted by the Senate and House of Representatives of the United States of America in Congress assembled,* That there shall be, and hereby is, annually appropriated. . . to each State and Territory for the more complete endowment and maintenance of colleges for the benefit of agri-

---

[33]United States Statutes, Volume 26, Chapter 841, pp. 417-18. The first Morrill Act (1862) made no reference to racial discrimination. Under the provisions of this second act (1890), separate land grant colleges for Negroes were established in the Southern states. The absence of any state matching requirement meant that states could distribute federal funds equally, but still discriminate with state funds. It should be noted that the second Morrill Act applied to funds appropriated in 1890 and afterward. Since the Hatch Acts which established experiment stations in the land grant colleges had been passed in 1887, the Negro land grant colleges did not receive them. The primary contribution of these schools was the preparation of teachers rather than scientifically trained workers in agriculture or the mechanic arts.

culture and the mechanic arts now established, or which may be hereafter established . . . the sum of fifteen thousand dollars for the year ending June thirteenth, eighteen hundred and ninety, and an annual increase . . . thereafter for ten years by an additional sum of one thousand dollars over the preceding year . . .: *Provided,* That no money shall be paid out under this act to any State or Territory for the support and maintenance of a college where a distinction of race or color is made in the admission of students, but the establishment and maintenance of such colleges separately for white and colored students shall be held to be a compliance with the provisions of this act if the funds received in such State or Territory be equitably divided as hereinafter set forth: *Provided,* That in any State in which there has been one college established in pursuance of the act of July second, eighteen hundred and sixty-two, and also in which an educational institution of like character has been established, or may be hereafter established, and is now aided by such State from its own revenue, for the education of colored students in agriculture and the mechanic arts, . . . the legislature of such State may propose and report to the Secretary of the Interior a just and equitable division of the fund to be received under this act between one college for white students and one institution for colored students . . ., which shall be divided into two parts and paid accordingly, and thereupon such institution for colored students shall be entitled to the benefits of this act and subject to its provisions, as much as it would have been if it had been included under the act of eighteen hundred and sixty-two, and the fulfillment of the foregoing provisions shall be taken as a compliance with the provision in reference to separate colleges for which and colored students.

## Argument for Industrial Education
### 1886[34]

We are in a large degree a landless, a tradeless and homeless race. We are too much absorbed by politics; the best talent of the Negro is engaged

---

[34]Philip H. Murry as quoted in William J. Simmons, *Men of Mark* (Cleveland: George M. Rewell and Company, 1887), p. 101, from a speech at the National Press Convention in Atlantic City, July, 1886. Murry was born in 1842 in Reading, Pennsylvania. He taught school in several states, finally settling in St. Louis where he was active in the school system and published the *St. Louis Advance.* Advocates of industrial education tended to emphasize the weaknesses and failures of Negroes as causing the plight of the race to a greater degree than did advocates of other educational programs.

in political machinations, scheming to elect some white man to office, or praying for the "New Jerusalem" to descend down out of heaven. Emigrants from the most fecund blood of Europe are marching by our doors in platoons of ten thousand deep, to the possession of the fertile lands of the West . . . We loiter about in the big cities, living on the offals of the wealthy that overawes and overshadows us at every turn. But we stay until some great city springs up in the West and the trains are burdened with the commerce of the new lands, then we go West with the broom and white jacket. We should have gone West with the hoe and plow. This is the age of material progress; the engineer has replaced the scholar; the mathematician instead of puzzling his brain over the problems of Euclid is wrestling with the "Bulls and Bears on 'change.' " The Greek grammarian has been supplanted by the machinist, and the man who would hunt for a hundred years to find out the meaning of a Hebrew dot only illustrates the intellectual fool of our times. Railroads, big farms, manufactories, steam engines, electric lights, cable cars, and the telegraph are the textbooks of today; and if the Negro will not study to understand, control and take possession of these, he cannot keep pace with the progress of the age.

## Henry Grady Proclaims the Southern Stand
### 1890[35]

First—That the whites shall have clear and unmistakable control of public affairs. They own the property. They have the intelligence. Theirs is the responsibility. For these reasons they are entitled to control. Beyond these reasons is a radical one. They are the superior race, and will not and cannot submit to the domination of an inferior race. . . .

Second—That the whites and blacks must walk in separate paths in the South. As near as may be, these paths should be made equal—but separate they must be now and always. This means separate schools, separate churches, separate accommodation everywhere—but equal accommodation where the same money is charged, or where the State provides for the citizen. Georgia gives her State University $8,000 a year; precisely the same sum to her colored university. When the colored university insisted on educating whites and blacks together, the Legislature withheld its appropriation, but the money was held in the treasury for two years, sacred to the uses of a colored university, and has just been voted in bulk to Morris-Brown College, which agreed to admit no white students, but to stand on separate education. . . .

## New York Authorizes Separate Schools
### *1894*[36]

The school authorities of any city or incorporated village, the schools of which are or shall be organized under the title eight of this act, or under special act, may, when they shall deem it expedient, establish a separate school or separate schools for the instruction of children and youth of African descent, resident therein, and over five and under twenty-one years of age; and such school or schools shall be supported in the same manner and to the same extent as the school or schools supported therein for white children, and they shall be subject to the same rules and regulations, and be furnished with facilities for instruction equal to those furnished to the white schools therein.

## The Supreme Court Approves "Separate but Equal"
### *1896*[37]

By the fourteenth amendment, all persons born or naturalized in the United States, and subject to the jurisdiction thereof, are made citizens of the United States and of the state wherein they reside; and the states are forbidden from making or enforcing any law which shall abridge the privileges or immunities of citizens of the United States, or shall deprive any person of life, liberty, or property without due process of law, or deny to any person within their jurisdiction the equal protection of the laws. . . .

[36]New York Laws, 1894, Volume 2, Chapter 556, Article 11, p. 1288. Repealed April 18, 1900. See New York Laws, 1900, Chapter 492. Note that the idea of equality, even though separate schools were allowed, is given much more emphasis than in the previously cited laws of Kentucky.

[37]Plessy v. Ferguson, 16 Supreme Court 1138 (1896). The case involved segregation on train coaches. The court referred incidentally to school segregation.

The object of the amendment was undoubtedly to enforce the absolute equality of the two races before the law, but, in the nature of things, it could not have been intended to abolish distinctions based upon color, or to enforce social, as distinguished from political, equality, or a commingling of the two races upon terms unsatisfactory to either. Laws permitting, and even requiring, their separation, in places where they are liable to be brought into contact, do not necessarily imply the inferiority of either race to the other, and have been generally, if not universally, recognized as within the competency of the state legislatures in the exercise of their police power. The most common instance of this is connected with the establishment of separate schools for white and colored children, which have been held to be a valid exercise of the legislative power even by courts of states where the political rights of the colored race have been longest and most earnestly enforced. . . .

We consider the underlying fallacy of the plaintiff's argument to consist in the assumption that the enforced separation of the two races stamps the colored race with a badge of inferiority. If this be so, it is not by reason of anything found in the act, but solely because the colored race chooses to put that construction upon it. . . .

## Washington Urges Education Based on Needs
### *1896*[38]

With this preliminary survey, let us examine with more care the work to be done in the South before all classes will be fit for the highest duties of citizenship. In reference to my own race I am confronted with some embarrassment at the outset because of the various and conflicting opinions as to what is to be its final place in our economic and political life. . . .

With all these conflicting opinions, and with the full knowledge of all our weaknesses, I know that only a few centuries ago in this country we went into slavery pagans: we came out Christians; we went into slavery pieces of property: we came out American citizens; we went into slavery without language: we came out speaking the proud Anglo-Saxon

---

[38]Booker T. Washington, "Democracy and Education," in E. Davidson Washington (ed.), *Selected Speeches of Booker T. Washington* (Garden City, New York: Doubleday, Doran and Co., Inc., 1932), pp. 62-67. Washington delivered this address in Brooklyn, New York, September 30, 1896. It is important to note that Washington did not originate the idea of practicality in education, nor did the idea originate out of race issues in education. He gave it an unusual twist at Tuskegee by abandoning some of the usual graduation oratory in favor of demonstrations before the audience of such skills as milking a cow and carpentry.

tongue; we went into slavery with the slave chains clanking about our wrists: we came out with the American ballot in our hands. My friends, I submit it to your sober and candid judgment, if a race that is capable of such a test, such a transformation, is not worth saving and making a part, in reality as well as in name, of our democratic government... It seems to me that the temptation in education and missionary work is to do for a people a thousand miles away without always making a careful study of the needs and conditions of the people whom we are trying to help. The temptation is to run all people through a certain educational mold regardless of the condition of the subject or the end to be accomplished. Unfortunately for us as a race, our education was begun, just after the war, too nearly where New England education ended. We seemed to overlook the fact that we were dealing with a race that has little love for labor in their native land and consequently brought little love for labor with them to America. Added to this was the fact that they had been forced for two hundred and fifty years to labor without compensation under circumstances that were calculated to do anything but teach them the dignity, beauty, and civilizing power of intelligent labor. We forgot the industrial education that was given the Pilgrim Fathers of New England in clearing and planting its cold, bleak, and snowy hills and valleys, in providing shelter, founding the small mills and factories, in supplying themselves with home-made products, thus laying the foundation of an industrial life that now keeps going a large part of the colleges and missionary effort of the world. May I be tempted one step further in showing how prone we are to make our education formal, technical, instead of making it meet the needs of conditions regardless of formality and technicality? At least eighty per cent of my pupils in the South are found in the rural districts, and they are dependent on agriculture in some form for their support. Notwithstanding in this instance we have a whole race depending upon agriculture, and notwithstanding thirty years have passed since our freedom, aside from what we have done at Hampton and Tuskegee and one or two other institutions, not a thing has been attempted by state or philanthropy in the way of educating the race in this industry on which their very existence depends. Boys have been taken from the farms and educated in law, theology, Hebrew, and Greek—educated in everything else but the very subject they should know the most about. I question whether or not among all the educated colored people in the United States you can find six, if we except the institutions named, that have received anything like a thorough training in agriculture. It would have seemed, since self-support and industrial independence are the first conditions for lifting up any race, that education in theoretical and practical agriculture, horticulture, dairying, and stock-raising should have occupied the first place in our system. Some time ago when we decided to make tailoring a part of our training at the Tuskegee Institute, I was amazed to find that it was almost impossible to find in the whole country an educated colored man who could teach the making of clothing. I could find them by the score who could teach astronomy, theology, Greek, or Latin, but almost none who could instruct in the making of clothing, something that has to be used by every one of us every day in the year. How often has my heart been made to sink as I have gone through the South and into the homes of the people and found women who could converse intelligently on Grecian history, who had studied geometry, could analyze the most complex sentences, and yet could not analyze the poorly cooked and still more poorly served bread and fat meat that they and their families were eating three times a day. It is little trouble to find girls who can locate Pekin and the Desert of Sahara on an artificial globe; but seldom can you find one who can locate on an actual dinner table the proper place for the carving knife and fork or the meat and vegetables. A short time ago, in one of our Southern cities, a colored man died who had received training as a skilled mechanic during the days of slavery. By his skill and industry he had built up a great business as a house contractor and builder. In this same city there are thirty-five thousand colored people, among them young men who have been well educated in languages and literature, but not a single one could be found who had been trained in architectural and mechanical drawing that could carry on the business which this ex-slave had built up, and so it was soon scattered to the wind. Aside from the work done in the institutions that I have mentioned, you will find no colored men who have been trained in the principles of architecture, notwithstanding the vast majority of the race is without homes. Here, then, are the three prime conditions for growth, for civilization—food, clothing, shelter—yet we have been the slaves of form and custom to such an extent that we have failed in a large measure to look matters squarely in the face and meet actual needs.

## Daniel C. Gilman Favors Industrial Education
*1896*[39]

Let us look toward the future. The education of a race is a very complex subject if we think of it as a whole; but if we remember that the education

---

[39]Daniel C. Gilman, *A Study in Black and White* (Baltimore: Trustees of The John F. Slater Fund, 1897), pp. 8-14. An address at Hampton, Virginia, Nov. 18, 1896. Gilman, organizer of Johns Hopkins University in 1876, voices here the almost unanimous view of the philanthropists whose efforts not only heavily financed Negro education but influenced the course it would take.

of a race means the education of the individuals in that race, the problem is simplified, for we quickly perceive that the training of every person involves three elements—the formation of habits, the acquisition of skill and the performance of work. Accordingly, that institution or school is best which enforces habits of order, attention, obedience, discrimination, memory; which then secures skill in handcraft and redecraft, and likewise shows how these habits and this skill may be applied in useful avocations.

Careful observers are agreed that among the blacks there is at this time the special need of well trained teachers, artisans, and tillers of the soil, and that Hampton and other Institutions engaged in kindred work should introduce, as far as possible, the methods of "the new education" which have been developed among the whites during the last half century. This "new education," as it is called, is largely the education of the hand.

During the present generation, there has been a remarkable change in the instruction of whites in schools of every grade, from the kindergarten to the University. In one form or another, handcraft has been restored to the place from which it was long excluded by redecraft. The change has not been accomplished without experiment, controversy, difficulty, and failure; but, at last, I think we may claim that the victory is won and that no scheme of study can be regarded as complete unless the study of books is constantly supplemented by the study of objects. The young must be taught to acquire knowledge by the observation of nature and her forces, as well as by reading the observation of others respecting nature; and the character must be developed not merely by the exercise of memory and by the interpretation of written documents, but also by the training of our youth to useful occupations. . . .

In concluding these remarks, let me express a belief that the distinction between the two races is as permanent as the distinction between the colors white and black; that this distinction is natural and cannot be set aside by human action; that the lessons of history make it clear that differences of race are ineffaceable, by legislation or volition. They are doubtless implanted in us for some purpose which our limited intelligence is unable to descry. It is of no consequence whether we 'like to think so' or not. The stars move in their orbits without regard to mortal wishes. Whites or Blacks, it is our duty to recognize what is true; to make each race as good as it can be made; to discover and develop such qualities as tend to its improvement; to eradicate those which are degrading; to help the people that are downcast, by giving them the uplifting influences of freedom, religion and education; and especially to teach them the uses of skilled labor; and then—it is our duty to leave the outcome to Providence—never forgetting and never hiding the fact and never fearing to say, that deeper than all distinctions of race, is the basis of human nature;

lower down than all the idiosyncracies by which human nature is differentiated we find the Brotherhood of man and the Fatherhood of God. . . .

## Negroes Should Teach Negroes
*1897*[40]

I confidently hold that no white teacher is competent to teach Negro children. . . . 1. The educational development of the Negro must be from within and by the race itself, and not solely through extraneous agencies. 2. The intellectual and moral dependence of the race should not be perpetuated. The Negro needs to be stimulated to independent activity. 3. As a teacher of his race, the Negro occupies a position of trust and honor, which he needs to quicken his sense of responsibility and to furnish him the incentives and the means for race elevation. 4. The teacher and the pupil must possess a common consciousness, whose historic processes have common elements, resulting in common institutions. The teacher must embody in his character the race epochs and processes represented in the child. 5. The instinct of race identity renders impossible the realization of an ideal relation between the white teacher and the Negro pupil. The teacher and the child must be coordinated.

## Industrial Education not Enough
*1897*[41]

Cheapness characterizes almost all the donations of the American people to the Negro:—Cheapness, in all the past, has been the regimen provided

---

[40]J.H. Phillips, "Negro Teachers for Negro Schools," *Liberia*, Bulletin No. 10 (February, 1897), p. 28. The history of Negro education indicates that Negro institutions have generally been relatively democratic and open. Nevertheless some Negroes have felt that self respect and race strategy required that exclusion be met by exclusion. By this date practically all white teachers had been replaced by Negroes in Negro elementary schools.

[41]Alexander Crummell, *Civilization The Primal Need of the Race*, American Negro Academy Occasional Papers No. 3 (Washington: The Academy, 1898), pp. 12-16. Crummell, with an A.B. (1853) from Queens College, Cambridge, was regarded as the leading intellectual among Negroes in the latter half of the nineteenth century. He spent 20 years in Liberia, but from 1879–1894 was a minister in Washington, D.C. As a strong proponent of race pride he took the lead in organizing the American Negro Academy.

for the Negro in every line of his intellectual, as well as his lower life. And so, cheapness is to be the rule in the future, as well for his higher, as for his lower life:—cheap wages and cheap food, cheap and rotten huts; cheap and dilapidated schools; cheap and stinted weeks of schooling; cheap meeting houses for worship; cheap and ignorant ministers; cheap theological training; and now, cheap learning, culture and civilization! . . .

Ask the great men of the land how this Negro problem is to be solved, and then listen to the answers that come from divers classes of our white fellow-citizens. The merchants and traders of our great cities tell us—"The Negro must be taught to work;" and they will pour out their moneys by thousands to train him to toil. The clergy in large numbers, cry out—"Industrialism is the only hope of the Negro;" for this is the bed-rock, in their opinion, of Negro evangelization! "Send him to Manual Labor Schools," cries out another set of philanthropists. "Hic, haec, hoc, is going to prove the ruin of the Negro" says the Rev. Steele, an erudite Southern Savan. "You must begin at the bottom with the Negro," says another eminent authority—as though the Negro has been living in the clouds, and had never reached the bottom. Says the Honorable George T. Barnes, of Georgia—"The kind of education the Negro should receive should not be very refined nor classical, but adapted to his present condition" as though there is to be no future for the Negro. . . .

One would suppose from the universal demand for the mere industrialism for this race of ours, that the Negro had been going daily to dinner parties, eating terrapin and indulging in champagne; and returning home at night, sleeping on beds of eiderdown; breakfasting in the morning in his bed, and then having his valet to clothe him daily in purple and fine linen—all these 250 years of his sojourn in this land. And then, just now, the American people, tired of all this Negro luxury, was calling him, for the first time, to blister his hands with the hoe, and to learn to supply his needs by sweatful toil in the cotton fields. . . .

It is not a mere negative proposition that settles this question. It is not that the Negro does not need the hoe, the plane, the plough, and the anvil. It is the positive affirmation that the Negro needs the light of cultivation; needs it to be thrown in upon all his toil, upon his whole life and its environments.

What he needs is CIVILIZATION. He needs the increase of his higher wants, of his mental and spiritual needs. *This*, mere animal labor has never given him, and never can give him. But it will come to him, as an individual, and as a class, just in proportion as the higher culture comes to his leaders and teachers, and so gets into his schools, academies and colleges; and then enters his pulpits; and so filters down into his families and his homes; and the Negro learns that he is no longer to be a serf, but that he is to bare his strong brawny arm as a laborer; *not* to make the white man a Croesus, but to make himself a man. He is always to be a laborer; but now, in these days of freedom and the schools, he is to be a laborer with intelligence, enlightenment and manly ambitions.

But, when his culture fits him for something more than a field hand or a mechanic, he is to have an open door set wide before him! And that culture, according to his capacity, he must claim as his rightful heritage, as a man:—not stinted training, not a caste education, not a Negro curriculum.

## Discrimination in Secondary Education Upheld
### *1899*[42]

The plaintiffs in error complain that the board of education used the funds in its hands to assist in maintaining a high school for white children without providing a similar school for colored children. The substantial relief asked is an injunction that would either impair the efficiency of the high school provided for white children or compel the board to close it. But if that were done, the result would only be to take from white children educational privileges enjoyed by them, without giving to colored children additional opportunities for the education furnished in high schools. The colored school children of the county would not be advanced in the matter of their education by a decree compelling the defendant board to cease giving support to a high school for white children. The board had before it the question whether it should maintain, under its control, a high school for about 60 colored children or withhold the benefits of education in primary schools from 300 children of the same race. It was impossible, the board believed, to give educational facilities to the 300 colored children who were unprovided for, if it maintained a separate school for the

---

[42]Cumming v. County Board of Education. 175 United States Supreme Court 528 (1899). This was the first case to be decided by the U. S. Supreme Court directly involving education and race. The court upheld the school board of Richmond County, Georgia, in closing its Negro high school while operating a white high school. Thus at a time when the high school was becoming a part of the common school system, Negroes were largely excluded from it except by private provision. The development of the colleges was hindered by the necessity of giving preparatory work to the vast majority of their students.

60 children who wished to have a high-school education. Its decision was in the interest of the greater number of colored children, leaving the smaller number to obtain a high-school education in existing private institutions at an expense not beyond that incurred in the high school discontinued by the board.

We are not permitted by the evidence in the record to regard that decision as having been made with any desire or purpose on the part of the board to discriminate against any of the colored school children of the county on account of their race. But if it be assumed that the board erred in supposing that its duty was to provide educational facilities for the 300 colored children who were without an opportunity in primary schools to learn the alphabet and to read and write, rather than to maintain a school for the benefit of the 60 colored children who wished to attend a high school, that was not an error which a court of equity should attempt to remedy by an injunction that would compel the board to withhold all assistance from the high school maintained for white children. If, in some appropriate proceeding instituted directly for that purpose, the plaintiffs had sought to compel the board of education, out of the funds in its hands or under its control, to establish and maintain a high school for colored children, and if it appeared that the board's refusal to maintain such a school was in fact an abuse of its discretion and in hostility to the colored population because of their race, different questions might have arisen in the state court. . . .

We may add that while all admit that the benefits and burdens of public taxaton must be shared by citizens without discrimination against any class on account of their race, the education of the people in schools maintained by state taxation is a matter belonging to the respective states, and any interference on the part of Federal authority with the management of such schools cannot be justified except in the case of a clear and unmistakable disregard of rights secured by the supreme law of the land.

## An Argument for Classical Education
### *1900*[43]

The white man needs classical training. The Negro is a man, and, therefore, needs whatever training any other man needs. But there are *special* reasons why the Negro needs classical training.

---

[43]R.S. Lovinggood, *Why Hic, Haec, Hoc For the Negro?* (Marshall, Texas: Wiley University, 1900), pp. 30-37. Lovinggood was Professor of Greek and Latin at Wiley College, 1894-1900, and President of Sam Houston College from 1900 until his death.

1.  He needs solidity of character. Slavery was not a good school to teach self-reliance. The slave relied on his master. His master did all the thinking and planning. There was no opportunity for developing in the Negro continuity of thought and purpose and stability of character. . . .

At present the masses of the colored people are too easily herded by political tricksters and designing speculators. Of course, we have strong characters among us. I speak here in general terms. Possibly no one will censure me if I suggest that the average American of whatever race lacks much of that steadiness of character necessary to a great people. He is excitable and changeable. . . . *We need a deeper education.* How shall we develop this solidity of character? There is no better way than by puttting as large a number as possible of our boys and girls through a long, severe, difficult course of instruction such as is furnished by the college course. Such a course develops individuality, strengthens the will-power, and gives self-control. It will test the Negro's power of endurance. It will give him an insight into a literature that is free from the chilling influences of race prejudice. It will make him feel that he is permitted to hold up his head. In the classics, he is not constantly coming upon Negro spelled with a little n and two g's.

2.  Such a course and the time required to complete it call the student away from the weakening, degrading desire for pleasure. When the Negro was emancipated, he began to celebrate his freedom and he has not yet finished. As Dr. Bowen puts it, he wants to have a "good time." He loves too much to be in "society." He is taken up too much with dress. He should desire cleanliness and decency. But he should not love dress, tinsel, powder, feathers, etc.

Now, no one can successfully pursue to completion a college course and yet be a leader in society. His difficult studies require all his thought and time. They call his mind from dress and society and he soon learns that there is something more in life than a silk hat, patent leather shoes, etc.

3.  The ex-slave, gazing upon the grandeur of Anglo-Saxon civilization will be inclined to believe that this glory is based upon banks, railroads, stocks and bonds. He does not fully realize that there can be no banks, stocks and bonds, unless back of them there is spirit, courage, thought, endurance. . . .

4.  The thousands of Negro teachers in the common schools need a fountain of knowledge. Shall these thirty thousand or more teachers have no source from which to draw that knowledge? Shall all Negro schools be placed on the level of the common school? If there is no wider, deeper source of knowledge, the supply of information of the public school teacher will soon be exhausted. . . .

5.  The Negro race is in special need of professional men. It is generally conceded that men who expect to be experts in their profes-

sions—medicine, law, science, theology, music, philosophy, literature—
should first of all complete the full A. B. course. Do those who are endeavoring to limit us to industrial education realize that they would practically shut us out from the learned professions? Shall we have no leaders
in the world of medicine? Do we not need more and better lawyers to
defend the interest of our poor and struggling people to keep them out
of the clutches of sharks? . . .

6.   There is a pleasure in scholarship which the Negro should seek.
At present, we have not Chatauquas, splendidly equipped libraries and
Y.M.C.A. reading rooms. We cannot hear the able lecturer that passes
through our city. Often we cannot go to hear the Shakespearean play and
maintain our self respect. We do not associate with the cultured of the
dominant race. Their great statesmen, religionists, musicians, and literary
men are, in the main, apart from the masses of our people. As their distinguished churchmen pass our way, they do not come into our homes;
we can scarcely touch the hem of their garments. Over the entrance to
many of the beautiful parks of the leading cities of the South, you will
see this sign. "No dogs and niggers allowed." . . .

If the effort to prevent the Negro's taking the classical course is
successful, scholarship among Negroes will be effectually crippled, for
industrial courses are not such as to produce scholars, and, in the second
place, it is impossible to produce scholars when the student's time is
about equally divided between literary studies and so-called industrial
pursuits. The majority of the graduates of these schools which give only
a limited amount of literary training, but put most stress on the industries,
go out, we are informed, and teach. As we have before intimated it would
be better that these schools do the work of industrial training alone. In
fact when the fad has played its part, they will come to this, for it is impossible for one school to do much along religious and literary lines and
at the same time make of the same students experts in the industrial profession. A little time will demonstrate the futility of such efforts.


## Negro Bishop Seeks Broad Education
### 1900[44]

Q.—You have quite a large knowledge of your own race and their capa-
bilities. Do you feel in your own mind that it is better to educate and

---

[44]Testimony of W.J. Gaines, Bishop, AME Church, Atlanta, in *Report of the
Industrial Commission* Vol. XV (Washington: Government Printing Office, 1901),
pp. 141, 142, 149, 150.

train them in the industrial schools and agricultural colleges, so that they are sure to make a living anyway, before they adapt themselves to the higher education? A.—I believe in industrial education just as strongly as you do, but I do not want to negelect the higher education by putting all the forces into industrial education. Of course we know our people are laborers generally. Our people are the poorer classes, and we can not at once hope to get up just where the white people are today; but it is our intention somewhere in the future to reach the highest standard of education and wealth that is occupied by the best white people of the country.

Q.—What is your opinion of the industrial schools for colored people in the South now? A.—Well, those that I know are very good, and they are doing good. I would not say a word to discourage them. I rather encourage them. But at the same time I do not want to speak so as to injure the idea of higher education. . . .

Q.—Do you not think . . . that if an education other than a purely industrial one were placed in the hands of the Southern colored man and he takes a political line or bias with it, that he is going to do more harm to his race and himself than he would if he remained unschooled? A.—I think the development of the human mind, with the same environments, the same associations, brings the same results; whatever would happen to any other people would happen to us. . . .

Q.—Is it not the best way, both for his moral and social condition, that a man should be educated a good deal on industrial lines, independent of these public questions and higher education? A.—I do not believe it can be done independent of public questions. A man that lives in a country where the newspapers are giving information all over the country can not be educated independent of public questions. I believe he ought to have industrial education . . . but I do not believe that that ought to be exclusive of the higher education.

## Georgia Governor on Negro Education
### *1900*[45]

Q.—For the betterment of the Negro race would you prefer an industrial education or a literary education? A.—Our situation is peculiar here. Industrial education is preferable, confined to certain lines. Now we have this difficulty to encounter: the poorer classes of white people engaged

---

[45]Testimony of A.D. Candler, Governor of Georgia, in *Report of the Industrial Commission* Vol. VII (Washington: Government Printing Office, 1901), p. 539.

in our industrial enterprises are jealous of the Negro. They do not work together well in the same factories. Now, I do not think it would be to the interest of either race to mix them in manufacturing establishments, because of these race prejudices which crop out. We may deny it, but they exist in every human being. The Negro is the best farm laborer I ever saw; no question about that. He is a skillful and successful farm laborer when under intelligent direction.

Q.—You believe that is his natural sphere? A.—I believe he is more useful there than anywhere else.

Q.—Do you believe it is a mistake for him to enter the professions? A.—Well, yes; I do. Of course he can preach; that is all right. He is useful there. There is no reason that I see why he should not practice medicine among his own race. . . .

Q.—You would prefer the establishment of manual schools for colored boys? A.—The best school I ever saw for the Negro, or the white boy either, was the corn patch to learn the art and science of farming.

Q.—I mean manual training for such occupations as bricklayers and carpenters. A.—I doubt if it would be in the interest of either race for them to be trained in these schools.

# Poor Education Protested
### *1901*[46]

It is a weak and mistaken policy which advocates meager provisions and facilities for the training and education of Negroes. . . . The Nation must treat the Negro fairly, must educate his head, heart and hand, or buy Gatling guns, drive him into the Gulf of Mexico as the Indian is being driven into his grave. . . . It would be a sin for the strong white man . . . to do one thing or say one thing, or insinuate one thing to cripple Negro education.

---

[46]William H. Councill, "Negro Development in the South." Address before the Southern Industrial Convention, Philadelphia, June 13, 1901, unpaged. Councill was head of the State Normal and Industrial School at Huntsville, Alabama.

# New York Editor Supports Industrial Education
## *1901*[47]

That education is best for a man, always, which stimulates most his peculiar genius and enables him to become the most useful citizen in the occupation he selects. A thorough acquaintance with the conditions which now rule in the Southern States, where a majority of Afro-Americans reside, convinces me that what the masses most need at this stage of their development, is skilled captains of industry. We have been making teachers and preachers and professional men for three decades . . . but a close observer sees plainly that they are in danger of starvation unless more attention shall be given to the industrial and commercial sides of life, unless these graduates of the higher schools of learning . . . have a commercial and industrial element to feed upon. . . . We need educated farmers, mechanics, and tradesmen in the South today more than we need graduates of higher schools of learning, because we have done little else than manufacture the latter since the war; and what to do with the learning after they have got it, is fast becoming a burning question.

# Education at Hampton
## *1901*[48]

*Q.* — Do you have what is known as a manual-training school? *A.* — Yes, we have connected with our academic department a manual-training school. From the time that the children commence in the kindergarten

---

[47]T. Thomas Fortune, *The Kind of Education the Afro-American Most Needs* (Tuskegee, Alabama: Tuskegee Institute Steam Print, 1901), pp. 10, 11. Fortune was a leading Negro journalist around the turn of the century and a Washington partisan. He published successively the *New York Rumor, Globe, Freeman,* and *Age.*

[48]Testimony of Hollis B. Frissell in *Report of the Industrial Commission* Vol. XV (Washington: Government Printing Office, 1901), pp. 79-81, 87. Two things are especially noteworthy in this extract. First, it indicates there was good reason for DuBois to fear that industrial education meant shortchanging the student in basic literary and academic skills. Second, it shows the desire to instill in students the ideal of community service which would cause them to go out as missionaries of intelligent work and good management.

until they graduate from the academic department they are having what we call manual training of some sort. . . . For instance, on Monday they have their washtubs; on Tuesday they have their ironing boards. They learn to do small pieces of carpentry work, even to make parts of houses. . . . We take them out on a little piece of ground in the springtime and they have their rakes and their hoes, and they cultivate radishes and cultivate flowers. . . . Then, as they grow up and take up books somewhat, they take up at the same time working in wood and working in iron and work in clay; and the girls commence working in cooking and in sewing, and that goes along through our preparatory departments; the two go right along together, but the emphasis is laid every time on the industrial side, on the manual training, and the book side is subordinated to the work side, because to us it seems that the doing is the important thing, and the knowledge ought to be harnessed in some way to the doing, and the knowing on the book side ought to be harnessed to the doing.

Q. — Is that the rule all through the course? A. — That is the rule all through the course. The majority of our students that come into our boarding department go into what is called our night school, where they work for a year 10 hours a day — in order to learn to do work, and to do it carefully. They are put into our various shops. We have 16 shops and a large sawmill, where they get a chance to work and very largely earn their board and clothes; and in that way they learn to work 10 hours a day, and they go to school 2 hours at night. . . . The first year is given up very largely with most of them to this work. Of course if they come with money they can go right into the classes; but most of them that come into the boarding department spend a year, in order to lay up enough credit so that they can go into the regular classes. . . . They can go into the academic department, and in that case they take certain studies in history and geography, and all the rest, but all related definitely to agriculture and trades; and they have manual training . . . that is, they go from one process to another just as they would in arithmetic. . . . Then there are some that do not go through the academic department at once. They want to go directly into the trades after they have been through their first year. Eventually I hope not to allow any boy or girl to go into a trade before he goes through the academic course. That is not true yet. But we allow them, after they have gone through the year and gotten some knowledge of English and some small knowledge of mathematics — we allow them to go directly into the trades. . . . There we teach blacksmithing, wheelwrighting, carpentry, painting, bricklaying, glass setting, together with work in shoemaking, carpentry and harness making; and then we have mechanical drawing for all that go into the trades. We have a 3-year

course at present in trades work. The first year they have regular instruction. . . . The second year . . . we put them out to work in our shops.
Then . . . we send them back for the third year in their trades, into the
trade school proper, where they have more of the theoretical side.

Q. — Would a larger number of your male graduates become farmers and mechanics if the demand for teachers was not so great? A. — I
suppose they would. We have thought in the past that the best thing that
our students could do would be to go into the public schools of the South,
where they get a salary usually of $25 a month for sometimes not more
than 3, 4, or 5 months, and there get a little work in the little church, and
at the same time build their houses and cultivate their little piece of land.
In that way they have a certain amount of money coming to them from
their salary, and they are able to present an object lesson to the community. . . . Our thought has been to establish these centers just as far as
possible, and we have established them in certain counties of Virginia, for
instance. . . . I could tell you of one county, for instance, where we sent
between 40 and 50 of our graduates. Most of them went in and started
schools such as I have spoken of, and cultivated their land. The result is
that where 16 years ago the colored people of that community owned
no land to speak of, today they pay one-fifth of the property tax of the
county, and where there has been that increase of property or land hold-
ings there has been a corresponding decrease in crime, and the character
of the houses and the churches and everything has correspondingly
increased.


# Discrimination in Agricultural Education
### *1901*[49]


. . . The great drawback and discouragement of the colored farmers is a
lack of a working knowledge of the soil and of improved farming implements. I think I am safe in saying that there is now little or no effort put

---

[49]Testimony of R.R. Wright in *Report of the Industrial Commission* (Washington: Government Printing Office, 1901), pp. 202-05 *passim*. Although agricultural
education was widely advocated for Negroes, the Negro land grant colleges were
unable to offer their students adequate training along these lines. The lack of experiment stations meant that they could not provide the usual extension services to the
community.

forth to improve the colored farmer. No farmers' institutes are held among them. Little or no agricultural literature reaches them. The agricultural experiment stations are of practically no benefit to them. . . . It seems to me that national aid for education is the thing for the South, and certainly for Georgia; and then, again, the duplication of experiment stations. If you will pardon me, the conditions that obtain in the South are such that the experiment stations as now placed can not possibly do the desired work for both races. . . .

*Q.* — What experiment stations do you want? *A.* — Say, one in connection with such a school as ours.

*Q.* — What are you going to experiment with? *A.* — Farming; carry out the very same idea that is carried out in the regular stations. . . .

*Q.* — What I wanted to get at was this: Don't you think the trouble with your people is more the lack of continued perseverance, rather than lack of knowledge as to how some of these crops are raised? *A.* — Well, you may take any class of people who are ignorant, and their ignorance is the cause of lack of perseverance. . . .

*Q.* — Am I mistaken in the thought that that experiment station is for all the people, and not for the white people alone? *A.* — It is for all the people; you are correct, sir. But I thought I stated that there are conditions that it is unnecessary for me to go into. . . . We want them to cause incitement and encouragement among the colored people along the line of farming, and it would be, as it were, a sort of inspiration, headquarters, as it were, for the advancement of that class of interests.

## A Northern Negro on Education in the South
### *1901*[50]

At the beginning of his free career two fundamental obstacles, blinding, bewildering, and insurmountable, were thrust in the pathway of the freedman. One was partisan politics, the other sectarian education. Each still clutches him with a remorseless grip, and what the outcome will be no

---

[50]William H. Thomas, *The American Negro* (New York: The Macmillan Company, 1901), pp. 245, 260, 273-76. Thomas, a mulatto, was born in 1843 in Ohio and served in the Union Army until wounded at Wilmington, North Carolina, in 1865. He moved to South Carolina in 1871 where he taught school, practiced law and served in the South Carolina legislature.

man can foresee. One thing is evident, with all our innumerable agencies and reformatory devices, we are not making headway in the regeneration of Negro mankind. While the school-taught generation of Negroes has acquired a veneer of intellectual superiority over their unlearned fathers and mothers, they have neither their strength of character nor sincerity of purpose, and are immensely below them in sober conduct and enduring worth. . . .

Before the time of Christ the Greek philosophers asked, "What shall we teach the young?" and the answer then, as it ought to be now, was, "Teach them what they will have to do when they are men." We have here the hint and key for the instruction of the Negro, — for whom the system of education should be primary and fundamental, and every step forward verified by actual proof of the intelligent discernment of the pupil. To this end, the best and most profitable elementary instruction for illiterate and submerged classes like the Negroes is, in our judgment, that which begins with what well-conducted kindergartens teach. We say this for the reason that children, coming from slovenly and disorderly homes, will there be taught to be deft of hand, gentle of touch, keen of vision, alert in action, tidy in habits, and modest in deportment, — acquirements that will prove of no small advantage to the future men and women of the race. In all the higher graded schools, public or private, there should be a well-defined system of daily industrial instruction, not with the view of teaching a trade (that cannot be done, and should never be undertaken in connection with mental training), but for the purpose of steadying and increasing the intellectual efficiency of pupils. . . .

A great defect in Negro institutional work is the forced insulation of the pupils from today's relations, and his subjection to an environment that, for the time being, dominates, but does not elevate or awaken his higher nature. We are therefore convinced that a feasible system of community education offers the most remunerative and satisfactory solution of the Negro question.

The establishment of such communities involves an authoritative oversight and capable supervision of all dependent members. It involves the creation of schools of instruction, which resident children within certain ages would be required to attend eight months in the year, and where they would be taught such lessons as are best calculated to instil a sound knowledge of elementary letters and Christian morality. It involves also the guidance of each individual in such industrial exercises as would give them a knowledge of household or of agricultural work. This system of education begins by creating a home for the homeless, and seeks to develop a love for it by inculcating sentiments of fraternal and filial obedience, by devising and promoting true family relations, and by undertaking to influence each and all of its members to habits of thrift, sobriety, reverence, and integrity in daily living. . . .

Many years have passed since reconstruction set in motion the machinery of popular education. The freedman were then eager to get knowledge, but are now indifferent to learning because the methods employed have neither reached nor interested the majority of that people. Three decades ago, when the Negro, then a physical and illiterate mendicant, overwhelmed with credulous benightedness, was begging for the bread of common understanding, we built universities and fettered his feeble brain with moth-eaten hieroglyphics. Today, after he has toiled through one generation of industrial servitude without making serious headway, we are making puerile attempts at his industrial development, much after the same manner that mistaken, but doubtless well-meaning people, are teaching millinery and lace-making to blanketed Indian women. Some people are prone to ask of what avail, in either case, are these senseless fads? But from the dawn of freedom the Negro has been deluged with false expectations. He was told that enfranchisement would make him a man, but he speedily awoke to that deception. He was told that education would lift him out of industrial bondage, but a taste of the fruit of the tree of knowledge has merely opened his eyes to the bitterness of his degradation. He is now told that industrial training in schools will transform the race into trade artisans, and that through industrial strife will come the redemption of the freed people. But this mirage of golden expectations is doomed to fade away, just as the others have done. It is not external, but internal, development that the Negro needs.

## Some Southern Impressions
### *1901*[51]

I shall not attempt any report of this Conference. A paragraph would be totally inadequate to indicate even the conclusions to which it pointed. I can only record impressions. It is always a matter of regret that those who attend such gatherings are those who least need their influence.

---

[51]Lyman Abbott, "Some Southern Impressions," *Outlook*, LXVII (April 27, 1901), pp. 947, 948. Abbott wrote these comments after attending the Fourth Annual Conference for Education in the South. This series of conferences brought together leaders from North and South to discuss educational problems of the southern states. His attitudes are typical of the northern "compromise" which accepted the premise that southern white leaders understood the situation best, and therefore should be left to handle it in their own way. Abbott doubtless had little contact with actual conditions or Negro leaders.

The audiences were mostly made up of progressive Southerners and open-minded Northerners. It would be a great advantage if representatives of the old South and of the radical North could have been there as listeners. The later would have been surprised at some aspects of public opinion in the South as expressed by leading citizens from the South. The Governor of the State of North Carolina evidently represented the general sentiment of all those present from his section when he referred to and repeated the pledges he had made before the election in campaign speeches, and after the election in his inaugural, committing the State, to the full extent of its financial ability, to a policy of education of all the people, black and white, in town and country. . . .

To sum up these impressions in a sentence: The Southerner has less prejudice against the Negro and more interest in his welfare than the Northerner has; he desires the Negroes' education, but believes that, whatever it may become in the future, it should now be industrial rather than literary; the South has spent on the Negroes' education between three and four times as much in school taxes as the North has spent in contributions; the work of the North among the Negroes should be carried on in fellowship with the Southern whites, not in antagonism to them; to attempt to force either political or social equality is to inflict incalculable injury on the Negro and on the Nation. In a word, the Northerner should recognize the fact that the Southern white man now wishes to befriend the Negro; but the Negro should recognize the fact that he has yet to earn the Southern white man's respect.

## Former Virginia Superintendent Speaks Out
### *1901*[52]

It is well known that I am, and always have been, in favor of educating the Negro race for public reasons, but it does not follow in respect to grades above the primary . . . that I should in all cases consider the methods or lines of education equally suited to both races. . . . Circumstances,

---

[52]"The School Question," *The Times*, Richmond, Virginia (November 17, 1901). Extract from a statement by William H. Ruffner regarding educational issues being debated by the Virginia Constitutional Convention. Ruffner was state superintendent in Virginia during Reconstruction and was popularly regarded as the "father" of Virginia's public school system. In most of the discussion over industrial *vs.* literary education for the Negro, the question of the level of education was ignored. Here it is obvious that to one leading educator, at least, industrial education meant that the Negro would be confined to elementary education. It did not mean the combination of advanced general education with vocational education as in the modern high school.

for example, might call for a regular high school for whites when there would be no need for a high school for blacks, whilst there might be a demand for some sort of industrial or composite school that would benefit the public more than the higher literary studies, but such changes in our school system should be allowed only under very carefully considered regulations.

## Southern Educator Opposes Discrimination
### *1901*[53]

The most serious question in the ordinance is the treatment of the Negro. This is a question in which the people of the whole country are deeply interested. I think every true Southerner has the right to expect the convention of old Virginia shall deal justly with the Negro. Virginia is the leading educational State and one to which all look for guidance in such matters. The people of the whole country have agreed to leave the Negro problem to the good people of the South to solve. It has been tacitly agreed that it shall be taken out of politics, and the conscience of the entire American people in regard to this question is for the time being left in the keeping of the men of the South.

It can't be possible that the noble men who make up the convention intend to leave any chance for either voters or counties or the officials of the State to treat the Negro unfairly in the division of school funds. This point should be most carefully guarded and the law on the subject should be above suspicion.

---

[53]"Finds Flaws in School Ordinance," *The Times*, Richmond, Virginia (November 16, 1901). The paper quoted the remarks of Charles W. Dabney of the University of North Carolina concerning the educational issues being debated at the Virginia Constitutional Convention. The specific issue was the apportionment of state educational funds in the local districts. Previously, the legislatures in southern states had apportioned and required the distribution to be on a pro rata basis to schools of each race. Several states changed this arrangement so that although legislatures continued to apportion money to local districts on a pro rata basis, the actual distribution was made by local officials on whatever basis they felt was most educationally desirable. Dabney realized that this would lead to deliberate discrimination and opposed any change in the law.

# Policies of the General Education Board
## *1902*[54]

The movement represented by the General Education Board and the Southern Education Board has proceeded upon certain definite assumptions. I speak of them again, after our year of work, not because I would imply that they have been forgotten, but because I think you will bear me witness that we have kept faith with them.

1.   This movement has assumed that when philanthropy comes into the South with an exclusive interest in the Negro, it is likely to fail in its service both to the South and to the Negro. The South, under the irritations of such a policy, is tempted to leave the Negro wholly to the care of voluntary forces. If the South is not to draw the race line against one element of the population, the North should not draw that line against another. Racial favoritism makes for inter-racial hatred. The educational policy of a genuine patriotism will include all the children of the unprivileged, white as well as black.

2.   We may next remember our assumption that, if broad educational policies are to be attempted in the South, they should be largely worked out by Southern men. Southern men are face to face with the conditions; and just as there should be the sympathetic recognition of the leadership of Northern men in Northern affairs, so there should be the sympathetic recognition of Southern men in the affairs of the South. This is simply a principle of statesmanship; it is self-evident.

3.   We have also worked in the conviction that the first appeal of the moment in our Southern States lies in the need, not of the noble few, but of the unprivileged masses. We wish to begin with the plain people. We wish to aid our educational development, not primarily where it ends, but where it starts. We believe in our colleges and universities. We hope to serve them. We rejoice in the many millions which have been given in late years to the cause of "higher education." But our distinctive interest is in the public school, in the rural public school, for the rural public school is the first school of the masses of our people. And we are espe-

---

[54]Edgar Gardner Murphy, *The Task of the South* (N.P.: N.P., N.D.), pp. 5-7, 8, 9. Murphy, who was executive secretary of the Southern Education Board, gave this address at the close of his first year's work. The Southern Education Board was an organization of educational propaganda to secure better local support and philanthropic aid for education. It worked closely with the General Education Board, created in 1902 as the agent of the Rockefeller philanthropies. By 1929, the General Education Board had given $21 million to Negro education.

cially interested in all those forms of education which look toward thrift, industry and usefulness.

4.   The second of the assumptions of which I have spoken carries with it a further assumption which should be obvious to all. The work performed through Southern men and through those who are in touch with Southern men will necessarily be performed in harmony with Southern conceptions and in conformity with the educational systems of our Southern States. Nothing has been attempted or can be attempted save through the accepted methods and the constituted authorities of the South.

There are certain things which the South has once for all decided, which she has a right to decide, and which I believe she has decided wisely. First, therefore, in dealing with the question of popular education, she has begun by placing her Negro children in one school house and her white children in another. That division, as Dr. Curry, the Supervising Director of our Southern Board, has said, will stand until the day of our children's children. No man now living, no child of any man now living, will ever see at the South these two races taught together in the same school-room and graduated together from the same institution. These races must be educated apart. The South, as one of our friends in Georgia has observed, is not ready to open or to discuss that question with anybody. It is a closed question.

# Industrial Education Considered
## *1902*[55]

In the case of the Negroes there were a number of mixed incentives to action which have not yet clearly worked themselves out today. *First*, there was the idea of working one's own way through school which many consider an excellent moral tonic; *secondly* there was the idea of educating children in the main according to the rank in life which they will in all probability occupy. This is a wide-spread theory of education and can be especially traced in the European schools. *Thirdly* there was the scheme of using student labor to reduce the expenses of maintaining the school; *fourthly* there was the idea of training girls for house-work; *fifthly* there

---

[55]William E. B. DuBois (ed.), *The Negro Artisan* (Atlanta: Atlanta University Press, 1902), pp. 28, 188.

was the idea of having the youth learn trades for future self-support, and *sixthly* there was the idea of "learning by doing" — of using things to enforce ideas and physical exercises to aid mental processes. All these distinct aspects of education have been loosely lumped together in popular speech as "Industrial Education" with considerable resulting confusion of thought. . . .

We have studied in considerable detail the history of the Negro artisan, the industrial schools, the condition of Negro mechanics throughout the country, the attitude of organized labor toward the Negro, the opinions of employers, and Negro inventions. On the whole the survey has been encouraging, although there is much to deplore and criticise. Our conclusions may be summed up as follows:

1.   Slavery trained artisans, but they were for the most part careless and inefficient. Only in exceptional cases were they first-class mechanics.

2.   Industrial schools are needed. They are costly and, as yet, not well organized or very efficient, but they have given the Negro an ideal of manual toil and helped to a better understanding between whites and Negroes in the South. Eventually they may be expected to send out effective artisans, as they have already begun to do.

3.   There are a large number of Negro mechanics all over the land, but especially in the South. Some of these are progressive, efficient workmen. More are careless, slovenly and ill-trained. There are signs of lethargy among these artisans and work is slipping from them in some places; in others they are awakening and seizing the opportunities of the new industrial south.

4.   The labor unions, with 1,200,000 members, have less than 40,000 Negroes, mostly in a few unions, and largely semi-skilled laborers like miners. Some labor leaders have striven against color prejudice, but it exists and keeps the mass of Negroes out of many trades. This leads to complicated problems, both industrial, political and social.

5.   Employers on the whole are satisfied with Negro skilled labor and many of them favor education as tending to increase the efficiency of Negroes. Others think it will spoil the docility and tractableness of Negro labor. The employment of Negro skilled labor is slowly increasing.

6.   The Negro evinces considerable mechanical ingenuity.

On the whole this study of a phase of the vast economic development of the Negro race in America but emphasizes the primal and emphatic need of intelligence. The situation is critical and developing swiftly. Deftly guided with the larger wisdom of men and deeper benevolence of great hearts, an outcome of good to all cannot be doubted. Muddled by half-trained men and guided by selfish and sordid interests and all the evils of industrial history may easily be repeated in the South. *"Wisdom"* then *"is the principal thing; therefore, get wisdom, and with all thy getting, get understanding."*


# Washington Defends Industrial Education
### *1903*[56]


But this is somewhat aside from my purpose, which is, I repeat, to make plain that in all political matters, there was for years after the war no meeting of agreement for the two races, or for the North and South. . . .

In matters of education the difference was much less sharp. The truth is that a large element in the South had little faith in the efficacy of the higher or any other kind of education of the Negro. They were indifferent, but did not openly oppose: on the other hand, there has always been a potent element of white people in all of the Southern states who have stood out openly and bravely for the education of all the people, regardless of race. This element has thus far been successful in shaping and leading public opinion, and I think that it will continue to do so more and more. This statement must not be taken to mean that there is as yet an equitable division of the school funds, raised by common taxation, between the two races in many sections of the South, though the Southern states deserve much credit for what has been done. In discussing the small amount of direct taxes the Negro pays, the fact that he pays tremendous indirect taxes is often overlooked.

I wish, however, to emphasize the fact that while there was either open antagonism or indifference in the directions I have named, it was the introduction of industrial training into the Negro's education that seemed to furnish the first basis for anything like united and sympathetic interest and action between the two races in the South, and between the whites in the North and those in the South. Aside from its direct benefit to the black race, industrial education has furnished a basis for mutual

---

[56]Booker T. Washington, "The Fruits of Industrial Training," *Atlantic Monthly*, XCII (October, 1903), pp. 453-62. Washington correctly points to the general American interest in industrial education, which had enjoyed popularity off and on since the 1820's. His claim that industrial education for Negroes was similar to what was being done at Cornell and Amherst should be evaluated in the light of Hollis Frissell's description of industrial education at Hampton Institute found in a preceding document.

faith and co-operation, which has meant more to the South, and to the work of education, than has been realized. . . .

From its first inception the white people of the South had faith in the theory of industrial education, because they had noted, what was not unnatural, that a large element of the colored people at first interpreted freedom to mean freedom from work with the hands. They naturally had not learned to appreciate the fact that they had been worked, and that one of the great lessons for freemen to learn is to work. They had not learned the vast difference between working and being worked. The white people saw in the movement to teach the Negro youth the dignity, beauty and civilizing power of all honorable labor with the hands, something that would lead the Negro into his new life of freedom gradually and sensibly, and prevent his going from one extreme of life to the other too suddenly. Furthermore, industrial education appealed directly to the individual and community interest of the white people. They saw at once that intelligence coupled with skill would add wealth to the community and to the state, in which both races would have an added share. Crude labor in the days of slavery, they believed could be handled and made in a degree profitable, but ignorant and unskilled labor in a state of freedom could not be made so. . . .

Many of the white people were wise enough to see that such education would enable some of the Negro youths to become more skillful carpenters and contractors, and that if they laid an economic foundation in this way in their generation, they would be laying a foundation for a more abstract education of their children in the future.

Again, a large element of people at the South favored manual training for the Negro because they were wise enough to see that the South was largely free from the restrictive influences of the Northern trade unions, and that such organizations would secure little hold in the South so long as the Negro kept abreast in intelligence and skill with the same class of people elsewhere. . . .

A careful investigation of the subject will show that it was not until after industrial education was started among the colored people, and its value proved, that it was taken up by the Southern white people.

Manual training or industrial and technical schools for the whites have, for the most part, been established under state auspices, and are at this time chiefly maintained by the states. An investigation would also show that in securing money from the state legislatures for the purpose of introducing hand work, one of the main arguments used was the existence and success of industrial training among the Negroes. It was often argued that the white boys and girls would be left behind unless they had the opportunities for securing the same kind of training that was being given the colored people. . . .

Beginning with the year 1877, the Negro in the South lost practically all political control; that is to say, as early as 1885 the Negro scarcely had any members of his race in the National Congress or state legislatures, and long before this date had ceased to hold state offices. . . . It was at this period in the Negro's development, when the distance between the races was greatest, and the spirit and ambition of the colored people most depressed, that the idea of industrial or business development was introduced and began to be made prominent. It did not take the more level-headed members of the race long to see that while the Negro in the South was surrounded by many difficulties, there was practically no line drawn and little race discrimination in the world of commerce, banking, storekeeping, manufacturing, and the skilled trades, and in agriculture; and in this lay his great opportunity. They understood that while the whites might object to a Negro's being a postmaster, they would not object to his being the president of a bank, and in the latter occupation they would give him assistance and encouragement. The colored people were quick to see that while the Negro would not be invited as a rule to attend the white man's prayer-meeting, he would be invited every time to attend the stockholders' meeting of a business concern in which he had an interest, and that he could buy property in practically any portion of the South where the white man could buy it. The white citizens were all the more willing to encourage the Negro in this economic or industrial development, because they saw that the prosperity of the Negro meant also the prosperity of the white man. They saw, too, that when a Negro became the owner of a home and was a taxpayer, having a regular trade or other occupation, he at once became a conservative and safe citizen and voter; one who would consider the interests of his whole community before casting his ballot; and, further, one whose ballot could not be purchased. . . .

It ought to be stated frankly here that at first, and for several years after the introduction of industrial training at such educational centres as Hampton and Tuskegee, there was opposition from colored people, and from portions of those Northern white people engaged in educational and missionary work among the colored people in the South. Most of those who manifested such opposition were actuated by the highest and most honest motives. From the first the rank and file of the blacks were quick to see the advantages of industrial training, as is shown by the fact that industrial schools have always been overcrowded. Opposition to industrial training was based largely on the old and narrow ground that it was something that the Southern white people favored, and therefore must be against the interests of the Negro. Again, others opposed it because they feared that it meant the abandonment of all political privileges, and the higher or classical education of the race. They feared that the final outcome would be the materialization of the Negro, and the smothering of his spiritual and aesthetic nature. Others felt that industrial education had for its object the limitation of the Negro's development, and the branding him for all time as a special handworking class.

Now that enough time has elapsed for those who opposed it to see that it meant none of these things, opposition, except from a very few of the colored people living in Boston and Washington, has ceased, and this system has the enthusiastic support of the Negroes and of most of the whites who formerly opposed it. All are beginning to see that it was never meant that all Negro youths should secure industrial education, any more than it is meant that all white youths should pass through the Massachusetts Institute of Technology, or the Amherst Agricultural College, to the exclusion of such training as is given at Harvard, Yale, or Dartmouth; but that in a peculiar sense a large proportion of the Negro youths needed to have that education which would enable them to secure an economic foundation, without which no people can succeed in any of the higher walks of life. . . .

Another reason for the growth of a better understanding of the objects and influences of industrial training, is the fact, as before stated, that it has been taken up with much interest and activity by the Southern whites, and that it has been established at such universities as Cornell in the East, and in practically all of the state colleges of the great West. . . .

To those who still express the fear that perhaps too much stress is put upon industrial education for the Negro, I would add that I should emphasize the same kind of training for any people, whether black or white, in the same state of development as the masses of the colored people.

## The Talented Tenth
### *1903*[57]

What, under the present circumstances, must a system of education do to raise the Negro as quickly as possible in the scale of civilization? The answer to this question seems to me clear: It must strengthen the Negro's character, increase his knowledge, and teach him to earn a living. Now it

---

[57]W.E.B. DuBois, "The Talented Tenth," in *The Negro Problem* (New York: James Pott and Company, 1903), pp. 57, 58, 60, 61, 63, 75. Differences in educational emphasis between DuBois and Washington apparently arose from different models for achieving racial advancement.

goes without saying, that it is hard to do all these things simultaneously or suddenly, and at the same time it will not do to give all the attention to one and neglect the others. . . . A system of education is not one thing, nor does it have a single definite object, nor is it a mere matter of schools. Education is that whole system of human training within and without the school house walls, which molds and develops men. . . . I would not deny, or for a moment seem to deny, the paramount necessity of teaching the Negro to work, and to work steadily and skilfully; or seem to depreciate in the slightest degree the important part industrial schools must play in the accomplishment of these *ends*, but I *do* say, and insist upon it, that it is industrialism drunk with its vision of success, to imagine that its own work can be accomplished without providing for the training of broadly cultured men and women to teach its own teachers, and to teach the teachers of the public schools. . . . I am an earnest advocate of manual training for black boys, and for white boys, too. I believe that next to the founding of Negro colleges, the most valuable addition to Negro education since the war has been industrial training for black boys. Nevertheless, I insist that the object of all true education is not to make men carpenters, it is to make carpenters men; there are two means of making the carpenter a man - - -: the first is to give the group and community in which he works, liberally trained teachers and leaders to teach him and his family what life means; the second is to give him sufficient intelligence and technical skill to make him an efficient workman; the first object demands a Negro college and college-bred men — not a quantity of such colleges, but a few of excellent quality; not too many college-bred men, but enough to leaven the lump, to inspire the masses, to raise the Talented Tenth to leadership; the second object demands a good system of common schools, well-taught, conveniently located . . . Education must not simply teach work — it must teach life. The Talented Tenth of the Negro race must be made leaders of thought and missionaries of culture among their people. No others can do this work and the Negro colleges must train men for it. The Negro race, like all other races, is going to be saved by its exceptional men.

# A Moderate Southerner's Views
## *1904*[58]

I know well all the arguments against educating the Negroes. I know the struggle that the South made in the days of her poverty to educate that

---

[58]Thomas Nelson Page, *The Negro: The Southerner's Problem* (New York: Charles Scribner's Sons, 1904), pp. 297-99, 303-06.

race, even at the expense of her white children; expending upon them, out of taxes levied by the whites on the property of the whites, over $110,000,000, though over a fifth of the whites were left in ignorance. I know the disappointment from which she has suffered. What is charged as to the educated Negro's being just educated enough to make him worthless as a laborer and leave him useless for anything else has in it often too much truth. I am well aware that often the young Negro thinks his so-called education gives him a license to be insolent, and that not rarely it is but an aid to his viciousness. . . .

We have the Negro here among us to the number of ten millions and increasing at a rate of about twenty-five percent every ten years. They are here; what must we do with them? One of three courses must be taken: We must either debase them, keep them stationary, or improve them.

Everyone will discard the first plan.

No one can make the second feasible. A race, like a class, is always in a state of change, at least under conditions like those in America.

Then, we must adopt the third course.

At this point, the question arises: How shall they be improved? One element says, Improve them, but only as laborers, for which alone they are fitted; another, with a larger charity, says, Enlarge this and give them a chance to become good mechanics, as they have shown themselves capable of improvement in the industrial field; a third class goes further yet, and says, Give them a yet further chance — a chance to develop themselves; enlighten them and teach them the duties of citizenship and they will become measurably good citizens. Yet another says, Give him the opportunity and push him till he is stuffed full of the ideas and the learning that have made the white race what it is.

The last of these theories appears to the writer as unsound as the first, which is certainly unsound. Keep them ignorant, and the clever and the enterprising will go off and leave to the South the dull, the stupid, and the degraded. . . .

It is undoubtedly, true that the apparent result of the effort to educate the Negro has been disappointing. There are a few thousand professional men, a considerable number of college or high school graduates, but, for the greater part, there is discernible little apparent breadth of view, no growth in ability, or tendency to consider great questions reasonably. . . .

Whatever disappointment, then, there may be, this much at least may be laid down: There are only two ways to solve the Negro problem in the South. One is to remove him; the other is to elevate him. The former is apparently out of the question. The only method, then, is to improve him.

In suggesting the method of education that will prove of greatest service, it is easier to criticize than to reform. Hitherto, the idea has been to educate the Negro race just as the white race is educated; that is, to give him book education and "turn him loose." There was, it is true, no field except the curious politics of the time in which the Negro could exercise his powers based on such an education. The whites did not want this; the Negroes could not use it; but this made no difference with those who had the matter in charge. Education was understood to be ability to show book-learning. With this meagre equipment, the "educated Negro" rushed into politics, or into the pulpit, which mainly was but another name for the same thing. Sentiment, however, demanded that the Negro should be placed on an equality with the whites, and other conditions were left out of account, with disheartening results.

It is axiomatic to say that the education given to the Negro should be of the kind which will benefit him most. A few plain principles may be stated: He should be taught that education consists of something more than a mere ability to read and write and speak; that education includes moral elevation as well as intellectual development; that religion includes morality and is more than emotional excitement. He should be taught that one of the strongest elements in racial development is purity of family life; he should be taught that the duties of citizenship are much more than the ability to cast a ballot, or even to hold an office; that elevation to superiority among the people of his own race is of far greater moment to him at this time than external equality with another race, and that true superiority is founded on character. He should be taught to become self-sustaining, self-reliant, and self-respecting.

## Realism in Education
### 1904[59]

My own experience in outdoor life leads me to hope that the time will soon come when there will be a revolution in our methods of educating

---

[59]Booker T. Washington, *Working With The Hands* (New York: Doubleday, Page, and Company, 1904), pp. 157-59. This extract, lacking the usual emphasis upon racial strategy and problems, suggests another frame of reference within which the educational thought of Washington and other Negro leaders can be examined.

children, especially in the schools of the smaller towns and rural districts. I consider it almost a sin to take a number of children whose homes are on farms, and whose parents earn their living by farming, and cage them up, as if they were so many wild beasts, for six or seven hours during the day, in a close room where the air is often impure.

I have known teachers to go so far as to frost the windows in a school-room, or have them made high up in the wall, or keep the window curtains down, so that the children could not even see the wonderful world without. For six hours the life of these children is an artificial one. The apparatus which they use is, as a rule, artificial, and they are taught in an artificial manner about artificial things. Even to whisper about the song of a mocking-bird or the chirp of a squirrel in a near-by tree, or to point to a stalk of corn or a wild flower, or to speak about a cow and her calf, or a little colt and its mother grazing in an adjoining field, are sins for which they must be speedily and often severely punished. I have seen teachers keep children caged up on a beautiful, bright day in June, when all Nature was at her best, making them learn — or try to learn — a lesson about hills or mountains, or lakes, or islands, by means of a map or globe, when the land surrounding the school-house was alive and beautiful with the images of these things. I have seen a teacher work for an hour with children, trying to impress upon them the meaning of the words *lake, island, peninsula,* when a brook not a quarter of a mile away would have afforded the little ones an opportunity to pull off their shoes and stockings and wade through the water, and find, not one artificial island or lake, on an artificial globe, but dozens of real islands, peninsulas, and bays. Besides the delight of wading through the water, and of being out in the pure bracing air, they would learn by this method more about these natural divisions of the earth in five minutes than they could learn in an hour in books. A reading lesson taught out on the green grass under a spreading oak tree is a lesson needing little effort to hold a boy's attention, to say nothing of the sense of delight and relief which comes to the teacher.

I have seen teachers compel students to puzzle for hours over the problem of the working of the pulley, when not a block from the school-house were workmen with pulleys in actual operation, hoisting bricks for the walls of a new building.

I believe that the time is not far distant when every school in the rural districts and in the small town will be surrounded by a garden, and that one of the objects of the course of study will be to teach the child something about real country life, and about country occupations.

## Southern Clergyman Urges Education
*1904*[60]

Mistakes that have become a tragedy were made by some misguided persons who came South after the war to be the political teachers and leaders of the Negroes. Representing themselves as the only friends of the recently emancipated race, they made denunciation of former slave-owners an apology for their presence, and a part of the Negro's education. That policy only complicated the difficult problem. . . .

Now let us consider some of the duties we owe these people, committed to us as a trust.

*First.* — They must be guaranteed the equal protection of the law. To do less would forfeit plighted faith and disrupt the very foundations of social order. . . .

*Second.* — The right education of the Negro is at once a duty and a necessity. All the resources of the school should be exhausted in elevating his character, improving his condition and increasing his capacity as a citizen. The policy of an enforced ignorance is illogical, un-American and un-Christian. It is possible in a despotism, but perilous in a republic. It is indefensible on any grounds of social or political wisdom, and is not supported by any standards of ethics or justice. If one fact is more clearly demonstrated by the logic of history than another, it is that education is an indispensable condition of wealth and prosperity. This is a universal law, without exemption or exception. Ignorance is a cure for nothing. . . .

Of course, educational methods may be unwise and inadequate, and educational auspices may be unfortunate and unwholesome. In such event the proper course is not to close the school, but to change the methods — not to stop the teaching, but to improve the teachers. . . .

We cannot have a democracy for one class of our population, and a despotism for the other. We cannot elevate and subjugate at the same time. And, above everything, let us be just. I am jealous for my people, that they be not amenable to the charge of injustice. We must keep our covenants. . . .

From the declaration that education has made the Negro more immoral and criminal, I am constrained to dissent. There are no data or figures on which to base such an indictment or justify such an assertion. On the contrary, indisputable facts attest the statement that education and its attendant influences have elevated the standard and tone of morals among the Negroes of the South. . . .

---

[60]Charles B. Galloway, *The South and The Negro* (New York: The Trustees of the John F. Slater Fund, 1904), pp. 7-15.

The true theory of Negro education in the South has been admirably stated in these words: "The rudiments of an education for all, industrial training for the many, and a college course for the talented few." . . .

To every man among them with the evident qualities of leadership, we should lend our Christian sympathy and a helping hand. . . .

## Discrimination Protested
### *1906*[61]

Of public educational funds the Southern Negro is being *robbed*. It is strong language to use, but . . . the Southern Negro is literally being robbed of three-fourths of his due. . . . Why should the white man seek such tremendous advantages if he is confident of "superiority?"

## Anna T. Jeanes Contributes to Negro Education
### *1907*[62]

*Item* — And now, trusting, and believing, in the practicable and far-reaching good, that may result from the moral and elevating influence of Rural Schools for Negros in the South taught by reputable teachers, I do hereby name and appoint Booker T. Washington, of Tuskegee, Alabama, and Hollis Burke Frissell, of Hampton, Virginia, to be Trustees of an Endowment Fund in Perpetuity of One Million of dollars to be devoted to the one purpose of assisting *in the Southern United States, Community, Country or Rural* Schools, for that great class of Negros, to whom *the*

---

[61]William Pickens, "The Educational Condition of the Negro in Cities," *Voice of the Negro*, III (October, 1906), p. 428.

[62]Will of Anna T. Jeanes, quoted in Arthur D. Wright, *The Negro Rural School Fund, Inc.* (Washington: The Negro Rural School Fund, Inc., 1933), p. iii. Jeanes' teachers, while paid by the Fund, were expected to work as members of local school systems. For many years they provided the only effective supervision for Negro schools. The mention of Booker T. Washington in the will suggests the significant role Washington played in channelling philanthropic aid to Negro schools. His power in these matters was the basis for DuBois's bitter complaint about the "Tuskegee machine."

*smaller* Rural or Community Schools are alone available, while the larger Colored Institutes are open to those who desire a more advanced education, and farther I request and direct that the said Booker T. Washington and the said Hollis Burke Frissell, do nominate and appoint a Board of Trustees to fulfill the office and duties of Trustees of the aforesaid Endowment Fund in Perpetuity and to ensure a succession of the Members of the Board thereof.

*Item* — Should, however, Booker T. Washington and Hollis Burke Frissell die or decline to become Trustees of the said Endowment Fund in Perpetuity or should a Board of Trustees not have been established within six months after my death, I request that the Trustees of Tuskegee Colored Institute, and the Trustees of Hampton Colored Institute, shall select from members of their own Boards, a special Board of Trustees who are willing to act as Trustees of said Endowment Fund in Perpetuity of One Million of dollars, to be devoted solely to the assistance of Rural, Community, or Country Schools for Southern Negroes, and not for the benefit or use of large Institutions, but for the purpose of rudimentary education and to encourage moral influence and social refinement which shall promote peace in the land, and good will among men.

## Report on Effects of Industrial Education
### *1907*[63]

One teacher says:—"The whole tone of the community has been changed. Homes have been bought and well furnished."

We estimate that 75 per cent of the homes belonging to the Negroes show this marked improvement.

Now, as to the children:

In 1896 hardly a single child of eight years of age knew how to thread a needle; among the older girls only about 10 per cent had any idea of sewing; none of them knew anything of cooking.

Now, every colored girl attending the public schools of Norfolk and its vicinity is taught sewing; some 70 per cent cooking; about 70 per cent fine sewing and dressmaking. This means that ignorance has been replaced by knowledge, and that, in 75 per cent of the colored homes of Norfolk, all the girls can sew, and many of them cook.

Among the boys, there has been manifested, since these classes were started, an increasing desire to learn trades. Knowing now the use of tools,

---

[63]Trustees of the John F. Slater Fund, *Report of the Society of the Southern Industrial Classes*, Occasional Papers No. 12 (Hampton: Hampton Industrial Press, 1907), pp. 8, 9.

the boys have saved their parents many a dollar, doing all the repair work about the house, mending fences, making chicken coops, building wood sheds, caning and upholstering chairs.

The interest manifested by the children and their parents in industrial work has increased the attendance at the schools about 10 per cent.

After leaving school, we roughly estimate that about 20 to 30 per cent of the girls go into domestic service, — 5 per cent the first year, more the next; 50 per cent do sewing and dressmaking at home; 20 per cent marry.

In the Normal Class, there have been in all 24 graduates, 19 of whom have become teachers.

All this in view of the fact that industrial work is taught now in 35 schools as against 1 in 1896; that there are 17 paid teachers as against 4 in 1896; volunteer teachers, 34 as against none in 1896, and that 3,247 children are now receiving instruction in these branches, while the first year marked an enrollment on its books of 105 only.

This spells progress in big letters and, we hope, will receive acknowledgement.

The teachers continue to do splendid work, and their interest never abates.

The district trained nurse continues her good work, nursing and instructing, and has earned the right to a place for herself, second to none in this scheme of benevolence.

As the work grows, the expenses augment, and it is hoped that former contributors will continue their donations, and that others, glancing over these pages, may feel inclined to give interest, co-operation and money.

To the people of Virginia a special appeal is made. Let those living in communities where the colored people are irresponsible, "trifling" and lazy, realize that those people cannot be useful without training; and then, through the medium of the Public School, let them provide, or get others to provide, at a small cost, an industrial education which will fit the next generation of Negroes for responsible service, for a better mode of life, and make them good citizens.

## Education and Economic Competition
### *1908*[64]

The South cannot, economically, eat its cake and have it too. It cannot adopt a policy and a code of laws to degrade its Negro labor, to hedge it

---

[64]Archibald H. Grimké, *Modern Industrialism and the Negroes of the United States* (Washington: The American Negro Academy, 1908), pp. 16-18.

about with unequal restrictions and proscriptive legislation, and raise it at the same time to the highest state of productive efficiency. But it must as an economic necessity raise this labor to the highest point of efficiency or suffer inevitable industrial feebleness and inferiority. What are the things which have made free labor at the North the most productive labor in the world and of untold value and wealth to that section? What, but its intelligence, skill, self-reliance and power of initiative? And how have these qualities been put into it? I answer unhesitatingly, by those twin systems of universal education and popular suffrage. One system trains the children, the other the adult population. The same wide diffusion of knowledge, and large and equal freedom and participation in the affairs of government, which have done so much for Northern labor, cannot possibly do less for Southern labor.

For weal or woe the Negro is in the South to stay. He will never leave it voluntarily, and forcible deportation of him is impracticable. And for economic reasons, vital to that section, as we have seen, he must not be oppressed or repressed. All attempts to push and tie him down to the dead level of an inferior caste, to restrict his activities arbitrarily and permanently to hewing wood and drawing water for the white race, without regard to his possibilities for higher things, is in this age of strenuous industrial competition and struggle an economic blunder, pure and simple, to say nothing of the immorality of such action. Like water, let the Negro find his natural level, if the South would get the best and the most out of him. If nature has designed him to serve the white race forever, never fear. He will not be able to elude nature; he will not escape his destiny. But he must be allowed to act freely; nature does not need our aid here. Depend upon it, she will make no mistake. Her inexorable laws provide for the survival of the fittest only. Let the Negro freely find himself, whether in doing so he falls or rises in the scale of life. . . .

The commercial and industrial rivalry of the nations of the world was never so sharp and intense as at the present time, and all signs point to increased competition among them during this century. In this contest the labor of each country is primarily the grand determining factor. It must from sheer necessity and stress of circumstances be brought in each instance to the highest state of economic efficiency by every resource in the possession of the respective world rivals. And this will be attempted in the future by each of these world rivals on a grandeur of scale and with a scientific thoroughness and energy in the use of educational means yet realized by the most progressive of them. For those nations who succeed best in this respect will prevail over those others which fail to raise their labor to an equally high grade of efficiency. Now, if Negro labor is the best for its climate and needs, the South must seek earnestly, constantly, by every means in its power, to raise that labor to the highest state of economic efficiency of which it is capable. That section must do so in spite of its chimerical fears of Negro domination, in spite of its rooted race prejudices. It must educate and emancipate this labor, all hostile sentiment of whatever nature to the contrary notwithstanding, if it will hold its own in that great cosmic struggle for existence in which it is now engaged with powerful rivals at home and abroad. Nor can the republic be indifferent on this head. No country in this age of strenuous commercial competition can forget with impunity its duty in this regard. Neglect here brings swift retribution to any nation which carries a vast horde of crude and relatively inefficient labor into an industrial struggle with the rest of the world, for the world's labor will henceforth assume more and more the character of vast standing armies engaged in world-wide industrial warfare. Each unit of these industrial armies will be ultimately trained and disciplined to the highest possible efficiency. . . .

The Negro has proved himself one of the best soldiers in the world; he will prove himself in this country, provided fair play be accorded him, one of the most productive laborers in the world also. He has the capacity for becoming one of the best all-round laborers and artisans in our industrial army of conquest and one of the best all-round citizens of the republic likewise. Overcome, then, your prejudices, ye white men of the South, and ye white men, too, of the North; trust the Negro in peace as ye have trusted him in war, nor forget that the freest and most intelligent labor is ever the best and most productive labor, and that liberal and equal laws and institutions are the one unerring way yet discovered by human experience and wisdom whereby modern industrialism and democracy may reach their highest development and the highest development of humanity at the same time.

# A Progressive Reports on Negro Education
## *1908*[65]

It keeps coming to me that this is more a white man's problem than it is a Negro problem. The white man as well as the black is being tried by fire. The white man is in full control of the South, politically, socially, industrially: the Negro, as ex-Governor Northen points out, is his helpless ward. What will he do with him? Speaking of the education of the Negro,

---

[65]Ray Stannard Baker, *Following The Colour Line* (Garden City: Doubleday, Page and Company, 1908), pp. 65, 85, 132, 247, 284, 300, 302, 306. Although Progressives urged many kinds of reform, Baker was one of the few to call attention to racial problems.

and in direct reference to the conditions in Atlanta which I have already described, many men have said to me:

"Think of the large sums that the South has spent and is spending on the education of the Negro. The Negro does not begin to pay for his education in taxes."

Neither do the swarming Slavs, Italians, and Poles in our Northern cities. They pay little in taxes and yet enormous sums are expended in their improvement. For their benefit? Of course, but chiefly for ours. It is better to educate men in school than to let them so educate themselves as to become a menace to society. The present *kind* of education in the South may possibly be wrong; but for the protection of society it is as necessary to train every Negro as it is every white man.

When I saw the crowds of young Negroes being made criminal — through lack of proper training — I could not help thinking how pitilessly ignorance finally revenges itself upon that society which neglects or exploits it. . . .

One illustration more and I am through. I met at Montgomery, Alabama, a lawyer named Gustav Frederick Mertins. We were discussing the "problem," and Mr. Mertins finally made a striking remark, not at all expressing the view that I heard from some of the strongest citizens of Montgomery, but excellently voicing the position of many Southerners.

"It's a question," he said, "who will do the dirty work. In this country the white man won't: the Negro must. There's got to be a mudsill somewhere. If you educate the Negroes they won't stay where they belong; and you must consider them as a race, because if you let a few rise it makes the others discontented." . . .

In New York I had a talk with William L. Bulkley, the coloured principal of Public School No. 80, attended chiefly by coloured children, who told me of the great difficulties and discouragements which confronted the Negro boy who wanted to earn his living. He relates this story:

"I received a communication the other day from an electric company stating that they could use some bright, clean, industrious boy in their business, starting them at so much a week and aiding them to learn the business. I suspected that they did not comprehend coloured boys under the generic term 'boys,' but thought to try. So I wrote asking if they would give employment to a coloured boy who could answer to the qualifications stated. The next mail brought the expected reply that no coloured boy, however promising, was wanted. I heaved a sigh and went on.

"The saddest thing that faces me in my work is the small opportunity for a coloured boy or girl to find proper employment. A boy comes to my office and asks for his working papers. He may be well up in the school, possibly with graduation only a few months off. I question him somewhat as follows: 'Well, my boy, you want to go to work, do you? What are you going to do?' 'I am going to be a door-boy, sir.' 'Well, you will get $2.50 or $3 a week, but after a while that will not be enough; what then?' After a moment's pause he will reply: 'I should like to be an office boy.' 'Well, what next?' A moment's silence, and, 'I should try to get a position as bell-boy.' 'Well, what next?' A rather contemplative mood, and then, 'I should like to climb to the position of head bell-boy.' He has now arrived at the top; further than this he sees no hope. He must face the bald fact that he must enter business as a boy and wind up as a boy." . . .

It is a fact of common knowledge in history that aristocracies cannot long survive when free education is permitted among all classes of people. Education is more potent against oligarchies and aristocracies than dynamite bombs. Every aristocracy that has survived has had to monopolise learning more or less completely—else it went to the wall. It is not surprising that there should have been no effective public-school system in the South before the war where the poor whites could get an education, or that the teaching of Negroes was in many states a crime punishable by law. Education enables the Negro, as Mr. Lane says, to "ascertain his rights and force his way to assert them." Therefore to prevent his ascertaining his rights he must not be educated. The undivided supremacy of the white party, it is clearly discerned, is bound up with Negro ignorance. Therefore we have seen and are now seeing in certain parts of the South continuous agitation against the education of Negroes. That is one reason for the feeling in the South against "Northern philanthropy" which is contributing money to support Negro schools and colleges.

"What the North is sending South is not money," says Vardaman, "but dynamite; this education is ruining our Negroes. They're demanding equality." . . .

The new leaders, then, of whom I have spoken, do not oppose Negro education: they favour it and will go forward steadily with the task of bringing it about. So far, the Negro public schools have felt little of the new impulse; in some states and localities, as I have shown in other chapters, the Negro schools have actually retrograded, where the white schools have been improving rapidly. But that is the continuing influence of the old leadership; the new men have not yet come fully into their own. . . .

So much for conditions; what of remedies? . . .

As a fundamental proposition, then, it will be found that the solution of the Negro problem lies in treating the Negro more and more as a human being like ourselves. Treating the Negro as a human being, we must judge him, not by his colour, or by any other outward symbol, but upon his worth as a man. Nothing that fails of that full honesty and fairness of judgment in the smallest particular will suffice. We disgrace and injure ourselves more than we do the Negro when we are not willing to admit virtue or learning or power in another human being because his face happens to be yellow or black. . . .

As in the case of the Jim Crow laws, separate schools in the South are necessary, and in one way I believe them to be of great advantage to the Negroes themselves. In Northern cities like Indianapolis and New York, where there are no separation laws of any kind, separate schools have appeared, naturally and quietly, in districts where the Negro population is dense. That the pupils in each should be treated with exact justice in the matter of expenditures by the state is axiomatic. And the Negro boy should have the same unbounded opportunity for any sort of education he is capable of using as the white boy; nothing less will suffice. . . .

## Self-Help

*1909*[66]

Three Times Ten Club, Tuscaloosa, Alabama.

We meet fortnightly at the homes of club members (alphabetically), when we attend to business and a literary and musical programme, is had. As our club is federated with the Alabama Federation of Colored Women's Clubs, we of course help to sustain the Colored Boys' Reformatory at Mt. Meigs; and we assist charitably those in Tuscaloosa who are deserving.

Our main object (locally) is to establish what we sorely need and have been striving to establish—a High School. With that purpose in view we purchased a plot of land for $200, but have never been able to build. A few months ago a Tuscaloosa Educational Association, composed of citizens of the county, was formed; to which organization we have donated the plot of land, with the understanding that they are to erect a High School. We have about $200 in our treasury now, and as soon as a building is assured we will no doubt make further donation, and shall continue to contribute.

---

[66]Cited from *Southern Workman* (October-November, 1909) in W.E.B. DuBois (ed.), *Efforts for Social Betterment Among Negro Americans* (Atlanta: Atlanta University Press, 1909), p. 32. The most significant feature in southern Negro education has not been segregation or poor quality of education, but the failure on the part of public officials to accept responsibility for incorporating fully and completely Negro education into the public educational system. As a result, Negro citizens in their private capacity have been forced, as the above document shows, to assume a burden which other Americans have not encountered within the framework of public education.

# North Carolina Educator
# Examines the Tax Question
*1909*[67]

I shall confine this paper to the investigation of the question, *"Is the Negro public school in the South a burden on the white taxpayer, and if so, to what extent?"* . . .

The South is spending $32,068,851 on her public schools, both white and black, but what part of this sum is devoted to Negro public schools, which must serve at least 40 per cent of her school population? It is not possible to answer this question with absolute accuracy. But it is possible, from the several State reports, to find out the whole amount spent for teachers, and, in all the States except Arkansas, what was spent for white and Negro teachers separately. The aggregate amount now being spent for public school teachers of both races in these eleven States is $23,856,914, or 74.4 per cent of the whole amount expended. Of this sum not more than $3,818,705 was paid to Negro teachers, or 12 per cent of the total expenditures. And here let me call your attention directly to the fact that nearly three-fourths of our total public school expendiures are for teachers, but that Negro teachers receive only 12 per cent of the total expended, while white teachers receive 62.4 per cent. It is also evident that the amount spent for Negro teachers is by far the largest item of expense of the Negro public schools. . . .

It is generally assumed in the discussion of the cost of the Negro public schools, that the white race bears all the cost or nearly all; that the Negroes of the South are truly the white man's burden when it comes to paying the bills for public education. Much of this unseasoned talk reminds me of the North Carolina farmer who was in the habit of asserting on all occasions that he could live and get along so much better if it were not for his large and oppressive doctor bills. But the doctor declared at the next term of the court, on oath, that this chronic complainer had not paid him a cent in fifteen years, and that he was the only doctor in the community.

And this brings me directly to the main inquiry: Is the Negro public school of the South a burden on the white taxpayer? But here again, complete data with which to work cannot be had. However, this question can be answered for Virginia, North Carolina, and Georgia, with some degree of accuracy. . . .

---

[67]Charles L. Coon, *Public Taxation and Negro Schools* (Cheyney, Pennsylvania: Committee of Twelve for the Advancement of the Interests of the Negro Race, 1909), pp. 3-11. Coon was Superintendent of Schools in Wilson, North Carolina. A common objection to Negro education was that it was almost entirely at the expense of whites.

I have shown before that Virginia is spending only about $489,228 on her Negro schools. If my figures are correct, then $18,077 of the amount which should be devoted to their schools, if we assume the race division of the funds, does not reach the Negro schools of Virginia. . . .

I have shown before that North Carolina is likely spending only $402,658 on her Negro schools. This leaves $26,539 of the North Carolina fund which never reached the Negro in 1908. . . .

I have shown that Negroes actually received about $506,170 of the Georgia school fund of 1907. This leaves $141,682.54 to the credit of the Negro fund, upon any fair race division. . . .

Time is not at hand to make a detailed study of this question for all the eleven States under consideration. What is true of the school funds of the three States considered above is probably true of all the others. A somewhat careful study of this question for several years leads me to the conclusion that the Negro school of the South is no serious burden on the white taxpayer. The same conclusion will be reached if the subject is approached from another standpoint. Suppose the Negro children of these States were all white. Then it will be found that it would cost to educate the present Negro school population on the basis they were all white, just about five times as much as it does now to give the same number of Negroes such education as they are getting. . . .

Such facts give us glimpes of the economic importance of the Negro and abundantly justify us in hoping that the senseless race prejudice which has for its object the intellectual enslavement of Negro children will soon pass away. I do not believe that any superior race can hope for the blessings of heaven on its own children while it begrudges more light and efficiency for those of an inferior race.

## Atlanta Conference Resolutions
### *1910*[68]

1.  There is an increased and pressing demand for college trained Negroes.
2.  The Negro graduates are at present, with few exceptions, usefully and creditably employed.
3.  The course of study in these colleges does not call for any peculiar modification, but should, on the whole, conform to the gen-

---

[68]"Resolutions of the Fifteenth Atlanta Conference," in W.E.B. DuBois and Augustus G. Dill (ed.), *The College-Bred Negro American* (Atlanta: Atlanta University Press, 1910), p. 7.

eral type of curriculum designed for the preparation of broadly educated men to take their places in modern civilization.

4. There should be at least one college for Negro students in each state, liberally endowed.

5. There should be every effort towards cooperation between colleges in the same locality, and towards avoidance of unnecessary duplication of work.

6. We believe that Negro public high schools in the South are greatly needed.

7. We believe in perfect honesty in living up to catalog requirements of admission.

8. We believe the amount of Greek and Latin in college should be gradually reduced.

9. We believe that the time given to Natural Science, English, History and Sociology should be increased.

10. We believe that vocational training is a pressing need of Negroes but that it should be preceded by as much cultural training as possible.

## DuBois Criticizes Negro Education
### *1911*[69]

From these and other evidences it seems fair to conclude:

1. That the overwhelming majority of Negro children of school age are not in school.

2. That the chief reason for this is the lack of school facilities; and a further reason is the poverty and ignorance of parents.

3. That those Negro children who are in school are as a rule poorly taught by half-prepared and poorly paid teachers and through short terms of three to six months a year.

4. That the school houses and equipment for Negro schools are for the most part wretched and inadequate.

---

[69]W.E.B. DuBois and Augustus A. Dill (ed.), *The Common School and the Negro American* (Atlanta: Atlanta University Press, 1911), pp. 137-38. DuBois, as here, was outspoken and forthright in discussing educational problems and especially in pointing out deficiencies. The dominant theme of those associated with the Hampton-Tuskegee pattern was that of steady improvement despite hardships and difficulties. One would scarcely learn of gross financial inequities in southern Negro education from the latter men, or if they were mentioned it would be in a context of a temporary aberration which would soon disappear.

5. That the Negro schools as a rule receive little or no helpful superintendence from the school authorities.
6. That the result and apparently one of the objects of disfranchisement has been to cut down the Negro school fund, bar out competent teachers, lower the grade and efficiency of the course of study and employ as teachers in the Negro schools those willing tools who do not and will not protest or complain.
7. That in the attempt to introduce much needed and valuable manual and industrial training there has been introduced into the curriculum of the Negro common school a mass of ill-considered, unrelated work which has overburdened the teacher and pushed into the background the vital studies of reading, writing and arithmetic.
8. That the forward movement in education in the South during the past ten years has been openly confined almost entirely to white people. . . In many cases the Negroes have been taxed for the improvement of white school facilities, while their own schools have not been allowed to share in these improvements.
9. That along with this curtailment of elementary public education for Negroes has gone a tendency to decry the work of those schools which are devoted to the higher training of the Negro youth, to lower their curricula, to cut off northern benevolence, and to decrease the supply of intellectual leaders for the Negro race.

# A Call for Racial Justice
## *1916*[70]

In this letter the Commission wishes to direct the attention of the college men to the educational aspect of the race question, inasmuch as the solution of all human problems ultimately rests upon rightly directed education. In its last analysis, education simply means bringing forth all the native capacities of the individual for the benefit both of himself and of society. It is axiomatic that a developed plant, animal, or man is far more valuable to society than the undeveloped. It is likwise obvious that

---

[70]"Open letter on Education by the University Commission, September 1, 1916," in *Five Letters of the University Commission on Southern Race Questions, 1927,* Occasional Papers, No. 24, (Trustees of the John F. Slater Fund), pp. 8, 9.

ignorance is the most fruitful source of human ills. Furthermore, it is as true in a social as in a physical sense that a chain is no stronger than its weakest link. The good results thus far obtained, as shown by the Negro's progress within recent years, prompt the Commission to urge the extension of his educational opportunities.

The inadequate provision for the education of the Negro is more than an injustice to him; it is an injury to the white man. The South cannot realize its destiny if one-third of its population is undeveloped and inefficient. For our common welfare we must strive to cure disease wherever we find it, strengthen whatever is weak, and develop all that is undeveloped. The initial steps for increasing the efficiency and usefulness of the Negro race must necessarily be taken in the school room. There can be no denying that more and better schools, with better trained and better paid teachers, more adequate supervision and longer terms, are needed for the blacks, as well as the whites. The Negro schools are, of course, parts of the school systems of their respective states, and as such share in the progress and prosperity of their systems. Our appeal is for a larger share for the Negro, on the ground of the common welfare and common justice. He is the weakest link in our civilization, and our welfare is indissolubly bound up with his.

Many means are open to the college men of the South for arousing greater public interest in this matter and for promoting a more vigorous public effort to this end. A right attitude in this, as in all other important public questions, is a condition precedent to success. For this reason the Commission addresses to Southern college men this special appeal.

# The Colored Girl Beautiful
## *1916*[71]

The colored child should be taught Negro history that she may be proud of her dark skin. . . . Let her know that the black man was the author of much of the world's history. . . . Tell her the record of the Negro as a soldier, statesman, and explorer. . . . The colored girl beautiful will select

---

[71]E. Azalia Hackley, *The Colored Girl Beautiful* (Kansas City: Burton Publishing Company, 1916), p. 28, 133-39. This is one of several books of self-culture designed to supplement school learning with advice on general culture, manners, posture, grooming, health and personal conduct. Azalia Hackley compiled her book from talks made to girls at boarding schools.

the school which fights flies, dirt, filth around back doors; the school which aims for sanitation before putting in electric lights . . . she will attend a school that buys books and takes care of them and which compels the students to read that they may grow into the reading habit, to pass it along to posterity. . . . The colored girl beautiful will be taught her duty and relationship to the race, that she may be a living example of what right education and right training will do. . . . She will learn that the aim of education is the aim of religion, that is, to lift one above the animal. . . . The colored girl beautiful will be taught the value and use of money, and the relative value of character, education, and other things, which money cannot buy. She will be taught the care and cleanliness of the body, simplicity of wearing apparel and appropriate becoming inconspicuous costumes for church, school, street and home. . . . She will be taught that it is unforgiveable not to walk erect, to talk in good English, and in a soft tone or voice. . . . She will be taught that the aim of education is to give good habits of reading along with book-knowledge. . . . She will be taught a trade, or some means of earning a livelihood, that she may be prepared, if circumstances should force her into the business arena.

# 3

# World War I to 1970

This chapter will illustrate the significant issues, events, and conditions in black education from World War I to the present. The first world war marked a turning point in the history of Negro education. The very act of fighting for democracy abroad inevitably forced some introspection concerning democracy at home. The cry for the schools to be consistent with basic American ideals was renewed. The death of Booker T. Washington, the establishment of the National Association for the Advancement of Colored People, and the National Urban League meant that the pattern of Negro leadership was moving away from individual leadership and toward corporate leadership. Changes in the income tax law, recognition of the need to encourage public responsibility for Negro education, and the growing unwillingness by blacks to be saddled with the accommodationist strategy and vocational education seemingly promoted by the philanthropists, were some factors that slowly brought an end to the huge philanthropic bequests which had so profoundly affected Negro education. States were forced to accept their responsibility for education, and philanthropy reflected less the interests of a single benefactor. Finally, with the prohibition of immigration during the war, Negro migration to the city was accelerated, and the black man encountered his first major opportunity for industrial employment. All these factors challenged and changed Negro education as it had existed.

The concept of democracy was probably the dominant normative concept affecting Negro education in this period. The readings in this chapter will illustrate the conscious application of democracy to the education of Negroes. An extract from a speech by William Pickens during World War I, will illustrate the way in which the popular notion of making the world "safe for democracy" was turned inward upon the nation and its largest minority group.

This theme is further explored in selections from J. Saunders Redding (1951), Dan Dodson (1962), and John H. Fischer (1964).

Perhaps the most visible issue in the history of Negro education has been segregation. Although school segregation was firmly fixed before World War I, the increasing racism following the war brought further attempts to solidify the barriers between the races.[1] In 1919, the Georgia legislature passed laws requiring segregation, while in 1927, the Arizona legislature passed laws making segregation optional. Thus segregation was removed from custom and became state law.

Not all Negro leaders have agreed on the importance of desegregated schools. Those who favored separate schools have done so for a variety of reasons and apparently have been a relatively small minority. Negro leaders who had opposed segregation, did so partly on the ground that it was inextricably linked with inferior educational opportunities. Following World War I, this opposition to the companion evils of segregation and inferior education greatly increased. Readings from Payne, Caliver, and Johnson will illustrate efforts to publicize school conditions and thereby eliminate them. The NAACP played a major role during this period by initiating in 1935, a long range attack first upon educational inequities and ultimately upon segregation itself. A selection by Charles Houston outlines the plans for this attack. The earliest result of the publicity and legal attacks were moves toward the equalization of teacher salaries as may be seen in the documents from West Virginia (1929) and Georgia (1937). The action taken by these states preceded the first court victory on this subject (Ann Arundel County, Maryland, 1939).[2]

From their initial attacks on elementary and secondary schools, NAACP lawyers quickly turned their attention to graduate and professional training. The results are illustrated in materials from the University of Maryland law school case (1935), and the McLaurin and Sweatt cases (1950). These latter cases are especially significant because of the willingness on the part of the court to consider intangible factors in evaluating equality of educational opportunity. The climax of this entire effort came with the 1954 Supreme Court decision prohibiting segregation.[3]

---

[1]On the racism of the period, see Idus A. Newby, *Jim Crow's Defense: Anti-Negro Thought in America*, 1900-1930 (Baton Rouge: Louisiana State University Press, 1965).

[2]For a discussion of this aspect of the NAACP program, see Herman H. Bozeman, "Attitudes of Selected Racial Leadership Organizations Towards Educational Policies and Practices for Negroes During the Twentieth Century," an unpublished doctoral dissertation, University of Michigan, 1956.

[3]For the background of the 1954 decision, see Loren Miller, *The Petitioners* (New York: Pantheon Books, 1966).

Even as the NAACP was beginning its program, other agencies were being brought to bear upon the problem of improving black education. The depression and the resulting plight of the South where most Negroes lived, served to focus national attention upon the problem. Testing programs connected with two world wars and increased Negro militancy served the same purpose. A number of selections in this chapter will indicate the wide variety of efforts to improve education for Negroes.[4] In 1921, North Carolina passed legislation to strengthen supervision in Negro schools, which had long been weak. Perhaps one of the strongest symobls of federal concern was the appointment of a black specialist in the Bureau of Education in 1930. Regular appropriations were authorized for Howard University in 1928, and various states (Missouri, 1921; Maryland, 1937) made arrangements for out-of-state graduate and professional education for blacks. Most southern states entered into a regional compact in 1948 which anticipated the development or adoption of certain schools as regional centers for the training of blacks in fields not available within individual states. None of these belated efforts to provide improved education, however, could stem the attack by Negroes themselves upon school segregation and discrimination.

Several documents in the readings trace the sequel to the 1954 desegregation decision.[5] The massive resistance attempted by Virginia is illustrated by various laws passed in 1956, 1958 and 1960. Prince Edward County, Virginia, closed its public school system to avoid integration, thus at long last carrying out the threat which had been used by opponents of mixed schools as far back as the Reconstruction Era. An extract is included from the court order requiring the reopening of Prince Edward County schools. Other examples of resistance to desegregation are given in materials relating to the entry to James Meredith into the University of Mississippi (1962) and the desegregation of Central High School, Little Rock, Arkansas (1957).

Despite the clear intent of the 1954 Supreme Court decision, school desegregation proceeded at a rate of about 1 percent of Negro children per year during the first decade. In 1964, Congress passed a civil rights bill requiring the withholding of federal funds from segregated schools. An extract from this bill is included in the readings. This bill, with the 1965 Elementary and Secondary Educa-

---

[4]Other efforts to improve schools are discussed in Russell A. Lane, "The Legal Trend Toward Increased Provisions for Negro Education in the United States Between 1920 and 1930," *Journal Of Negro Education*, I (October, 1932), pp. 396-99.

[5]There is a great deal of literature dealing with events following the 1954 decision. Two general works are: Benjamin Muse, *Ten Years of Prelude* (New York: Viking Press, 1964), and Reed Sarratt, *The Ordeal of Desegregation* (New York: Harper & Row, Publishers, 1966). A detailed account of events in Virginia is found in Benjamin Muse, *Virginia's Massive Resistance* (Bloomington: Indiana University Press, 1961).

tion Act, providing massive federal aid to education, dramatically increased the rate of desegregation.[6]

What had been declared unconstitutional in 1954 was segregation based upon state law (*de jure*). Since segregation frequently was due to housing patterns, there arose the question of the schools' obligation to eliminate *de facto* segregation. Extracts from certain court cases (Briggs, 1955; Bell, 1963; Balaban, 1964; Jackson, 1963) illustrate the varying stands taken by the courts on this issue. Quite apart from legal requirements, some school systems adopted the policy of deliberately promoting racial integration. An extract from a statement by the New York City Board of Education illustrates this viewpoint. The Coleman report on equality of educational opportunity disclosed not only the fact that segregation remained twelve years after the Supreme Court decision, but also that the racial composition of schools was strongly related to student achievement.

The reaction of Negroes to the desegregation decision and succeeding events was determined by the length of time that had elapsed. The statement by a conference of southern black educators illustrates their immediate reaction. Renewed demands for drastic improvement of education even if still in a segregated setting came with the glacial pace of desegregation. Indeed, the critique of American education which has developed from this reaction is much more profound than the earlier statistical demonstrations of inferior buildings, budgets, or teachers. The writings of Charles S. Johnson in the 1940's drew attention to the failure of the school to help the black child. The work of Kenneth Clark has continued this theme. Efforts to improve educational opportunities for Negroes and other minorities have gone beyond the technical equalization of objective features and now include a wide range of "compensatory" programs and even proposals that teachers be held accountable for the educational output of their efforts.[7] At the same time, there has been an increasing scepticism and cynicism about desegregation efforts. By 1970, as

---

[6]The most authoritative record of the progress of desegregation is found in the publications of the Southern Education Reporting Service, especially its *Southern School News.* See also Yearbook issues of *The Journal of Negro Education,* especially "The Relative Progress of the American Negro Since 1950," XXXII (Fall, 1963), and "Race and Equality in American Education," XXXVII (Summer, 1968).

[7]The most comprehensive study of compensatory programs can be found in Edmund W. Gordon and Doxey A. Wilkerson, *Compensatory Education for the Disadvantaged* (New York: College Entrance Examination Board, 1966). Plans for a massive study of such programs at the college level were announced by Edmund Gordon and Charles L. Thomas in "Brief: A Study on Compensatory Collegiate Programs for Minority Group Youth," Teachers College, Columbia University, 1969, ERIC Document 028 746.

illustrated by the Whitney Young selection, some Negroes felt that the vision of equality which seemed bright in 1954, had somehow become the same nightmare over again.

While the twin issues of segregation and equality of opportunity were surely the most visible issues within this period, there are other readings which suggest certain important developments. Prior to World War I, the myth of white racial supremacy not only enjoyed popular vogue among lay whites, but also had wide support among scientists and scholars as well. In the twenties and thirties, scholars began to reevaluate the assumptions and methods which underlay these racist conclusions.[8] In addition to the objective considerations presented in scholarly articles, the association of racism with Nazi Germany as well as a more sensitive appreciation for the implications of the democratic creed brought about a gradual shift in majority group attitudes.

Throughout this period, an interest in studies relating to Negro life has developed, indeed, becoming more intense with the passing of time. Some readings in this chapter will reflect this interest on the part of Negroes, and the corresponding response on the part of school systems. One important aspect of the development of race consciousness and pride has been the continued interest in Africa and the study of black peoples wherever they are.

The debate over the kind of education needed by the Negro, at least in the traditional terms of industrial vs. liberal academic was moribund after World War I. In its place, rose the question of the role of the predominantly (or historically) Negro college. As one document will indicate, relatively few Negroes received industrial or vocational education at any level. Thomas Jesse Jones published a survey of Negro colleges in 1916 for the U.S. Bureau of Education which seriously criticized these schools. Another Bureau of Education survey was made by Arthur J. Klein and published in 1928. It reported only slight improvement. Attempts to have Negro colleges accredited by the Southern Association of Colleges and Secondary Schools covered the period from 1930 to 1957, when the first group of Negro colleges was admitted to regular membership. These factors, among others, stimulated frequent criticism of the education provided by the Negro college. Articles by Hughes, Miller, Woodson, and Lomax present examples of the criticism frequently leveled at

---

[8]See Thomas F. Gossett, *Race: The History of an Idea in America* (Dallas: Southern Methodist University Press, 1963). Subsequently published in paperback by Schocken Books.

the Negro college.[9] Also a part of this debate over the kind of education needed by Negroes are the views of various nationalistic groups. Extracts from representatives of three groups are included in the readings. The common thread that seems to run through all the debates is the belief that Negro colleges have a unique mission in serving a particular constituency. This mission, some think, imparts a public service function to the Negro college not unlike that characteristic of the land grant colleges. In this situation, however, there is much less agreement on the nature and manner of that service.

After 350 years of educational history, every fundamental issue in the education of blacks in the United States still remains a topic of current debate. The basic democratic ideals which have informed education in the United States remain largely unrealized for black Americans. It is these facts, and the moral obligations that they impose, which make a study of the history of Negro education relevant to every American.

## Democracy in Education
### 1916[10]

Democracy in Education. This is fundamental. No other democracy is practicable unless all of the people have equal right and opportunity to develop according to their individual endowments. There can be no real democracy between two natural groups, if one represents the extreme of ignorance and the other the best intelligence. The common public school and the state university should be the foundation stones of democracy. If men are artificially differentiated at the beginning, if we try to educate a "working class" and a "ruling class," forcing different race groups into different lines without regard to individual fitness, how can we ever hope for democracy in the other relations of these groups? Individuals do differ, but in democracy of education peoples living on the same soil should not be widely diverged in their training on mere racial lines. This would be illogical, since they are measured by the same standards of life. Of

---

[9]Christopher Jencks and David Riesman stimulated a lively discussion of the Negro college with their *The Academic Revolution* (New York: Doubleday & Company, 1968). A verson of Chapter X, "Negroes and Their Colleges," appeared in the *Harvard Educational Review*, XXXVII (Winter, 1967), pp. 3-60.

[10]William Pickens, "The Kind of Democracy the Negro Race Expects," in Carter G. Woodson, *Negro Orators and Their Orations*, (Washington: Associated Publishers, 1925), p. 655. No date is given for this address but internal evidence indicates that it was given during World War I.

course, a group that is to live in Florida should be differently trained from a group that is to live in Alaska; but that is geography and general environment, not color or caste. The Negro believes in democracy of education as first and fundamental: that the distinction should be made between individual talents and not between colors and castes.

## The Curriculum in Negro Schools
### *1916*[11]

An examination of the secondary courses of the schools . . . shows the large place given to foreign languages and especially the ancient languages. This emphasis on ancient languages is greatest in the schools owned and managed by the colored denominations. This devotion to the old rigid curriculum, with Latin four years, Greek two or three years, and mathematics two or three years, is not difficult to explain. The majority of the schools were established at a time when the old curriculum was the current practice. This practice has continued somewhat longer in the South than in other sections of the country and the Negroes naturally adopted the educational forms of their neighbors. The persistence of the colored people in their faith in the languages is mainly due to a lack of contact with the progressive educational movements of the day and to the small school income, which limits the possibility of electives. So far as the needed changes are in the direction of larger recognition of industrial and agricultural instruction, the opposition of the Negroes is based on a suspicion that the white people are urging caste education which confines them to industrial pursuits.

## Segregation Required in Georgia
### *1919*[12]

. . . It shall also be the duty of said Board of Education to make arrangements for the instruction of the children of the white and colored races in

---

[11]Thomas Jesse Jones, *Negro Education*, Department of Interior, Bureau of Education, Bulletin I, 38 (Washington D.C.: Government Printing Office, 1917), 42, 43. It is interesting to note that despite the widespread advocacy of industrial education for Negroes both by southern whites and northern philanthropists, most Negro children were never exposed to it.

[12]Statutes of Georgia, Part I, Title 6, Article VIII, Sections 84 and 110, 1919.

separate schools. They shall, as far as practicable provide the same facilities for both races in respect to attainments and abilities of teachers
and for a minimum of six months length of term time; but the children
of the white and colored races shall not be taught together in any common
or public school of this State. . . .

Colored and white children shall not attend the same school; and no
teacher receiving or teaching white and colored pupils at the same school
shall be allowed any compensation at all out of the common school fund.


# The Object of Education
## *1920*[13]


Many . . . feverishly argue the relative values of Greek, mathematics, and
manual training, but fail with singular unanimity in pointing out the fundamental cause of our failure in human education: that failure is due to
the fact that we aim not at the full development of the child, but that the
world regards and always has regarded education first as a means of
buttressing the established order of things rather than improving it. . . .
We may teach frankly that this world is not perfection, but development:
that the object of education is manhood and womanhood, clear reason,
individual talent and genius and the spirit of service and sacrifice, and
not simply a frantic effort to avoid change in present institutions. . . .
Given as the ideal the utmost possible freedom for every human soul, with
slavery for none, and equal honor for all necessary human tasks, then our
problem of education is greatly simplified: we aim to develop human
souls; to make all intelligent; to discover special talents and genius. With
this course of training beginning in early childhood and never ceasing
must go the technical training for the present world's work according
to carefully studied individual gifts and wishes. On the other hand, if we
arrange our system of education to develop workmen who will not strike
and Negroes satisfied with their present place in the world, we have set
ourselves a baffling task. We find ourselves compelled to keep the masses
ignorant and to curb our own thought and expression so as not to influence the ignorant. We force moderate reformers and men with new and
valuable ideas to become red radicals and revolutionists, since that hap-

---

[13]W.E.B. DuBois, "The Immortal Child," in *Darkwater: Voices From Within the
Veil* (New York: Harcourt, Brace and Howe, 1920), pp. 205-10 *passim*.

pens to be the only way to make the world listen to reason. . . . Above all we must not forget that the object of all education is the child itself and not what it makes or does. It is here that a great movement in America has grievously sinned against the light. There has arisen among us a movement to make the Public School primarily the hand-maiden of production. . . . Consequently, the public schools are for training the mass of men as servants and laborers and mechanics to increase the land's industrial efficiency. Those who oppose this program, especially if they are black, are accused of despising common toil and humble service. . . . Without wider, deeper intelligence among the masses Democracy cannot accomplish its greater ends. Without a more careful conservation of human ability and talent the world cannot secure the services which its greater needs call for. . . . Who goes to college, the Talented or the Rich? Who goes to high school, the Bright or the Well-To-Do? Who does the physical work of the world, those whose muscles need the exercise or those whose souls and minds are stupefied with manual toil? . . . We cannot base the education of future citizens on the present inexcusable inequality of wealth nor on physical differences of race. . . . Colored Americans must then with deep determination educate their children in the broadest, highest way. They must fill the colleges with the talented and fill the fields and shops with the intelligent. . . . Is not the problem of their education simply an intensification of the problem of educating all children?

## Missouri Provides Higher Education for Negroes
*1921*[14]

SEC. 1 . . . The name of the Lincoln institute is hereby changed to Lincoln university . . .

SEC. 3 The board of curators of the Lincoln university shall be authorized and required to reorganize said institution so that it shall

[14]Laws of Missouri, 1921, pp. 86, 87. Approved April 15, 1921. Lincoln was established after the Civil War largely through the efforts of a group of Negro soldiers. One of the early NAACP cases involved Lloyd Gaines, a graduate of Lincoln, who sought admission to the University of Missouri in the absence of the desired courses at Lincoln. The U.S. Supreme Court held that the provision of out-of-state facilities, as contemplated in the above law, did not meet constitutional requirements.

afford to the Negro people of the state opportunity for training up to the standard furnished at the state university of Missouri whenever necessary and practicable in their opinion.

SEC. 7 Pending the full development of the Lincoln university, the board of curators shall have the authority to arrange for the attendance of Negro residents of the state of Missouri at the university of any adjacent state to take any course or to study any subjects provided for at the state university of Missouri, and which are not taught at the Lincoln university and to pay the reasonable tuition fees for such attendance; provided that whenever the board of curators deem it advisable they shall have the power to open any necessary school or department.

## Better Supervision of Negro Schools
*1921*[15]

There shall be annually appropriated from the State Public School Fund the sum of fifteen thousand dollars, or so much of this amount as may be necessary, to secure better supervision of Negro education in all normal schools, training schools, high schools, elementary schools, and teacher training departments in all colleges for Negroes over which the State now or hereafter may have any control.

The State Board of Education is hereby authorized, upon the recommendation of the Superintendent of Public Instruction, to employ a Director of Negro Education, and such supervisors, assistants, both clerical and professional, as may be necessary to carry out the purposes of this section not inconsistent with the amount of the appropriation, and to define the duties of the same.

---

[15]North Carolina Public Laws and Resolutions, 1921, Chapter 146, Sec. 17, pp. 420, 421. Despite gross inequities in funds and buildings, one of the most harmful but widespread types of discrimination was the failure to provide effective supervision of Negro schools. Often there grew up a quasi-political arrangement in which a Negro school principal was designated unofficially as the "supervising principal" through whom appointments and requests for materials and even buildings were handled. The Jeanes Fund and the General Education Board used much of their funds to pay the salaries of persons who would supervise Negro schools as agents of the state department of education. Gradually states assumed responsibility for paying these supervisors.

# Purpose of the Negro Colleges
*1924*[16]

Any segregated or semi-segregated group is doomed unless it develops and sustains its own leadership and wise self-direction. . . . The segregation of the Negro makes it necessary that his professional and higher needs be met by professional men of this own race. . . . Just in proportion as the spirit of segregation increases, the demand for internal leadership becomes intensified. . . . The function of the Negro college is to prepare the choice men and women of the race to fill the high places of intellectual, moral and spiritual authority as guide, philosopher and friend of their less fortunate brethren.

# A Plea for Negro History
*1925*[17]

But whatever general history, ancient or modern, may have to say of the Negro, American history cannot be truthfully written without giving the Negro some creditable roles. . . . What we need is an historical knowledge that will paint us as we are. . . . We want a literature of truth and inspiration that will embalm the deeds of our heroes and encourage the lives of our children. . . . The American Negro is *sui generis*. . . . Oh! for a Negro

---

[16]Kelly Miller, "The Practical Value of Higher Education," in *Why Go To College*, a pamphlet published by Alpha Phi Alpha Fraternity, (May, 1924), p. 21. Miller (1863–1939), long time Howard University professor, was a prolific propagandist and essayist rather than scholar. Here he seems to accept DuBois' assumption that only a small proportion (perhaps the "talented tenth") can profit from college work. The theme of race leadership was nearly universal, but with differences respecting the nature of that leadership. Miller stresses the professional services of college trained men, but in view of his attempt to convene a "Negro Sanhedrin" to provide race guidance, it is probably correct to think that he had racial political leadership also in mind.

[17]Charles Victor Roman, "A Knowledge of History Conductive to Racial Solidarity," in Carter G. Woodson, *Negro Orators and Their Orations* (Washington: Associated Publishers, 1925), pp. 648-51. Roman practiced medicine in Clarksville, Tennessee, then taught at Meharry Medical College. He was long time editor of the *Journal of the National Medical Association*. He delivered this speech on various occasions.

pen to record the lives of our great men and women! I would not circumscribe the fields of learning nor rob the white children of their pride of lineage, but I would teach Negro children the glorious deeds of Negro men and women *FIRST*. . . . I am not preaching ethnic antagonism nor endeavoring to give a racial tinge to the facts of history, but I do wish to widen sufficiently the fields of *taught* history to include the Negroes who just belong there.

A diffusion of such knowledge among the masses of our people will stimulate race pride, strengthen their consciousness of kind without lessening their patriotism, and furnish an atmosphere of mutual cooperation and helpfulness that will change the winter of our discontent into the glorious summer of racial solidarity.

It is my hope that Negro scholarships will become self-luminous with a brilliancy that will give our race correct historical perspective, and lead us to that ethnological respectability and racial solidarity which the floods of prejudice have so persistently washed beyond our grasp.

## Arizona Provides Segregation by Petition and Vote
### *1927*[18]

The powers and duties of the board of trustees of school districts are as follows:

2.   To prescribe and enforce rules not inconsistent with law or those prescribed by the State Board of Education for their own government and the government of the schools. They shall segregate pupils of the African race from pupils of the Caucasian race in all schools other than high schools, and to that end are empowered to provide all accommodations made necessary by such segregation.

Whenever there shall be registered in any high school, union high school, or county high school in the State of Arizona, twenty-five or more pupils of the African race, the board of trustees of any such high school shall, upon petition of fifteen per cent of the school electors . . . call an election to determine whether or not such pupils of the African race shall be segregated from the pupils of the Caucasian race. The question . . . shall be in substantially the following form: Are you in favor of segre-

---

[18]Laws of Arizona, 1927, Chapter 88, Paragraph 2733, pp. 235, 236.

gating the pupils of the African race from pupils of the Caucasian race on condition that the board of trustees shall provide equal accommodations and facilities for pupils of the African race as are now or may be hereafter provided for pupils of the Caucasian race; it being understood that the estimated cost of segregation at the present time will be $_____ over and above the cost of maintaining the school without such segregation? . . . If a majority of the electors voting at such election vote in favor of such segregation, then the school trustees of any such high school are hereby authorized and directed to segregate the pupils of the African race from the pupils of the Caucasian race and shall provide equal accommodations and facilities. . . .

## Status of Negro Education in the North
### *1928*[19]

Some general conclusions are obvious from the data herein presented:

1.  The rapid influx of the southern Negro into the North has created a serious problem of adjustment which will tax the intelligence of best educational leadership to solve.

2.  The problem of incorporating the Negro into the social and civic life of the North is complicated by a variety of factors such as color, customs, and previous history of the Negro. The solution of this problem is the one that the educator must face, because the welfare of both races depends upon its solution.

3.  The solution of the race problem will remain impossible, as long as the white race assumes that the Negro comprises an inferior group and he must remain the ward of the white man. This fact may postpone the solution indefinitely.

4.  Equal educational opportunity is not present in the North. The critical problem of the educator is to provide for every child, white or black, the opportunity for personal growth and social adaptation in the interest of the general social welfare. From this point of view one can face educational and racial situations only with extreme pessimism.

---

[19]E. George Payne, "Negroes in the Public Elementary Schools of the North," *Annals of the American Academy of Political and Social Science,* CXXXX (November, 1928), p. 233.

# Federal Support for Howard University
### 1928[20]

*Be it enacted by the Senate and House of Representatives of the United States of America in Congress assembled,* That section 8 of an Act entitled "An Act to incorporate the Howard University in the District of Columbia," approved March 2, 1867, be amended to read as follows:

"SEC. 8. Annual appropriations are hereby authorized to aid in the construction, development, improvement, and maintenance of the university, no part of which shall be used for religious instruction. The university shall at all times be open to inspection by the Bureau of Education and shall be inspected by the said bureau at least once each year. An annual report making a full exhibit of the affairs of the university shall be presented to Congress each year in the report of the Bureau of Education."

Approved, December 13, 1928.

# Psychologist Questions Conclusions From Racial Testing
### 1928[21]

As tests have made progress in accuracy and have gradually gained the confidence of scientists, questions of the comparative abilities of different race-groups have come to the fore, and a good deal of race-testing activity has manifested itself. Much of the work in this line has been premature and untrustworthy; nevertheless many testers have been ready with conclusions. A number of workers in this field have naively assumed that all differences of race medians are innate differences. It can, on the contrary, be said today that the experience of the testees is a large factor in determining their scores on all group tests, whether verbal or nonverbal. . . .

Many of the available tests, especially group tests, are of such a nature that the scores are considerably influenced by certain cultural sets or attitudes; such as habitual slow rate of work, carelessness about accu-

---

[20]An Act To Amend Section 8 of an Act Entitled "An Act to Incorporate the Howard University in the District of Columbia," Seventieth Congress, II Session, Chapter 26, Dec. 13, 1928.

[21]Joseph Peterson, "Methods of Investigating Comparative Abilities in Races," *Annals of the American Academy of Political and Social Science* CXXXX (November, 1928), pp. 178, 184.

racy, tendency to skip hard items in the test and therefore to waste time in finding the easy ones (practices seemingly common among Negroes), to state the matter somewhat negatively. . . .

Individuals are moved not only by present contacts and stimuli as are mere physical objects, but they gradually build up "sets," or attitudes (ideals, in subjective terminology) from contact with many situations whose effects are somehow carried over and become organized into more or less permanent tendencies of the kind mentioned. A set for working as rapidly as possible for a given period of time at a high degree of accuracy, is a thing that does not result merely from instructions and a few exercises given just before a test; it is built up gradually by means of various competitive exercises, reports on the accomplishment of others as compared with one's own record, praise and rewards, and other kinds of stimulation by members of the group. . . .

Differences obtained by means of tests, if these factors have not been equalized with the greatest care, cannot be set down uncritically as native differences. Indeed we are finding that testing for the solution of problems as to native differences, especially the testing of groups under different educational conditions, is beset with difficulties so great as to make the hasty drawing of conclusions a precarious adventure. . . .

It cannot be emphasized too much that the main object in testing various races is not merely to find differences: this should not be an end in itself. If well-established differences can be shown to exist between the mean abilities (either "general abilities" or any special aptitudes) of two races, sub-races, or national groups, that is of course, an important bit of information from many standpoints. But what can be done about it? You cannot kill off, sell, or otherwise dispose of the "inferior" group! It consists of individuals who have neither produced themselves nor the conditions that contributed to their measured inferiority, individuals that are here in the world to be dealt with. The testing is only the means— though probably one of the most important means—to some better adjustment.

## Teacher Salaries Equalized in West Virginia
### *1929*[22]

Salaries of Negro teachers shall be the same as the salaries of other teachers in the same district, independent district, city or town, with the same training and experience, and holding similar credentials.

---

[22]Acts of the West Virginia Legislature, 1929, Chapter 35, Section 67(a), pp. 167-68.

## U. S. Office of Education
## Appoints Specialist in Negro Education
### *1930*[23]

A new position of considerable importance has recently been created in the United States Office of Education and a specialist in Negro education has been assigned to the office. Its specific and immediate function is to serve as a clearing house of information concerning Negro education; to conduct, direct, and encourage educational research; to stimulate interest in the present status and future possibilities of Negro education; and to assist in coordinating the various researches, activities, and interests of Negro schools and of persons concerned in Negro education and related matters.

In realizing these purposes the office will endeavor to collect facts of all kinds bearing directly and indirectly on Negro education; and make periodic digests of educational literature dealing with or which may be of use to Negro education. The specialist in this office will visit schools and communities throughout the country; make contacts with school officials and others who are interested in Negro education; attend and address meetings of educational and other organizations on topics relating to his specialty; and will act as consultant on Negro education with educators and others desiring his services. In performing his duties the specialist will endeavor to confer with and utilize the services of specially qualified persons in the various fields throughout the country; and will attempt to focus on the problems of Negro education all of the expert knowledge, techniques, and educational forces available in the Nation.

The Secretary of the Interior, on the recommendation of the Commissioner of Education, has appointed Dr. Ambrose Caliver to this new and very important post. Professor Caliver has recently completed his work for the Ph.D. degree at Teachers College, Columbia University, where he majored in College Administration and Instruction and minored in Educational Personnel Research. He is the first Negro in the country to meet the requirements for the Ph.D. degree in this field. He has had wide experience in both public and private education, and in elementary and secondary schools, as well as in collegiate work, and his experience in matters of a social and civic nature has been broad. . . .

---

[23]"United States Government Recognizes Negro Education," (Department of the Interior memorandum for the press, September 11, 1930), P. N. 446625.

# Status of Negro Secondary Education
*1932*[24]

From the evidence assembled and analyzed for this report the following inferences may be drawn:

1.  The Negro has shown remarkable avidity in accepting the secondary-school facilities available to him.

2.  A close relationship is apparent between availability and popularization of secondary education among Negroes.

3.  Although the trend of the Negro population is from rural to urban centers, the fact that two-thirds still live in the rural centers suggests the need for a larger share of the secondary-school facilities in these localities.

4.  Since, as demonstrated in the National Survey of the Education of Teachers most of the Negro elementary teachers receive all their training in secondary schools, the improvement and extension of elementary education among Negroes and the reduction of the high percentage of illiteracy depends on the improvement and extension of secondary-school facilities.

5.  The accessibility of Negro high schools to the pupils they serve is a problem of serious proportions.

6.  The large school is far superior to the small school in offering the advantages of secondary education.

7.  The reorganized school is in general superior to the regular school in offering secondary-school facilites.

8.  The small Negro high school seems to be making an effort to simplify its program of studies.

9.  Although foreign language holds first place as an elective and fifth place as a required subject, it is gradually losing ground.

10.  Despite the fact that there seems to be a growing interest among Negro schools in studying Negro history, the offering in this subject is extremely meager.

11.  A definite tendency is observed in Negro high schools to change their programs of study to meet modern conditions.

12.  Negro girls appear to be favored over boys in the proportion who are sent to high school.

---

[24]Ambrose Caliver, *Secondary Education For Negroes*, U. S. Office of Education Bulletin, 1932, No. 17 (Washington: Government Printing Office, 1933), pp. 117-19.

13.   The fact that larger percentages of Negro pupils enrolled in small and regular high schools than in large and reorganized schools are graduated is probably a result of the pupils' objectives rather than of superior offerings of the schools.

14.   A direct relationship exists between the size of place, size of school, amount of training, and salaries of Negro high-school teachers.

15.   The typical Negro high-school teacher has a fair degree of academic and professional training, but is greatly overburdened and underpaid.

16.   The typical principal of the Negro high school is a teaching principal rather than a supervisory and administrative officer.

17.   A large proportion of Negro high schools are inadequately provided with equipment and facilities to maintain and promote health.

18.   In view of the lack of public-school facilities for Negroes and of the preponderance of Negro public-school teachers graduated from them the private colleges and universities still have a strong relationship and a responsibility to the education of the Negro.

19.   The differences in secondary-school facilities between the white and colored races are in most factors noticeable and in practically every instance of major importance in favor of the whites. This is true whether the colored schools of the Southern States are compared with the white schools of the same States or with the white schools for the country at large.

20.   The great progress made in secondary education for the colored race has been largely the result of an increasingly sympathetic attitude toward Negro education in the States maintaining separate schools.

21.   In spite of the progress made in secondary education for Negroes, they have a long way to go before they reach the optimum point in the matter of high-school enrollment. Meanwhile, a great source of wealth and power is going to waste in the thousands of Negro youth of high-school age who are not in school because of the absence of facilities.

22.   Because of the lack of educational facilities and the general inadequacy of secondary-school offerings, the Negro race is facing the competition of American life at an enormous disadvantage.

23.   If the educational chasm existing between the two races is ever bridged or lessened, improvement in school conditions must go forward at a much more rapid rate than it has in the past. Negroes can not meet the exacting standards of modern civilization with intelligence, skill, and courage, and keep pace with the tempo of American life with an education which lags behind 10, 15, or 20 years.

24.  That a growing number of persons in every section of the country is becoming conscious of the problems in Negro education is evidenced by many of the facts gathered during this study.

# Criteria for Racial Testing
*1932*[25]

From the analysis of these three major conditions basic for valid interpretations, a check list seems desirable which one may use as a criterion for accepting an experimental study as valid for generalizations regarding comparative differences in mental ability of races. The following check list in the form of questions requiring affirmative answers is proposed:

1.  Have the individuals tested had identical or very similar opportunities for gaining familiarity with the materials of the test which are assumed to be common?

2.  Were the provisions for formal education of the groups compared functioning on the same standard?

3.  Has the investigator checked the results of his measure of mental ability to ascertain their probable correlation with the results of some scientific measure of social status?

4.  Does the investigator base his comparison on differences more valid than the norms in the commonly used tests which reflect national standards for whites with educational conditions different from the Negroes tested?

5.  Are the scores or intelligence quotients used in the comparison the results obtained from the same test?

6.  If the study utilizes quotients obtained from different tests, has the investigator statistically equated the quotients?

7.  Is the test used one of unquestionable validity as a measure of mental ability?

---

[25]Robert P. Daniel, "Basic Considerations for Valid Interpretations of Experimental Studies Pertaining To Racial Differences," *Journal of Education Psychology*, XXIII, 1 (January, 1932), 26, 27. For a critical analysis of specific studies, see Charles H. Thompson, "The Educational Achievements of Negro Children," *Annals of the American Academy of Political and Social Science*, CXXXX (November, 1928), pp. 193-208. Discussion of these issues was renewed with great intensity in the late 1960's, stimulated especially by the writing of Arthur Jensen who contended that test differences along racial lines might indicate genetic differences.

8. Is the test reliable?

9. Has the investigator utilized a sufficiently large number of cases as to practically assure including a fair representation in distribution of abilities, if the groups offer such possibilities?

10. Has the investigator chosen enough cases as to eliminate differences of marked disproportionate magnitude between the number of cases in the samples compared?

11. Does the investigator indicate the probable variation in results due to the accidental conditions of sampling?

12. Has the investigator checked the reliability of an obtained difference with respect to the formulae for calculating the standard deviation or probable error of the difference between two measures?

13. Was the sampling random?

14. Does the investigator report the extent of variability as well as the central tendency of his data?

15. Does the investigator report sufficient of the primary data in some form as to permit verification of the statistical treatment and interpretation of his data?

16. Does the investigator report the conditions under which the tests were given in sufficient detail to permit one to know whether the conditions were standard, and were comparable for the different groups tested?

In the light of these criteria we may conclude that (1) most studies so far reported are worthless as indicating anything regarding the comparative mental ability of races; (2) most of our present techniques give measures of differences due to weaknesses in educational opportunities rather than of differences in mental ability; (3) there is need of a re-evaluation of the problems and methods of studies pertaining to racial differences.

## Journal of Negro Education Begins
### *1932*[26]

The justification for launching another publication in the field of education is found in the fact that such services, though needed, are not being

---

[26]Charles H. Thompson, "Why a Journal of Negro Education," *Journal of Negro Education*, I, 1 (April, 1932), 1-4.

adequately provided by existing agencies. Evidence of this need is found in the following facts.

In the first place, there are no general means of collecting and disseminating facts about educational activities among Negroes. . . .

In the second place, there is a need for continuous, critical appraisal and discussion of the present and proposed practices relating to the education of Negroes. It is obvious that the mere collection of facts is only the first step in developing an understanding upon which to base the same direction of any movement or institution. It can be truthfully said that proposals affecting the education of Negroes have not been subjected to an abundance of critical investigation and thinking. If one is familiar with the meetings of various organizations whose discussions are devoted, wholly or partially, to the education of the Negro, he does not need to be convinced that very little critical appraisal has been present in their "deliberations." Most of the discussions have consisted of inspirational talks rather than critical appraisals of the assumptions underlying certain basic procedures and proposals.

In the third place, there is need for some agency to stimulate and sponsor investigation of problems incident to the education of Negroes as was implied in the preceding section. . . .

Moreover, it should be pointed out here that leadership in the investigation of the problems incident to the education of Negroes should be assumed to a greater extent by Negro educators. . . .

Thus, it is believed that the launching of this project will stimulate Negroes to take a greater part in the solution of the problems that arise in connection with their own education.

A fourth and final reason for launching this publication is found in the fact that it meets a need that is not adequately met by any other agency at the present time. . . .

The JOURNAL is edited and published at Howard University under the sponsorship of the Faculty of the College of Education. There are many reasons which might be given in support of this policy, but it is only necessary to mention two of them in this connection. In the first place, the College of Education of Howard University has just been officially authorized to organize a "Bureau of Educational Research." . . . In the second place, the Faculty of the College of Education of Howard University, consisting of the largest single group of professionally trained Negroes in the field of education in the United States, feel that one of their first responsibilities as a part of a University, devoting its major efforts to the education of Negroes, is to make a concerted attempt to study some of the problems arising out of educational efforts among Negroes. . . .

# The Depression and Negro Education
*1933*[27]

During the past there were many deficiencies in the education of Negroes; the facilities provided in schools were very meager; there was considerable lack of financial support; and the margin upon which schools operated was exceedingly narrow. Since this was the situation before the depression, it is obvious that drastic cuts cannot be made now without doing irreparable damage. In many localities where reductions are made, the schools for white children still have sufficient facilities left to provide a fairly good minimum program of education; but if equal or proportional cuts are made in the education of Negroes, it frequently will mean the abolishment of schools, or *all* the facilities in some essential fields of activity. . . .

The following is a brief statement of the status of Negro education before the depression and its bearing on the present retrenchment programs.

1. *Short school term.* As the shortening of school terms is contemplated as an economy measure, it should be remembered that already the average term in schools for Negroes is only four-fifths as long as that for whites.

2. *Increase in class size.* Savings also are being effected by increasing the size of classes. The Negro child and teacher are now suffering from too large classes. In 1929–30 the class-size in Negro schools was on the average 50 per cent greater than that for the white schools in the same states.

3. *Abandoning schools.* A third means being employed to effect economies is the abandoning of schools. Several things should be taken into consideration before schools for Negroes are abandoned. (a) At present the inaccessibility of schools to Negro children in rural communities presents a serious problem. Of 44,000 Negro children studied in 1930, 17 per cent lived 3 miles or more, and 39 per cent lived 2 miles or more from their schools. Only 1 per cent of these children were transported at public expense. . . . (b) In 1930 there were 230 counties in

---

[27]Ambrose Caliver, "The Negro and the Emergency in Education," Circular No. 123, (United States Department of the Interior, Office of Education, 1933). Here Caliver warns of the effect of financial retrenchment upon Negro schools, already seriously behind white schools. Despite southern reluctance to provide first class education for Negroes, the total southern educational effort led the nation if one compares expenditures to resources.

15 Southern States which had no high-school facilities at all for Negroes, and 195 other counties had no four-year high schools. (c) Already more than one million (or one-third) of the Negro boys and girls of school age are out of school.

4. *Reduction of teaching force.* Many states and communities are attempting to economize by reducing the teaching force. It should be remembered in this connection that before the depression Negro schools were greatly undermanned. It was estimated in 1930–31 that more than 30,000 Negro public school teachers were needed.

5. *Reduction of salaries.* While drastic cuts are being made in the salaries of teachers, attention should be called to the already narrow subsistence margin upon which Negro teachers live. In 1930 the average annual salary of rural white teachers was $945, for colored teachers it was $388. In some rural communities colored teachers received as little as $200 per year.

During American Education Week special effort should be made to inform Negro and white citizens ... and ... to prevent the present retrenchment programs from so handicapping the Negro children that they will be unable to participate effectively in our future society.

## Criticism of Negro Colleges
### *1934*[28]

To set foot on dozens of Negro campuses is like going back to mid-Victorian England, or Massachusetts in the days of the witch-burning Puritans. To give examples, let us take the little things first. On some campuses grown-up college men and women are not allowed to smoke, thus you have the amusing spectacle of twenty-four year old men sneaking around to the back doors of dormitories like little boys to take a drag on a forbidden cigarette. At some schools, simple card playing is a wicked abomination leading to dismissal for a student—even though many students come from homes where whist and bridge are common amusements. At a number of schools, dancing on the campus for either faculty or students is absolutely forbidden. ...

[28]Langston Hughes, "Cowards From The Colleges," *Crisis*, XLI, 8 (August, 1934), 226-28.

Accompanying this mid-Victorian attitude in manners and morals, at many Southern schools there is a great deal of official emphasis placed on heavy religious exercises, usually compulsory, with required daily chapels, weekly prayer meetings, and Sunday services. Such a stream of dull and stupid sermons, uninspired prayers, and monotonous hymns— neither intellectually worthy of adult minds nor emotionally exciting in the manner of the old time shouts—pour into students' ears that it is a wonder any young people ever go to church again once they leave college. The placid cant and outworn phrases of many of the churchmen daring to address student groups today makes me wonder why their audiences are not bored to death. I did observe many young people going to sleep.

But there are charges of a far more serious nature to bring against Negro schools than merely that of frowning on jazz in favor of hymns, or their horror of friendly communication between boys and girls on the campuses. To combine these charges very simply: Many of our institutions apparently are not trying to make men and women of their students at all—they are doing their best to produce spineless Uncle Toms, uninformed, and full of mental and moral evasions. . . .

Freedom of expression for teachers in most Negro schools, even on such unimportant matters as to rouge or not to rouge, smoke or not smoke, is more or less unknown. Old and mossbacked presidents, orthodox ministers or missionary principals, control all too often what may or may not be taught in the class rooms or said in campus conversation. Varied examples of suppression at the campuses I visited are too numerous to mention in full in a short article, but they range all the way from an Alabama secondary school that permitted no Negro weeklies like the *Chicago Defender* or the *Pittsburgh Courier* in its library because they were "radical", to the great university of Fisk at Nashville where I asked a nationally known Negro professor and author of several books in his field what his attitude toward communism was, and received as an answer, "When I discuss communism on this campus, I will have a letter first from the president and the board of trustees."

There is at the Negro schools in the South, even the very well-endowed and famous ones that I have mentioned, an amazing acquiescence to the wishes of the local whites and to the traditions of the Southern color-line. When programs are given, many schools set aside whole sections in their own auditoriums for the exclusive use of whites. Often the best seats are given them, to the exclusion of Negro visitors. . . .

Even where there is no official campus segregation (such as Tuskegee's white guest house, or Hampton's hospital where local whites are given separate service) both teachers and students of Negro colleges accept so sweetly the customary Jim-crowing of the South that one feels sure the race's emancipation will never come through its intellectuals. . . .

And can it be that our Negro educational institutions are not really interested in turning out leaders at all? Can it be that they are far more interested in their endowments and their income and their salaries than in their students?

And can it be that these endowments, incomes, gifts—and therefore salaries—springing from missionary and philanthropic sources and from big Northern boards and foundations—have such strings tied to them that those accepting them can do little else (if they wish to live easy) but bow down to the white powers that control this philanthropy and continue, to the best of their ability, to turn out "Uncle Toms?"

## NAACP Launches Campaign
### 1935[29]

The National Association for the Advancement of Colored People is launching an active compaign against race discrimination in public education. The campaign will reach all levels of public education from the nursery school through the university. The ultimate objectives of the association is the abolition of all forms of segregation in public education, whether in the admission or activities of students, the appointment or advancement of teachers, or administrative control. The association will resist any attempt to extend segregated schools. Where possible it will attack segregation in schools. Where segregation is so firmly entrenched by law that a frontal attack cannot be made, the association will throw its immediate force toward bringing Negro schools up to an absolute equality with white schools. If the white South insists upon its separate schools, it must not squeeze the Negro schools to pay for them. . . .

At the present time the N.A.A.C.P. educational program has six specific objectives for its immediate efforts: (a) equality of school terms; (b) equality of pay for Negro teachers having the same qualifications and doing the same work as white teachers; (c) equality of transporta-

---

[29]Charles H. Houston, "Educational Inequalities Must Go!", *Crisis* (October, 1935), Vol. 42, Whole No. 298, pp. 300, 301, 316.

tion for Negro school children at public expense; (d) equality of buildings and equipment; (e) equality of *per capita* expenditure for education of Negroes; (f) equality in graduate and professional training.

The first five objectives relate to segregated and separate school systems. Equality of educational opportunity in separate school systems is the greatest immediate educational problem of the Negro masses. But the problem of Negro education would not stand completely solved even if segregated schools were suddenly abolished. There would still be the question of the Negro's position in the unified system. . . . The N.A.A.C.P. expects to fight race prejudice in nonsegregated systems just as hard as it fights for equality in separate school systems.

The sixth objective: equality in graduate and professional training, is essentially a problem of the South. . . . For purely technical reasons the first problem the association attacked in court was the exclusion of qualified Negroes from graduate or professional training in state-supported universities, solely on account of race or color. . . . As regards primary, secondary and collegiate education in the South, there is a system, albeit inadequate, of separate primary and secondary schools and colleges for Negroes supported from public funds. . . . But in the case of the graduate or professional training there are *no* facilities whatsoever provided for Negroes by the state, and the question narrows down to a simple proposition of law: whether the state can appropriate public money for graduate and professional education for white students exclusively. . . .

The N.A.A.C.P. appreciates the magnitude of the task ahead of it, but it has its duty to its constituency and to the America of the future. It conceives that in equalizing educational opportunities for Negroes it raises the whole standard of American citizenship, and stimulates white Americans as well as black. Fundamentally the N.A.A.C.P. is not a special pleader; it merely insists that the United States respect its own Constitution and its own laws.

## Court Orders Desegregation of
## Maryland Law School
### *1935*[30]

As a result of the adoption of the Fourteenth Amendment to the United States Constitution, a state is required to extend to its citizens of the two

---

[30]University of Maryland v. Donald G. Murray 169 Maryland, 478 (October, 1935).

races substantially equal treatment in the facilities it provides from the public funds. . . .

The requirement of equal treatment would seem to be clearly enough one of equal treatment in respect to any one facility or opportunity furnished to citizens, rather than of a balance in state bounty to be struck from the expenditures and provisions for each race generally. We take it to be clear, for instance, that a state could not be rendered free to maintain a law school exclusively for whites by maintaining at equal cost a school of technology for colored students. . . .

Equality of treatment does not require that privileges be provided members of the two races in the same place. The State may choose the method by which equality is maintained. . . .

Separation of the races must nevertheless furnish equal treatment. The constitutional requirement cannot be dispensed with in order to maintain a school or schools for whites exclusively. . . .

As has been stated, the method of furnishing the equal facilities required is at the choice of the State, now or at any future time. At present it is maintaining only the one law school, and in the legislative provisions for the scholarships that one school has in effect been declared appropriated to the whites exclusively. The officers and members of the board appear to us to have had a policy declared for them, as they thought. No separate school for colored students has been decided upon and only an inadequate substitute has been provided. Compliance with the Constitution cannot be deferred at the will of the State. Whatever system it adopts for legal education now must furnish equality of treatment now.

The case, as we find it, then, is that the State has undertaken the function of education in the law, but has omitted students of one race from the only adequate provision made for it, and omitted them solely because of their color. If those students are to be offered equal treatment in the performance of the function, they must, at present, be admitted to the one school provided.

## Negroes Need Separate Schools
### *1935*[31]

The proper education of any people includes sympathetic touch between teacher and pupil, . . . and such contact between pupils, and between

---

[31]W.E.B. DuBois, "Does the Negro Need Separate Schools?", *Journal of Negro Education*, IV (July, 1935), pp. 328-35, *passim.*

teacher and pupil, on the basis of perfect social equality, as will increase this sympathy and knowledge. . . . If the public schools of Atlanta, Nashville, New Orleans and Jacksonville were thrown open to all races tomorrow, the education that colored children would get in them would be worse than pitiable. It would not be education. And in the same way, there are many public school systems in the North where Negroes are admitted and tolerated, but they are not educated; they are crucified. . . . Under such circumstances, there is no room for argument as to whether the Negro needs separate schools or not. . . . To endure bad schools and wrong education because the schools are "mixed" is a costly if not fatal mistake. . . . As it is today, American Negroes almost universally disparage their own schools. They look down upon them; they often treat the Negro teachers in them with contempt. . . . As long as the Negro student wishes to graduate from Columbia, not because Columbia is an institution of learning, but because it is attended by white students; as long as a Negro student is ashamed to attend Fisk or Howard because these institutions are largely run by black folk, just so long the main problem of Negro education will not be segregation but self-knowledge and self-respect.

So far, I have noted chiefly negative arguments for separate Negro institutions of learning. . . . But beyond this, there are certain positive reasons due to the fact that American Negroes have, because of their history, group experiences and memories, a distinct entity, whose spirit and reactions demand a certain type of education for its development. . . . Negroes must know the history of the Negro race in America, and this they will seldom get in white institutions. . . . They ought to study intelligently and from their own point of view, the slave trade, slavery, emancipation, Reconstruction, and present economic development.

Beyond this, Negro colleges ought to be studying anthropology, psychology, and the social sciences from the point of view of the colored races. . . . In history and the social sciences the Negro school and college has an unusual opportunity and role. It does not consist simply in trying to parallel the history of white folk with similar boasting about black and brown folk, but rather an honest evaluation of human effort and accomplishment, without color blindness, and without transforming history into a record of dynasties and prodigies. . . .

Thus, instead of our schools being simply separate schools, forced on us by grim necessity, they can become centers of a new and beautiful effort at human education, which may easily lead and guide the world in many important and valuable aspects. It is for this reason that when our schools are separate, the control of the teaching force, the expenditure of money, the choice of textbooks, the discipline and other administrative matters of this sort ought, also, to come into our hands, and be incessantly demanded and guarded.

I know that this article will forthwith be interpreted by certain illiterate "nitwits" as a plea for segregated Negro schools and colleges. It is not. . . . It is saying in plain English: that a separate Negro school, where children are treated like human beings, trained by teachers of their own race, who know what it means to be black in the year of salvation of 1935, is infinitely better than making our boys and girls doormats to be spit and trampled upon and lied to by ignorant social climbers. . . . I say, too, that certain studies and discipline necessary to Negroes can seldom be found in white schools.

## Progressive Criticism of Traditional Education
## Reaches Negro Schools
*1937*[32]

This is the story of efforts in the South to drive rote teaching from the school system and to put some education in its place. Especially it is the story of cooperative activities by Southern teachers and one of the phil-anthropic foundations—the Julius Rosenwald Fund—to lift rural schools out of the formal routine into which so many of them have fallen. . . .

At first we thought this mumbo jumbo of rote recitation might simply be the mark of Negro schools, but when we enlarged our explorations to include white schools in the same communities we found little to choose between the two. In general the Negro teachers had less training, worked for smaller salaries and with shabbier equipment. Yet, in spite of handicaps, occasionally the zest and ingenuity of this hearty race resulted in activities and interests above the practice in the white schools.

We became convinced that the curse of American education is rote teaching, the continuous meaningless drill in formalistic studies. . . .

In a Negro school a teacher holding a health catechism read from the text, 'Why should we wash and comb our hair?' And the row of little Negroes droned back the answer, 'So it will not get stringy and fall down in our eyes.'

---

[32]Edwin R. Embree, "Little Red Schoolhouse—1938 Model," *Atlantic Monthly*, CLX, 5 ( November, 1937), pp. 636-38, 642. Copyright © 1937, 1965, by The Atlantic Monthly Company, Boston, Massachusetts. Reprinted with permission.

Neither teacher nor pupils seemed to think this a surprising answer from pupils whose hair was so kinky that it never could get into strings or hang down anywhere. This was the lesson; all that teacher or pupils had to do was to recite it. As with Tennyson's Six Hundred, 'theirs not to reason why, theirs but to do and die.' . . .

In a number of individual rural schools, both white and colored, experiments have been going forward during the past two years to see how typical units in the regular public school system may become lively influences upon the minds of the pupils and the attitudes and practices of the community. With the approval of the local authorities special teachers have been supplied and given a free hand to explore the various possibilities for giving a sound and stimulating education to country children. While in general these experimental public schools have followed the policies outlined in this paper, the only fixed principle has been to drive out rote teaching and to put in its place a learning process in which the pupil takes an active part and in which the stimulating environment of the countryside is used as much as possible.

## Maryland Arranges Out-of-State Education for Negroes
### 1937[33]

Whenever any bona fide Negro resident and citizen of this State, possessing the qualifications of health, character, ability and preparatory education required for admission to the University of Maryland desires to obtain an education not provided for either in Morgan College or Princess Anne College, he may make application for a scholarship provided by the funds mentioned in the foregoing section, so that he may obtain aid to enable him to attend a college or university where equal educational facilities can be provided or furnished, whether or not such an agency or institution is operated by the State or under some other arrangement, and whether or not such facilities are located in Maryland or elsewhere. Under such conditions, it shall be provided that out of the scholarship funds . . . , the applicant, if he possesses the proper qualifications, may have paid to

---

[33]Laws of the State of Maryland, 1937, Chapter 506, Section 5, pp. 1071-72. Some states provided only an amount of tuition equivalent to that in the home state university. In this regard, the Maryland law was somewhat more liberal than other states.

him or direct to the institution which he is to attend, such sum, if any, as may be necessary to supplement the amount which it would cost him to attend the University of Maryland, so that such person will be enabled to secure educational facilities, training, and opportunities equal to those provided otherwise for white students, without additional cost to such person . . . In determining the comparative costs of attending any of the institutions to which scholarships may be provided, there shall be taken into consideration tuition charges, living expenses, and costs of transportation.

## Georgia Calls for Educational Equality
*1937*[34]

It is hereby declared to be the public policy of the State of Georgia that educational opportunities for all of the children of school age in this State shall be equalized throughout the State by the State Board of Education, so far as possible.

## On the Mis-Education of Negroes
*1938*[35]

Practically all of the successful Negroes in this country are of the uneducated type or of that of Negroes who have had no formal education at all. The large majority of the Negroes who have put on the finishing touches of our best colleges are all but worthless in the development of their people. . . .

When a Negro has finished his education in our schools, then, he has been equipped to begin the life of an Americanized or Europeanized white man, but before he steps from the threshold of his alma mater he

---

[34]Georgia Laws, 1937, Part I, Title 7, Section 1, p. 883. Approved February 10, 1937.

[35]Carter G. Woodson, *The Mis-Education of the Negro* (Washington: The Associated Publishers, 1938), pp. 2, 5, 6, 29, 149.

is told by his teachers that he must go back to his own people from whom he has been estranged by a vision of ideals which in his disillusionment he will realize that he cannot attain. . . .

For the arduous task of serving a race thus handicapped, however, the Negro graduate has had little or no training at all. The people whom he has been ordered to serve have been belittled by his teachers to the extent that he can hardly find delight in undertaking what his education has led him to think is impossible. Considering his race as blank in achievement, then, he sets out to stimulate their imitation of others. The performance is kept up a while; but, like any other effort at meaningless imitation, it results in failure.

Facing this undesirable result, the highly educated Negro often grows sour. He becomes too pessimistic to be a constructive force and usually develops into a chronic fault-finder or a complainant at the bar of public opinion. Often when he sees that the fault lies at the door of the white oppressor whom he is afraid to attack, he turns upon the pioneering Negro who is at work doing the best he can to extricate himself from an uncomfortable predicament.

In this effort to imitate, however, these "educated people" are sincere. They hope to make the Negro conform quickly to the standard of the whites and thus remove the pretext for the barriers between the races. They do not realize, however, that even if the Negroes do successfully imitate the whites, nothing new has thereby been accomplished. You simply have a larger number of persons doing what others have been doing. The unusual gifts of the race have not thereby been developed, and an unwilling world, therefore, continues to wonder what the Negro is good for.

These "educated" people, however, decry any such thing as race consciousness; and in some respects they are right. They do not like to hear such expressions as "Negro literature," "Negro poetry," "African art," or "thinking black"; and, roughly speaking, we must concede that such things do not exist. These things did not figure in the courses which they pursued in school, and why should they? "Aren't we all Americans? Then, whatever is American is as much the heritage of the Negro as of any other group in this country." . . .

Real education means to inspire people to live more abundantly, to learn to begin with life as they find it and make it better, but the instruction so far given Negroes in colleges and universities has worked to the contrary. In most cases such graduates have merely increased the number of malcontents who offer no program for changing the undesirable conditions about which they complain. One should rely upon protest only when it is supported by a constructive program. . . . We should not close any accredited Negro colleges or universities, but we should reconstruct the whole system. We should not eliminate many of the courses now being offered, but we should secure men of vision to give them from the point of view of the people to be served. We should not spend less money for the higher education of the Negro, but should redefine higher education as preparation to think and work out a program to serve the lowly rather than to live as an aristocrat.

## Negro Representation on Indiana Board
### *1939*[36]

Sec. 1   Be it enacted by the General Assembly of the State of Indiana, that in filling vacancies hereafter occurring on the State Board of Education, . . . the governor shall so arrange appointments to such board that the legislative objective to have on said board at all times at least one member of the Negro race shall be realized.

## Graduate Education for Negroes
### *1941*[37]

The Negro's desire for graduate study is actuated by the same forces that would make any human being seek it. In some instances he wants the prestige given by an advanced degree; in others, he desires a better economic return on his educational investment which may come about as a result of possession of graduate training. In others still, he is motivated by the urge to acquire the attributes that will make him an original contributor to the world of thought. Of late, Negroes have felt a definite urge to marshal their best thinking on problems of their own group: problems relating to the administration of justice, to the adequacy of income, to the

---

[36]Acts of the Indiana General Assembly, 1939, Chapter 82, Section 1, pp. 474, 475.

[37]Felton G. Clark, "The South, The Supreme Court and Negro Education," in *The South . . . Child Rich . . . Dollar Poor* (Atlanta: Commission on Interracial Cooperation, Inc., 1942), p. 19.

availability of employment, to the facilities for appropriating leisure, to the maintenance of health, to the preservation of a well-balanced personality, to the sound development of character, to the facilities to grow in enlightenment. There is no doubt that never before has the Negro group in America been as cognizant of the problems envisaging it as now. To this same extent is there a tendency to procure scientific techniques for analyzing and, if possible, solving these problems. It follows that the desire for graduate instruction should be enhanced by these factors. And since approximately nine million Negroes live in the Southern states, the problem of graduate instruction for Negroes, if it is to be justly and logically considered, weighs heavily upon the doorstep of the South.

## Selective Service Testing and Education
### *1941*[38]

An alarming number of men have been rejected for army service because of educational deficiency. It was found last Spring that the Army was receiving too high a percentage of men of inferior intelligence. . . .

The intelligence tests conducted last Spring showed that less than 1 per cent of the Negro selectees were classified as of superior intelligence against 9½ per cent of the white selectees, while more than 50 per cent of the Negro selectees were classified as of inferior intelligence and only 8 per cent of the white selectees.

The fourth grade educational standard established by the Army has resulted in more than 150,000 men being rejected for military service. The Negro rate of rejection is much higher than the white. In some states it has reached more than 21 per cent of all those examined. . . .

Two, of the several important inferences to be drawn from the high rate of rejection of both white and Negro selectees for educational deficiency, are:

1.    Whether a state provides educational facilities for its citizens is no longer a state matter but is a matter of *national* concern. It has a definite bearing upon the ability of the state to provide its quota of manpower for National Defense.

---

[38]Campbell C. Johnson, "Implications of Selective Service Facts to Leaders in the Field of Education," *Proceedings of the Nineteenth Annual Conference of the Presidents of the Negro Land-Grant Colleges* (Chicago, 1941), pp. 19, 20.

2. Since the need for military manpower is not diminished by the higher standards required by the Army, states with low rejection rates for educational deficiency, may find themselves making up deficits in manpower unless an educational program can be established immediately that will increase the availability of men in states with high rejection rates. This comes very close home to you as educators. It is a challenge to you to devise programs that will make the Negro equally as available as the white citizen of your states for military service to his country.

## An Alabama Boy Quits School
### *1941*[39]

I started to school when I was 8 or 9, but I didn't get to go much. I had to work most of the time. I just went about two years straight, but I didn't go every day then 'cause I had to stop sometimes and plow and cut wood. . . . No, I didn't want to stop. I liked school. I want to go back to school and learn some more before I get grown. I want to learn how to keep folks from beatin' you out of things you own. I'd like to go to school up to the twelfth grade anyhow. I don't know if I can. I'd have to go to some high school I reckon. I could go to Normal if I had some money. Right smart of the children go to Normal when they finish up here. My father wouldn't send me. I guess I won't get to go no farther than I have. I went to the fourth grade. I want to try to go back this fall after pickin' but don't guess I'll get to go ever any more.

## Statement by Southern Negroes
### *1942*[40]

The war has sharpened the issue of Negro-white relations in the United States, and particularly in the South. A result has been increased racial tensions, fears, and aggressions, and an opening up of the basic questions

---

[39]Quoted in Charles S. Johnson, *Growing Up in the Black Belt* (Washington, D.C.: American Council on Education, 1941), p. 132.

[40]"A Basis For Interracial Cooperation and Development in the South: a Statement by Southern Negroes," quoted in *The Southern Regional Council: Its Origin and Purpose* (Atlanta: Southern Regional Council, Inc., 1944), pp. 7, 10, 12.

of racial segregation and discrimination, Negro minority rights, and democratic freedom, as they apply practically in Negro-white relations in the South. . . .

As equal opportunity for all citizens is the very foundation of the democratic faith, and of the Christian ethic which gave birth to the ideal of democratic living, it is imperative that every measure possible be taken to insure an equality of education to Negroes and, indeed, to all underprivileged peoples.

1. Basic improvement in Negro education is better schools, which involves expenditures by States of considerably more funds for the Negro schools. This group believes that a minimum requirement now is (a) equalization of salaries of white and Negro teachers on the basis of equal preparation and experience; (b) an expanded school building program for Negro schools designed to overcome the present racial disparity in physical facilities; this program to begin as soon as building materials are available; (c) revision of the school program in terms of the social setting, vocational needs and marginal cultural characteristics of the Negro children; and (d) the same length of school term for all children in local communities. Our growing knowledge of the effect of environment upon the intelligence and social adjustment of children, in fact leads us to believe that to insure equality of educational opportunity it is not enough to provide for the under-privileged child, of whatever race, the *same* opportunities provided for those on superior levels of familial, social, and economic life. We feel it a function of Government to assure equalization far beyond the mere expenditure of equivalent funds for salaries and the like.

2. The education of Negroes in the South has reached the point at which there is increased demand for graduate and professional training. This group believes that this training should be made available equally for white and Negro eligible students in terms defined by the United States Supreme Court in the decision on the case of Gaines versus the University of Missouri.

3. Where it is established that States cannot sustain the added cost of equalization, Federal funds should be made available to overcome the differentials between white and Negro facilities and between Southern and national standards.

4. It is the belief of this group that the special problems of Negro education make demands for intelligent and sympathetic representation of these problems on school boards by qualified persons of the Negro race.

5. The education of Negro youth can be measurably aided by the use of Negro enforcement officers of truancy and compulsory education laws. . . .

The effect of the war has been to make the Negro, in a sense, the symbol and protagonist of every other minority in America and in the world at large. Local issues in the South, while admittedly holding many practical difficulties, must be met wisely and courageously if this Nation is to become a significant political entity in a new international world. The correction of these problems is not only a moral matter, but a practical necessity in winning the war and in winning the peace. Herein rests the chance to reveal our greatest weakness or our greatest strength.

## Illinois Allows Teaching Negro History
### 1945[41]

History of the Negro race may be taught in all public schools and in all other educational institutions in this State supported or maintained, in whole or in part, by public funds.

## Report of President Truman's Committee on Civil Rights
### 1947[42]

The failure to give Negroes equal educational opportunities is naturally most acute in the South, where approximately 10 million Negroes live. The South is one of the poorer sections of the country and has at best only limited funds to spend on its schools. With 34.5 percent of the country's population, 17 southern states and the District of Columbia have 39.4 percent of our school children. Yet the South has only one-fifth of the taxpaying wealth of the nation. Actually, on a percentage basis, the South spends a greater share of its income on education than do the wealthier states in other parts of the country. For example, Mississippi, which has the lowest expenditure per school child of any state, is ninth in

---

[41]Laws of Illinois, 1945, Section 27-23, pp. 1581, 1852.
[42]President's Committee on Civil Rights, *To Secure These Rights* (Washington: U. S. Government Printing Office, 1947), pp. 63-65, 166.

percentage of income devoted to education. A recent study showed Mississippi spending 3.41 percent of its income for education as against New York's figure of only 2.61 percent. But this meant $400 per classroom unit in Mississippi, and $4,100 in New York. Negro and white school children both suffer because of the South's basic inability to match the level of educational opportunity provided in other sections of the nation.

But it is the South's segregated school system which most directly discriminates against the Negro. This segregation is found today in 17 southern states and the District of Columbia. Poverty-stricken though it was after the close of the Civil War, the South chose to maintain two sets of public schools, one for whites and one for Negroes. With respect to education, as well as to other public services, the Committee believes that the "separate but equal" rule has not been obeyed in practice. There is a marked difference in quality between the educational opportunities offered white children and Negro children in the separate schools. Whatever test is used—expenditure per pupil, teachers' salaries, the number of pupils per teacher, transportation of students, adequacy of school buildings and educational equipment, length of school term, extent of curriculum—Negro students are invariably at a disadvantage. Opportunities for Negroes in public institutions of higher education in the South—particularly at the professional graduate school level—are severely limited. . . .

In spite of the improvement which is undoubtedly taking place, the Committee is convinced that the gap between white and Negro schools can never be completely eliminated by means of state funds alone. The cost of maintaining separate, but truly equal, school systems would seem to be utterly prohibitive in many of the southern states. It seems probable that the only means by which such a goal can finally be won will be through federal financial assistance. The extension of the federal grant-in-aid for educational purposes, already available to the land-grant colleges and, for vocational education, to the secondary school field, seems both imminent and desirable.

Whether the federal grant-in-aid should be used to support the maintenance of separate schools is an issue that the country must soon face.

In the North, segregation in education is not formal, and in some states is prohibited. Nevertheless, the existence of residential restrictions in many northern cities has had discriminatory effects on Negro education. In Chicago, for example, the schools which are most crowded and employ double shift schedules are practically all in Negro neighborhoods. . . .

V. *To strengthen the right to equality of opportunity, the President's Committee recommends:*

1. *In general:*
   *The elimination of segregation, based on race, color, creed, or national origin, from American life.*

The separate but equal doctrine has failed in three important respects. First, it is inconsistent with the fundamental equalitarianism of the American way of life in that it marks groups with the brand of inferior status. Secondly, where it has been followed, the results have been separate and unequal facilities for minority peoples. Finally, it has kept people apart despite incontrovertible evidence that an environment favorable to civil rights is fostered whenever groups are permitted to live and work together. There is no adequate defense of segregation.

*The conditioning by Congress of all federal grants-in-aid and other forms of federal assistance to public or private agencies for any purpose on the absence of discrimination and segregation based on race, color, creed, or national origin.*

We believe that federal funds, supplied by taxpayers all over the nation, must not be used to support or perpetuate the pattern of segregation in education, public housing, public health services, or other public services and facilities generally. We recognize that these services are indispensable to individuals in modern society and to further social progress. It would be regrettable if federal aid, conditioned on non-segregated services, should be rejected by sections most in need of such aid. The Committee believes that a reasonable interval of time may be allowed for adjustment to such a policy. But in the end it believes that segregation is wrong morally and practically and must not receive financial support by the whole people.

# Texas Establishes a Negro University
## *1947*[43]

Sec. 2    To provide instruction, training, and higher education for colored people, there is hereby established a university of the first class in two divisions: the first, styled 'The Texas State University for Negroes' to be located at Houston . . .; the second, to be styled 'The Prairie View Agri-

---

[43]General and Special Laws of Texas, 1947, Chapter 29, pp. 36-41. Effective March 3, 1947. The "emergency" referred to at the end of this selection was a suit brought by Hemon Sweatt to compel his admission to the law school of the University of Texas. For the outcome, see p. 000.

cultural and Mechanical College of Texas' . . . originally established in 1876 . . . At the Prairie View Agricultural and Mechanical College shall be offered courses in agriculture, the mechanic arts, engineering, and the natural sciences connected therewith . . . The Texas State University for Negroes shall offer all other courses of higher learning, including, but without limitation, . . . arts and sciences, literature, law, medicine, pharmacy, dentistry, journalism, education, and other professional courses, all of which shall be equivalent to those offered at The University of Texas. . . .

Sec. 11    In the interim between the effective date of this Act and the organization, establishment, and operation of the Texas State University for Negroes at Houston . . . the Board of Regents of the University of Texas is authorized and required to forthwith organize and establish a separate school of law at Austin for Negroes to be known as the 'School of Law of the Texas State University for Negroes.' . . .

Sec. 14    The fact that the people of Texas desire that the state meet its obligation of equal educational opportunities for its Negro citizens from state supported institutions, and the fact that a separate and equivalent university of the first class for Negroes cannot be established and maintained under . . . the Constitution of Texas if such institution were made a college or branch of the University of Texas, and . . . the fact that interim courses must be established immediately by existing schools for the education of Negroes prior to the establishment and operation of said university . . . creates an emergency and imperative public necessity. . . .

## Southern Regional Educational Compact
### 1948[44]

WHEREAS, the States who are parties hereto have during the past several years conducted careful investigation looking toward the establishment and maintenance of jointly owned and operated regional educational institutions in the Southern States in the professional, technological, scientific, literary and other fields, so as to provide greater educational advantages and facilities for the citizens of the several States who reside within such region; and

---

[44]*Quoted in Alabama Acts, 1949, Act No. 227, p. 328. The regional compact was viewed by some as a device to relieve pressure for the integration of southern graduate and professional schools. Such a role was repudiated by a spokesman for the Southern Regional Council. See *The Baltimore Afro-American*, (June 17, 1950), p. 3.

WHEREAS, Meharry Medical College of Nashville, Tennessee, has proposed that its lands, buildings, equipment, and the net income from its endowment be turned over to the Southern States, or to an agency acting in their behalf, to be operated as a regional institution for medical, dental and nursing education . . .

WHEREAS, The said States desire to enter into a compact with each other providing for the planning and establishment of regional educational facilities;

NOW, THEREFORE, in consideration of the mutual agreements, covenants and obligations assumed by the respective States who are parties hereto . . ., the said several States do hereby form a geographical district or region consisting of the areas lying within the boundaries of the contracting States which, for the purposes of this compact, shall constitute an area for regional education supported by public funds derived from taxation by the constituent States and derived from other sources for the establishment, acquisition, operation and maintenance of regional educational schools and institutions for the benefit of citizens of the respective States residing within the region so established as may be determined from time to time in accordance with the terms and provisions of this compact.

## Southern Schools Seek Accreditation
### *1949*[45]

For approximately twenty years the schools which hold membership in this Association have benefitted by the excellent work of accreditation which has been carried on by the Committee on Approval of Negro Schools appointed by the Association of Colleges and Secondary Schools of the Southern States. We appreciate the work of this Committee and the great benefit which has come to us by virtue of its activity.

We feel, however, that, in the meantime, we have missed the opportunity for greater progress because of our inability to hold membership in the Southern Association. We feel that closer contact among all educators in our region will be mutually beneficial.

---

[45]*Proceedings of the Association of Colleges and Secondary Schools for Negroes, 1949*, p. 42. The Southern Association had maintained a listing of Grade A (meeting accreditation requirements) and Grade B (not quite meeting accreditation requirements) Negro colleges, but membership in the Association was withheld. No such grades were applied to member colleges and consequently it was not clear just what those designations meant.

We think that the time has come when all of us engaged in the same work should regularly share our experiences and jointly face our common problems. We request, therefore, that the separate members of the Association of Colleges and Secondary Schools be considered for full membership in said Southern Association; and that this Association authorize its Liaison Committee to work towards this end without hesitation and with our complete endorsement.

## Educational Equality Includes Intangible Factors
### *1950*[46]

In the instant case, petitioner filed an application for admission to the University of Texas Law School for the February, 1946 term. His application was rejected solely because he is a Negro. Petitioner thereupon brought this suit for mandamus against the appropriate school officials, respondents here, to compel his admission. At that time, there was no law school in Texas which permitted Negroes. . . .

The State trial court recognized that the action of the State in denying petitioner the opportunity to gain a legal education while granting it to others derived him of the equal protection of the laws guaranteed by the Fourteenth Amendment. The court did not grant the relief requested, however, but continued the case for six months to allow the State to supply substantially equal facilities. At the expiration of the six months, in December, 1946, the court denied the writ on the showing that the authorized university officials had adopted an order calling for the opening of a law school for Negroes the following February. While petitioner's appeal was pending, such a school was made available, but petitioner refused to register therein. . . .

The University of Texas Law School, from which petitioner was excluded, was staffed by a faculty of sixteen full-time and three part-time professors, some of whom are nationally recognized authorities in their field. Its student body numbered 850. The library contained over 65,000 volumes. Among the other facilities available to the students were a law review, moot court facilities, scholarship funds, and Order of the Coif affiliation. The school's alumni occupy the most distinguished positions

---

[46]Sweatt v. Painter et al., 70 S. Ct. 848 (June 5, 1950).

in the private practice of the law and in the public life of the State. It may properly be considered one of the nation's ranking law schools.

The law school for Negroes which was to have opened in February, 1947, would have had no independent faculty or library. The teaching was to be carried on by four members of the University of Texas Law School faculty, who were to maintain their offices at the University of Texas while teaching at both institutions. Few of the 10,000 volumes ordered for the library had arrived; nor was there any full-time librarian. The school lacked accreditation.

Since the trial of this case, respondents report the opening of a law school at the Texas State University for Negroes. It is apparently on the road to full accreditation. It has a faculty of five full-time professors; a student body of 23; a library of some 16,500 volumes serviced by a full-time staff; a practice court and legal aid association; and one alumnus who has become a member of the Texas Bar.

Whether the University of Texas Law School is compared with the original or the new law school for Negroes, we cannot find substantial equality in the educational opportunities offered white and Negro law students by the State. In terms of numbers of the faculty, variety of courses and opportunity for specialization, size of the student body, scope of the library, availability of law review and similar activities, the University of Texas Law School is superior. What is more important, the University of Texas Law School possesses to a far greater degree those qualities which are incapable of objective measurement but which make for greatness in a law school. Such qualities, to name but a few, include reputation of the faculty, experience of the administration, position and influence of the alumni, standing in the community, traditions and prestige. It is difficult to believe that one who had a free choice between these law schools would consider the question close.

Moreover, although the law is a highly learned profession, we are well aware that it is an intensely practical one. The law school, the proving ground for legal learning and practice, cannot be effective in isolation from the individuals and institutions with which the law interacts. Few students and no one who has practiced law would choose to study in an academic vacuum, removed from the interplay of ideas and the exchange of views with which the law is concerned. The law school to which Texas is willing to admit petitioner excludes from its student body members of the racial groups which number 85% of the population of the State and include most of the lawyers, witnesses, jurors, judges, and other officials with whom petitioner will inevitably be dealing when he becomes a member of the Texas Bar. With such a substantial and significant segment of society excluded, we cannot conclude that the education offered petitioner is substantially equal to that which he would receive if admitted to the University of Texas Law School.

## Court Requires Removal of Racial Restrictions in University of Oklahoma
### *1950*[47]

Appellant is a Negro citizen of Oklahoma. Possessing a Master's degree, he applied for admission to the University of Oklahoma in order to pursue studies and courses leading to a Doctorate in Education. At that time, his application was denied, solely because of his race. . . .

Citing our decisions . . . a statutory three-judge District Court held, 87 F. Supp. 526, that the State had a constitutional duty to provide him with the education he sought. . . .

Appellant was thereupon admitted to the University of Oklahoma Graduate School. . . . Thus he was required to sit apart at a designated desk in an anteroom adjoining the classroom; to sit at a designated desk on the mezzanine floor of the library, but not to use the desks in the regular reading room; and to sit at a designated table and to eat at a different time from the other students in the school cafeteria. . . .

Our society grows increasingly complex, and our need for trained leaders increases correspondingly. Appellant's case represents, perhaps, the epitome of that need, for he is attempting to obtain an advanced degree in education, to become, by definition, a leader and trainer of others. Those who will come under his guidance and influence must be directly affected by the education he receives. Their own education and development will necessarily suffer to the extent that his training is unequal to that of his classmates. State-imposed restrictions which produce such inequalities cannot be sustained.

It may be argued that appellant will be in no better position when these restrictions are removed, for he may still be set apart by his fellow students. This we think irrelevant. There is a vast difference—a Constitutional difference—between restrictions imposed by the state which prohibit the intellectual commingling of students, and the refusal of individuals to commingle where the state presents no such bar. The removal of the state restrictions will not necessarily abate individual and group

---

[47]McLaurin v. Oklahoma State Regents, 70 S. Ct. 851 (June 5, 1950).

predilections, prejudices and choices. But at the very least, the state will not be depriving appellant of the opportunity to secure acceptance by his fellow students on his own merits.

## Integration No Guarantee of Democratic Education
### *1951*[48]

In general, Negro-educated Negroes have never learned to live with Freedom and this is why they are almost totally missing from the ranks of those who apply the privileges and the tools of democracy to the construction of Freedom's spacious house. Where they have taken over as leaders of Negro communities there rises a nauseating reek of devious and oily obsequiousness. It is a kind of fascism in reverse.

A group of Negro parents in a Virginia city wished to equalize the facilities of the Negro school with those of white schools. One of the things that the colored schools lacked was a cafeteria. This was particularly noticeable because the city school board had just added such a convenience (at a cost of $20,000) to the only white school without it. The Negro parents went to the principal of their own school. As an ambitious and hard-working educator, less complacent and time-serving than most of his type, he had ideas, and the chief one was that the parents' group solicit funds (he thought $2,500 would do it!) in Negro homes, churches, and other racial institutions. By a show of initiative and energy, he thought, it might be brought home to the white people that Negro citizens were worthy of consideration.

Naturally among those to whom the project was first presented was the Negro acknowledged as the colored community's leader — a lawyer, graduate of a Negro college and a white law school. The esteem he commanded among his own people and the attention he could get from the whites were very real.

A friend of mine happened to be in the lawyer's office when the committee of parents went there. Whether out of boorishness, as my friend thinks, or because of the very human desire to prove his influence, or because he clearly saw his duty as a leader, the lawyer took over completely. "We'll get in touch with some real money," he said. "No point in piddling around with the colored folks' two cents' worth." Then, picking

---

[48]From *On Being A Negro In America,* copyright © 1951, by S. Saunders Redding, reprinted by permission of the publishers, The Bobbs-Merrill Company, Inc.

up the telephone, he called several of his "White friends" — a peanut-produce manufacturer (he carefully identified them between calls), a banker and an insurance broker, among others — and explained to them the Negro parents' project for the school. In ten minutes of "the most consummate fawning," my friend said afterward, the lawyer had solicited pledges of more than a thousand dollars. He typed out an identifying statement for the parents and sent them off to collect from his white friends.

My friend said she watched open mouthed during this masterly performance. "It was like being at the theater, when you're so struck by the skill of the star that you don't think of the play itself until after the curtain falls. Or maybe it isn't skill that strikes you. Maybe it's personality. I remember Katharine Cornell in _____ Well, it was exactly like that," my friend said, with something very like awe in her voice and in her pale face. She recovered after the curtain had fallen.

"Mr. So-and-So," she asked, "do you mean to tell me you're begging white people in this community to give you things that everybody ought to have and that you have as much right to as they? This is 1951! Haven't you heard what's going on — the legal suits for equalization and all?"

"Oh," the lawyer said, laughing blandly, "they don't want to sue. They just want a cafeteria like the white schools have."

Thurgood Marshall, chief legal counsel of the National Association for the Advancement of Colored People, has said that the hardest job his staff has had in bringing equal-education suits has been to persuade Negro teachers and representative Negro parents to stand as plaintiffs. They have to be bludgeoned out of their childish faith in the short-term profits of their minority middle-class position. They have to be taught, with pain and patience, that democracy is a legitimate enterprise, that its institutions must make for their dignity, and that they cannot save themselves without forgetting themselves in the struggle to save the rights of man. Negro colleges are doing almost none of this teaching. . . .

The only point is that the condition does exist, and it is not healthy. Nor can it be cured, it seems to me, by the superficial therapy of integration on special levels — the graduate and professional-school level, for instance — which is now being hailed as a cure-all. It is not. Integration on this level is at best a victory for the method of democracy, and method and spirit are not necessarily one. For years upper middle-class American Negroes have been going to graduate and professional schools with whites without learning, and without stimulating by their presence there, the inclusive kind of thinking that is necessary to the fulfillment of the spirit of democracy.

## Segregated Education Opposed
*1952*[49]

In the end and near future we look forward to the disappearance of the Negro college as a *Negro* college. Meanwhile, it is imperative that these institutions should be, in the interest of American education, adequate and vital colleges of the first order now. . . . The Negro college can make a special and invaluable contribution . . . because . . . it is much less hampered in its approach to many Southern problems than are those institutions whose energies are divided and objectives confused by allegiance to regional habits out of line with national principles. The Negro college . . . can serve the region both in the studies which it undertakes and in the kind of life it can create on its campus. . . . Just as the Negro Americans may have a special mission in history to bring America back to its first principles of freedom and equal opportunity, so the Negro college may have a mission to serve as a spur and an example to the South on the road to democratic education.

## Supreme Court Declares
## Segregation Unconstitutional
*1954*[50]

These cases come to us from the States of Kansas, South Carolina, Virginia, and Delaware. They are premised on different facts and different local conditions, but a common legal question justifies their consideration together in this consolidated opinion. . . .

The plaintiffs contend that segregated public schools are not "equal" and cannot be made "equal," and that hence they are deprived of the equal protection of the laws. Because of the obvious importance of the question presented, the Court took jurisdiction. Argument was heard in the 1952 Term, and reargument was heard this Term on certain questions propounded by the Court.

---

[49]Charles S. Johnson, "Negro Education in the National Economy," a speech delivered April 15, 1952, at Dayton, Ohio. Typescript in the Charles S. Johnson Papers, Fisk University, Nashville, Tennessee. p. 10.

[50]Brown et al. v. Board of Education of Topeka, Kansas, 74 S. Ct. 686 (May 17, 1954). The decision applied to four cases originating in Kansas, South Carolina, Virginia, and Delaware. The Brown case merely appears first in alphabetical order. A fifth case involving the District of Columbia was decided at the same time, but a separate decision was issued since the legal grounds rested in the Fifth rather than the Fourteenth Amendment.

Reargument was largely devoted to the circumstances surrounding the adoption of the Fourteenth Amendment in 1868. . . .

In approaching this problem, we cannot turn the clock back to 1868 when the Amendment was adopted, or even to 1896 when Plessy v. Ferguson was written. We must consider public education in the light of its full development and its present place in American life throughout the Nation. Only in this way can it be determined if segregation in public schools deprives these plaintiffs of the equal protection of the laws.

Today, education is perhaps the most important function of state and local governments. Compulsory school attendance laws and the great expenditures for education both demonstrate our recognition of the importance of education to our democratic society. . . .

We come then to the question presented: Does segregation of children in public schools solely on the basis of race, even though the physical facilities and other "tangible" factors may be equal, deprive the children of the minority group of equal educational opportunities? We believe that it does. . . .

Such considerations apply with added force to children in grade and high schools. To separate them from others of similar age and qualifications solely because of their race generates a feeling of inferiority as to their status in the community that may affect their hearts and minds in a way unlikely ever to be undone. . . .

Whatever may have been the extent of psychological knowledge at the time of Plessy v. Ferguson, this finding is amply supported by modern authority. Any language in Plessy v. Ferguson contrary to this finding is rejected.

We conclude that in the field of public education the doctrine of "separate but equal" has no place. Separate educational facilities are inherently unequal.

## Desegregation—The Right Thing to Do
### *1954*[51]

We welcome the decision and look upon it as another significant milestone in the nation's quest for a democratic way of life and in the Negro's long struggle to become a first class citizen. . . . It was the right and moral thing to do. . . . We hail the decision again because it dramatically distinguishes

---

[51]Conference of Southern Negro Educators, *It Was the Right and Moral Thing To Do* (n.p.: Phelps-Stokes Fund, 1954), p. 10. The conference, held in Hot Springs, Arkansas, brought together 64 Negro leaders in education for the purpose of clarifying and eliminating "conflicts often appearing in comments on how the Negro people of the South viewed the decision" of the Supreme Court in the Brown case. (p. 3)

our way of life in a democracy from that in such totalitarian countries as Nazi Germany and Communist Russia. Here in the United States great social wrongs can be and are righted without bloodshed and without revolutionary means. . . . The nation cannot consistently stand as leader of the democratic forces of the world and harbor the undemocratic practice of racial segregation at home.

The effort on the part of some leaders and some school officials to intimidate Negro teachers and other citizens under threat of loss of jobs if they express approval of the Court's decision and if segregation is not maintained is shortsighted, vindictive, and contrary to the fundamental sense of fair play of the American people. . . . We regret that some public officials have sought to persuade Negro educators and other leaders to evade the decision by agreeing to voluntary segregation. This cannot be decently done. . . .

Good statesmanship in a democracy requires that all segments of the population participate in the implementation of the Court's decision, which is of common concern. . . . Some public officials speak as if only white Americans are involved. We are all, Negro and white, deeply and equally involved. . . . Negroes are able and willing to serve on boards of education, on other policy-making bodies and in administrative capacities throughout the South. . . .

The Court's decision makes possible a single school system with the opportunity for the people in the region to marshall their educational resources and develop a philosophy that brings to education generally a new perspective and to the nation a new spirit. This cannot be done in a dual system of education. Let it be clearly understood that we are not pleading for Negroes alone. We are concerned about the best education that can be made available to every child in the South. . . . We want the white child to have the best and we want the Negro child to have the best. It is the opinion of the Supreme Court that there cannot be equality of educational opportunity for the Negro child in a segregated system. Moreover, it is the opinion of the Social Scientists that it is not possible for the white child to receive the best education in a segregated system.

## Problems of Integration
### *1955*[52]

Yes, integration is upon us and with it comes a challenge which will expose us to a competition we have never known. . . . There will be no

---

[52]Joe S. Johnson, "The Challenge," in *The Journal* (organ of the Oklahoma Association of Negro Teachers), (July, 1955), p. 1.

more top positions labeled "Negro". Our children won't be on the debating teams, in the chorus, hold offices, play on the athletic teams, represent their school just for the asking. To be recognized, we must work . . . a little harder and a little longer. . . . Let us pray that this inevitable transition will not be so hectic that we find ourselves confused and wandering aimlessly in the wilderness of hopelessness and frustration. Be vigilant that we lose not our identity as a capable and ingenious race nor lose a single phase of our cultural heritage.

## Voluntary Segregation Allowed
### *1955*[53]

Whatever may have been the views of this court as to the law when the case was originally before us, it is our duty now to accept the law as declared by the Supreme Court.

Having said this, it is important that we point out exactly what the Supreme Court has decided and what it has not decided in this case. It has not decided that the federal courts are to take over or regulate the public schools of the states. It has not decided that the states must mix persons of different races in the schools or must require them to attend schools or must deprive them of the right of choosing the schools they attend. What it has decided, and all that it has decided, is that a state may not deny to any person on account of race the right to attend any school that it maintains. This, under the decision of the Supreme Court, the state may not do directly or indirectly; but if the schools which it maintains are open to children of all races, no violation of the Constitution is involved even though the children of different races voluntarily attend different schools, as they attend different churches. Nothing in the Constitution or in the decision of the Supreme Court takes away from the people freedom to choose the schools they attend. The Constitution, in other words, does not require integration. It merely forbids discrimination. It does not forbid such segregation as occurs as the result of voluntary action. It merely forbids the use of governmental power to enforce segregation. The Fourteenth Amendment is a limitation upon the exercise of power by the state or state agencies, not a limitation upon the freedom of individuals.

---

[53]Briggs v. Elliott, 132 Federal Supplement 776 (July 15, 1955).

# Virginia's Massive Resistance
### *1956*[54]


From and after September 29, 1956, and in conformity with the public policy of the Commonwealth of Virginia as herein established . . . and specifically invoking the police powers of the Commonwealth and the constitutional powers of the General Assembly, the Commonwealth of Virginia assumes direct responsibility for the control of any school, elementary or secondary, in the Commonwealth, to which children of both races are assigned and enrolled by any school authorities acting voluntarily or under compulsion of any court order. The making of such an assignment, and the enrollment of such child, or children, shall automatically divest the school authorities making the assignment and the enrollment of all further authority, power, and control over such public school; . . . and such school is closed and is removed from the public school system, and such authority, power and control over such school . . . shall be and is hereby vested in the Commonwealth of Virginia to be exercised by the Governor of Virginia in whom reposes the chief executive power of the state.


# Federal Troops Integrate Little Rock's Central High School
### *1957*[55]


Central High School is a five-story building built on seven different levels and with six city blocks of lawn and athletic fields. Inside, many corridors are long and narrow and, in so large a building, difficult to supervise. I spent most of the night of Tuesday, September 24, talking with my administrative staff and Jess Matthews, the Central High principal, about the problem of protecting nine Negro students who would be widely scattered among some two thousand white pupils moving from class to class in

---

[54]Virginia School Laws, 1958, Chapter 9.1, Article 1, Section 22-188.5, p. 107. The law was passed in 1956 and refers specifically to the "unprecedented obstacles" which would "destroy the efficiency" of the schools as a result of the 1954 desegregation decision.

[55]Virgil T. Blossom, *It Has Happened Here* (New York: Harper & Row Pub. Inc., 1959), pp. 120-23, 134, 142, 147, 151, 201, 202. Copyright © 1959.

all parts of the building. I ended up by writing a letter to General Walker suggesting various measures that should be taken for the protection of all students, including guards at the entrances and thirty guards in the various corridors. We also arranged to keep all unauthorized persons out by having teachers and students use their library cards as passes to the school.

On Wednesday morning sidewalk and street-corner barricades were erected and about 350 men of the 357th Airborne Battle Group took strategic positions around the school before the first "sightseers" appeared in automobiles. As the soldiers kept traffic moving, one man stuck his head out of a car window and yelled: "Hi ya, Hitler!" It was significant that throughout the day most of the automobiles parked in the vicinity of the school were from outside Little Rock. A count showed twenty-five out-of-state cars and forty-two from other counties in Arkansas. . . .

But to get back to Tuesday's developments, it was just before nine-thirty that morning when an Army station wagon, followed by a jeep, screeched around the corner and stopped in front of the school. The helicopter circled overhead. The nine enrolled Negro students got out of the station wagon and, with twenty-two armed soldiers surrounding them, walked into the building. A few minutes later several white students walked out. . . .

Inside the school there was comparative calm. Only 1,250 of the 2,000 students were present, but we knew that many had been kept at home because their parents feared there might be violence. The day began with General Walker addressing the student body. He said they had nothing to fear from the soldiers, but he warned that anyone who attempted to interfere with the proper administration of the school "will be removed by the soldiers." There would be no exceptions to enforcement of the law, he added, because "if it were otherwise we would not be a strong nation but a mere unruly mob.". . .

The first signs of organized resistance to federal troups began mildly enough near the end of the first week of what Governor Faubus had called the "occupation" of Little Rock. The Mothers League of Central High School appealed to the Governor to close the school, and the League's vice-president, Mrs. Margaret Jackson, said they had an "unquestionable right" to demand closure because the schools "are supported by our tax money." . . .

I don't know whether these changes had a psychological effect on the segregationist-minded students, but on Friday a group of them greeted the arrival of the Negro students with shouts which the newspaper reporters variously described as "jeers" or "cheers." They were probably the former, because shortly thereafter some of the white students began a campaign of petty harassment of the Negroes inside the school. The trouble-makers, and again I want to emphasize that they were very few in number, began throwing pencils or pebbles at some of the Negroes as students thronged through the halls. There were also many opportunities for them to make remarks when the guards or teachers were out of ear-shot. For the most part the Negro students attempted to ignore such harassment, and the school staff repeatedly counseled them not to reply. . . .

The segregationists were prolific letter writers. My mail was full of denunciations day after day. The letters came from all over the country, although most of them were from southern states. They rather monoton-ously repeated the segregationist propaganda with occasional variations. One extreme example was a letter from a woman, who obviously had money and social position, suggesting that the best solution to the school integration problem would be to have all Negroes "chained, piled in one huge pile and burned alive." . . .

An important and perhaps the most vicious, phase of the segrega-tionist campaign to close Central High School was harassment of school officials with anonymous telephone calls, often in the middle of the night. Members of the School Board and members of the high school staff all were victims of these tactics over a period of many weeks, but I suppose I was the target more than anyone else.

It was obvious soon after federal troops were stationed at the high school that the telephone campaign was carefully organized so that it would cause us the greatest possible distress. The telephone at my office and at my home rang with great regularity throughout the day, and in the evening the calls were scheduled so that there was at least one every half hour without fail. Sometimes this schedule was continued until three or four o'clock in the morning. . . .

In addition to nuisance telephone calls, there were repeated anony-mous threats that the high school would be bombed, or tips that a bomb had been planted in the school. These were a part of the campaign to force closure of the integrated school, and in a period of several months we received at least forty-three such bomb-scare telephone calls. In general, they followed a set pattern. The anonymous call would first be made to one of the newspapers or radio stations or to all of them, presum-ably to be sure there would be maximum publicity and that parents would worry about sending their children to the school. Then the anonymous caller would get in touch with the police or one of the school officials and repeat the threat or the "tip" that a bomb had been planted. On some days during October and November we had several such calls on one day and once we had five.

. . . the people of the South must come to realize that, with desegre-gation the law of the land, every school district will be better off if it com-plies intelligently by planning its own program instead of delaying until the federal government steps in to enforce school integration. There cannot be any single, standardized program for all. Each community is different and each plan should be unique. Some may find it best to start integration in the primary grades as was done at Nashville. Others may prefer to start at college levels and work down through secondary and elementary grades, as was done in St. Louis. Or complete immediate integration — as at Louisville — may be the best solution. However it may be done, I am confident that local planning in line with local conditions will be essential to preserve standards of education, to protect the rights of the community and the state and to maintain the dignity of Americans.

I do not want to leave any impression that school integration in the South will be easy or rapid. Far from it. Progress is seldom easy; the transformation of a traditional way of life in which millions of persons sincerely believe is impossible without pain and anguish. There will be resistance, sometimes bitter resistance. In some areas today the people will not consider any kind of integration. They won't even talk about compliance with the law. But the law is still there, and it won't disappear no matter how tightly they close their eyes or their minds.

Little Rock was a classic example of what a community should not let extremists do to it. I did not believe it could happen. It did happen, despite the untiring efforts of members of the School Board, members of the school staff and many others with whom I am proud to have been associated. It can happen again, somewhere, some way.

But I don't believe it will happen again in the same way. It is no longer possible to escape the realization that the future of our system of public education is at stake, that the future of thousands upon thousands of wonderful young people depends on respect for the law. I hold a fundamental conviction that the South will intelligently and ably face, not to the illusory past, but to the high promise of our nation's future.

## Virginia Schools to Close
## Under Federal Intervention
### 1958[56]

The General Assembly declares and establishes it to be the policy of the Commonwealth that no public school shall be operated whenever any

---

[56]Virginia School Laws, 1958, Chapter 9.2, Article 1, p. 112. Passed February 17, 1958. Declared unconstitutional by Harrison v. Day, 200 Va. 439 (January 19, 1959) in which the Virginia Supreme Court ruled that the Governor could not legally assume control of public schools since the Constitution placed supervision of local schools in local school boards.

military forces or personnel are employed or used upon the order or direction of any federal authority for the purpose of policing its operation, or to prevent acts of violence or alleged acts of violence.

## Virginia's Pupil Placement Law
*1960*[57]

The State Board of Education shall promulgate rules and regulations to be used and applied by school boards in their respective jurisdictions in making placement of individual pupils in particular public schools so as to provide for the orderly administration of such schools, the competent instruction of the pupils enrolled and the health, safety, best interests, and general welfare of such pupils.

## The Place of the Negro College
*1961*[58]

Its identity as a Negro college . . . was imposed from its Negro student body, rather than growing out of the essential meaning and purpose of the institution. Obviously there is no educational uniqueness in racial designation alone. . . . Until the transition goes far beyond its present state the private Negro colleges are not only important, they are essential. As institutions searching out talented Negro youth and developing them into constructive leaders, they are making a significant contribution to the nation and must continue to do so through the long period ahead. When the transition to integration comes to a close, the Negro private colleges will operate simply as American institutions of higher learning. They will not seek a future existence on the basis of sentiment for the past. . . . The private colleges for Negroes will be needed in the future, but only in the sense that any college is needed: to serve with quality, and on a non-racial basis the educational needs of the largest student population which

---

[57]Virignia School Laws, 1960 Cumulative Supplement, Chapter 12, Article 1.2, Section 22-232.18, p. 35. Effective March 1, 1960.

[58]W. J. Trent, Jr., *The Private Negro College*. Pamphlet published by the United Negro College Fund, c. 1961, pp. 3, 11, 13.

this nation has seen. . . . Beyond the period of transition, the private Negro
colleges will seek suport and future existence on the basis of those factors
in their heritage that would enrich the total stream of American education
and on the basis of the same factors that every good American college
would emphasize as its needs and contributions.


# Talking About Africa
## 1961[59]


The great need in teaching today is to develop an understanding of people
throughout the world. The African people have been victims of misunder-
standing for many centuries, as a result of deliberate misrepresentation.
. . . Today, African leaders and Negro Americans are expressing the close-
ness of relationship and the identity of their common struggles and aspirations. Pride, human dignity and individual worth may result from effective
teaching of African contributions and achievements.


# James Meredith at the
# University of Mississippi
## 1962[60]


There was no lingering or turning back now. At eight o'clock the three of
us — McShane, Doar, and Meredith — with a retinue of marshals and
soldiers left Baxter Hall for the Lyceum Building to get on with the long-
delayed business of my registering as a student at the University of Mississippi. The signs of strife and warfare from the night before were everywhere. But at this moment the power of the United States was supreme.

---

[59]Walter G. Daniel in Virginia Teachers Association *Newsletter* (August 18,
1961). Appeals had been made for many years that schools incorporate more
teaching about black history, literature, and culture. The study of Africa came to
be seen as an essential part of this ethnic curriculur emphasis.

[60]James Meredith, *Three Years in Mississippi* (Bloomington: Indiana University
Press, 1966), pp. 212, 213, 217, 218, 274, 323.

. . . The border patrol car in which we rode to the administration building was a shattered example of the violence of social change. We had used this car to make our first attempt to enroll on September 20, 1962, and then it had been a spotless, unmarred specimen. Now it was battered and smashed: bullet holes had riddled the sides; the windows were all shot out. . . . We entered through the back door of the Lyceum Building. Fortunately, I did not know that it was the back door at the time; otherwise, I would have had to confront the question of whether this was a concession to the Mississippi "way of life." . . . Inside the room behind a desk sat Ellis, the Registrar. He was a lone stand-out, the only man on the scene with spirit — a spirit of defiance, even of contempt, if not hatred. Doar stated our purpose and the Registrar pointed to a group of forms to be filled out by me. I looked at them and filled out all but one — my class-schedule form. As I studied it, obviously Ellis knew what was on my mind. One course on my schedule not only was a duplicate of one with the same title which I had already completed with the grade of A, but when I got to class, I found that the instructor was using the very same textbook. Ellis said to me, "Meredith (he is the only official at the university who did not address me with the usual title of courtesy), you may as well sign." . . .

A quotation from Theodore Roosevelt was perhaps more important than anything else in helping me make the critical decisions. . . . At various times different parts of that quotation have been important to me, but when I made the decision to return to Mississippi to try to gain admission to the university, the part I kept remembering was the "cold and timid souls who know neither victory nor defeat." I did not want to be one of those.

I would usually awaken around five-thirty or a quarter to six to the click of the steel-plated heels of the soldier walking his post in the hallway from one end of my apartment to the other. . . . At seven I would walk out the only way open, through the living room (the Marshal's head-quarters). All the other doors had been blocked. The team of marshals for the day would join me, and I would head down the long flight of steps outside the dorm toward the sidewalk. When I reached the second step one of my watchers would yell, "Hey, Nigger. There's that Nigger!" I had been at the university ten months before I ever descended the fifteen or twenty steps without someone calling me nigger. They must have kept their eyes on those steps twenty-four hours a day. As I walked the two blocks down the hill to the cafeteria, I could hear the routine window-to-window comments. . . .

Perhaps the most remarkable achievement of my three years in Mississippi fighting the system of "White Supremacy" is that I survived.

## Next Steps in Providing
## Equal Educational Opportunity
### *1962*[61]

The board non-litigation tactics involved in implementing the Supreme Court decision seem to fall in three categories. The first includes those strategies designed to bring private power and privilege, whether held by groups or persons, ever under social regulation. In many local communities, this means a continued operation utilizing pressure, the weight of public opinion, etc., to change policies of agencies, organizations, and businesses so that all the people of the community participate in services, employment opportunities, and other advantages on a common basis of privilege.

The second aspect of strategy involves perhaps the psychological integration of the people of local communities into a common sense of identification and belonging. Undoubtedly the greatest barrier to participation in the American dream that a person will be rewarded according to his abilities and energies, is the psychological sense on the part of minority group members of being shut off; the never being quite certain that one is accepted; the continuous question mark as to whether even special opportunities are offered because of justly earned merit or because of racial status. This is illustrated, for instance, in many northern communities where Negro children still constitute a small proportion of school classes but are elected to offices out of all proportion to their numbers. The Negro student is never quite sure whether he is elected because he merits it or because he is a Negro. The strategy for dealing with this problem is complex but exceedingly important.

The third aspect of strategy is much more positive. It involves "taking up the slack" that has been caused by the patterns of the past. Equality of opportunity is not enough if it is conceived as simply giving an equal chance to every person as he is presently constituted. There is no equality of opportunity for the person who has been shut out of the main stream of American life, whose ancestors before him were shut out, if he must compete with persons who have had superior advantages. This is as true within groups as between groups. This is treacherous, dangerous ground ideologically, but it is a problem that must be faced realistically. . . .

---

[61]Dan W. Dodson, "Beyond Legislation and Litigation—What?", in Virgil Clift (ed.), *Negro Education In America* (New York: Harper & Row Pub. Inc., 1962), pp. 275, 276, 286.

The strategies for the improvement of minority groups in the future will be increasingly less those which "plead the cause." Undoubtedly they will be those which make "common cause." The great challenge to America today is how to go beyond mere "equal chance for everybody" and to bring all disprivileged peoples through the sociocultural gate into full participation in the common community life. In this responsibility, intelligent community action, education that gives direction to the social process, religion that reinterprets basic spiritual values, an economic system that assumes an obligation for the well being of all, a dynamic jurisprudence — all must lend a hand in the creation of new designs of community life if democracy is to prove that people have basic concerns for each other that transcend a raw power struggle for economic status.

## Court Upholds Neighborhood School
### *1963*[62]

The neighborhood school which serves the students within a prescribed district is a long and well established institution in American public school education. It is almost universally used, particularly in the larger school systems. It has many social, cultural and administrative advantages which are apparent without enumeration. With the use of the neighborhood school districts in any school system with a large and expanding percentage of Negro population, it is almost inevitable that a racial imbalance will result in certain schools. Nevertheless, I have seen nothing in the many cases dealing with the segregation problem which leads me to believe that the law requires that a school system developed on the neighborhood school plan, honestly and conscientiously constructed with no intention or purpose to segregate the races, must be destroyed or abandoned because the resulting effect is to have a racial imbalance in certain schools where the district is populated almost entirely by Negroes or whites. On the other hand, there are many expressions to the contrary, and these expressions lead me to believe that racial balance in our public schools is not constitutionally mandated. . . .

The Court finds no support for the plaintiffs position that the defendant has an affirmative duty to balance the races in the various schools

---

[62]Bell v. School City of Gary, 213 Federal Supplement 819 (1963).

under its jurisdiction, regardless of the residence of students involved. Indeed their own evidence is that such a task could not be accomplished in the Gary schools. Their expert, Dr. Wolff, submitted a proposal for balancing the races in most of the schools by eliminating four of the eight high schools now existing and building three new high schools and by transferring approximately 6,000 students from their neighborhood school to other schools, some of them great distances away. Even if his plan were adopted, Roosevelt School would still be 100% Negro and Bailly, by his definition, would continue to be a segregated white school. In developing his plan, Dr. Wolff, in effect, admitted that he considered only the desirability of creating a racial balance in the schools and that costs, safety factors and other considerations were at least secondary to his main objective.

Unfortunately, the problems confronting the school administration are not as simple as Dr. Wolff's solution. For example, the financial burden of transporting 6,000 students from their home neighborhood to another would be a matter of considerable concern to the administrators of an already heavily taxed and indebted school district. Moreover, the administrative problem of choosing those who would be transferred and those who would not in a rapidly growing school system where the racial complexion of the various neighborhoods is constantly changing would be almost impossible to solve.

Furthermore, requiring certain students to leave their neighborhood and friends and be transferred to another school miles away, while other students, similarly situated, remained in the neighborhood school, simply for the purpose of balancing the races in the various schools would in my opinion be indeed a violation of the equal protection clause of the Fourteenth Amendment.

## California Court Rejects Attendance Boundaries that Foster Segregation
### *1963*[63]

The constitutional rights of children not to be discriminated against in school admission on the grounds of race or color cannot be nullified by

---

[63]Jackson v. Pasadena City School District, 31 Cal. Rptr. 606 (June 27, 1963).

state action either openly and directly or indirectly by evasive schemes for segregation, and the Fourteenth Amendment is violated where zoning is merely a subterfuge for producing or perpetuating racial segregation in a school. . . .

Although it is alleged that the board was guilty of intentional discriminatory action, it should be pointed out that even in the absence of gerrymandering or other affirmative discriminatory conduct by a school bard, a student under some circumstances would be entitled to relief where, by reason of residential segregation, substantial racial imbalance exists in his school. So long as large numbers of Negroes live in segregated areas, school authorities will be confronted with difficult problems in providing Negro children with the kind of education they are entitled to have. Residential segregation is in itself an evil which tends to frustrate the youth in the area and to cause antisocial attitudes and behavior. Where such segregation exists it is not enough for a school board to refrain from affirmative discriminatory conduct. The harmful influence on the children will be reflected and intensified in the classroom if school attendance is determined on a geographic basic without corrective measures. The right to an equal opportunity for education and the harmful consequences of segregation require that school boards take steps, insofar as reasonably feasible, to alleviate racial imbalance in schools regardless of its cause.

## Louis Lomax Criticizes Negro Education
### 1963[64]

The generation of young Negroes that is doing so much to win new opportunities for itself is ill-equipped to use those opportunities. With splendid courage these youngsters are breaking down barriers of prejudice. Yet they are not qualified for the new jobs in industry and government now open to them. . . .

The need is crystal clear to any Negro who is courageous enough to be honest about our problem: The Negro community must launch crash programs — which might be called "study-ins" — that involve both vocational guidance and academic preparation. These study-ins

---

[64]Louis E. Lomax, "Young Negroes Aren't Ready," *Saturday Evening Post*, (September 21, 1963), pp. 12, 14. Copyright © 1963 by The Curtis Publishing Company.

must be soul meetings; like the sit-ins, they must become an article of faith, a folk covenant between the students and their teachers, and they must be carried out with the same new and inspired militancy that ushered legalized segregation to its belated death.

There is a basic reason why our students are so academically unprepared. Today's Negro-college students are the products of 300 years of slavery plus an additional century of life in a virtually separate and totally unequal socio-economic structure. Apartness and inequality involve more than the broad denial of opportunities and freedoms. They prescribe the inferior standards exacted of us by white people, and they serve as excuses as we Negroes fail to demand higher standards of ourselves. . . .

Another vital step in preparing students for the reality of today's job market is to overhaul the curricula of Negro colleges. Born during Reconstruction and nurtured under segregation, Negro colleges have graduated teachers, preachers, social workers and—all too infrequently—doctors for service in the *Negro community*. One has but to take a hard look at the 20,000 students graduating from Negro colleges each year to realize that they are still afflicted by *Negro education*, that peculiar concept of the liberal arts that dooms, rather than dedicates, students to service in the Negro world.

This course of study is much too narrow for today's job demands. . . .

Not only must the curricula of Negro colleges be overhauled but also academic standards must be raised. Evidences of this burning need are abundant. Many Negro students cannot cope with the Graduate Record examination. Several Negro-college administrators are disturbed because white students who withdrew from Ivy League schools and enrolled on their campuses in order to participate in the sit-in demonstrations have walked away with practically all the academic honors. Even more Negro-college administrators are disturbed over the fact that their students failed the State Department's Foreign Service entrance examination while Negro students from integrated colleges passed with little difficulty. All of us became concerned in 1961 when two of the three prizes awarded in the *Reader's Digest* writing contest for Negro-college students went to Africans studying on Negro campuses. But the most disturbing failure of the Negro colleges is the alarming number of graduates who cannot think deeply, speak properly or work effectively in the fields they are alleged to have mastered. . . .

Yet I refuse to abandon this generation of Negro-college students to Negro mediocrity. These are the young people who staged the sit-ins and the freedom rides. They are neither stupid nor irreparably mangled. These students *can* be taught, they *can* be inspired. In the words of the sit-in theme song, these students will overcome one day — *provided* their teachers do some overcoming themselves; *provided* these teachers set proper standards and demand good performances of the student; *provided* both teachers and students enter into a covenant of good scholarship for the sake of the race and the nation as a whole. . . .

As *Negro* schools they cannot survive much longer than another decade or so; but if they launch study-ins — crash programs calling for better instruction, broader curricula and higher academic standards — they will take their places among the centers of learning where students of all races prepare for life and labor in the general American Society. . . .

## Policy on Integration of New York City Board of Education
### *1963*[65]

It has been said, correctly, that the schools alone cannot eliminate prejudice, discrimination, and segregation. It is equally true that this task will not be accomplished with less than an all out effort of the schools.

Our schools must not be neutral in the struggle of society to better itself. We must not overlook the harmful effects of discrimination on the education of all children. Moreover, within the limits of our control, we must not acquiesce in the undemocratic school patterns which are a concomitant of segregated housing. Furthermore, we must continue our policy of not tolerating racial or religious prejudice on the part of any member of our staffs. If education is to fulfill its responsibility, it must recognize that the school world has a significant influence on each child's attitudes and affects the future of democracy.

To further its integration policy, the school system has responsibilities to its pupils and personnel and to the communities.

1. For pupils — We must seek ways to give every child an optimum opportunity for fulfillment and success:

(a) Our school system must vigorously employ every means at its disposal to desegregate schools and classrooms and to bring about true integration as soon as possible.

---

[65]Board of Education, New York City Public Schools, "Responsibility of the Schools In Integration," as quoted in Gordon J. Klopf and Israel A. Laster (ed.), *Integrating The Urban School* (New York: Bureau of Publications, Teachers College, Columbia University, 1963), pp. 125, 126.

(b)    We must continue to develop educational programs which prepare all pupils to live constructively in a pluralistic society.

(c)    We must provide whatever services and materials are essential to meet the special educational needs of those pupils whose progress has been impaired by an accumulation of the ills of discrimination. Simultaneously we must lift the goals of those whose environment has kept their aspirational levels at a low plane.

2.    For School Personnel — We must develop personnel practices which will maximize the success of the integration program:

(a)    We must provide appropriate education and training for school personnel so that every staff member may gain an appreciation of the strengths inherent in the variety of backgrounds that compose our total population.

(b)    In recognition of the value to the children of association with professionals of different backgrounds, our staffing procedures must provide for better ethnic heterogeneity in school faculties.

(c)    It is essential that capable and experienced teachers and supervisors be distributed in accordance with educational needs.

3.    With Communities — We must work closely and cooperatively with communities:

(a)    We must support the efforts of those communities which are struggling to overcome past frustration and failure and to surmount present deprivation.

(b)    We consider it our obligation to help develop the kind of community attitudes which will help in the implementation of the integration policies of the City public schools.


## The End of Massive Resistance
### *1964*[66]


On May 17, 1954, ten years ago, we held that the Virginia segregation laws did deny equal protection. . . .

Efforts to desegregate Prince Edward County's schools met with resistance. In 1956 Section 141 of the Virginia Constitution was amended to authorize the General Assembly and local governing bodies to appro-

---

[66]Griffin v. County School Board of Prince Edward County. 84 S. Ct. 1226 (1964).

priate funds to assist students to go to public or to nonsectarian private schools, in addition to those owned by the State or by the locality. The General Assembly met in special session and enacted legislation to close any public schools where white and colored children were enrolled together, to cut off state funds to such schools, to pay tuition grants to children in non-sectarian private schools, and to extend state retirement benefits to teachers in newly created private schools. . . . In April 1959 the General Assembly abandoned "massive resistance" to desegregation and turned instead to what was called a "freedom of choice" program. The Assembly repealed the rest of the 1956 legislation, as well as a tuition grant law of January 1959, and enacted a new tuition grant program. At the same time the Assembly repealed Virginia's compulsory attendance laws and instead made school attendance a matter of local option.

Having as early as 1956 resolved that they would not operate public schools "wherein white and colored children are taught together," the Supervisors of Prince Edward County refused to levy any school taxes for the 1959–1960 school year, explaining that they were "confronted with a court decree which requires the admission of white and colored children to all the schools of the county without regard to race or color." As a result, the county's public schools did not reopen in the fall of 1959 and have remained closed ever since, although the public schools of every other county in Virginia have continued to operate under laws governing the State's public school system and to draw funds provided by the State for that purpose. A private group, the Prince Edward School Foundation, was formed to operate private schools for white children in Prince Edward County and, having built its own school plant, has been in operation ever since the closing of the public schools. An offer to set up private schools for colored children in the county was rejected, the Negroes of Prince Edward preferring to continue the legal battle for desegregated public schools, and colored children were without formal education from 1959 to 1963, when federal, state, and county authorities cooperated to have classes conducted for Negroes and whites in school buildings owned by the county.

Virginia law, as here applied, unquestionably treats the school children of Prince Edward differently from the way it treats the school children of all other Virginia counties. Prince Edward children must go to a private school or none at all; all other Virginia children can go to public schools. Closing Prince Edward's schools bears more heavily on Negro children in Prince Edward County since white children there have accredited private schools which they can attend, while colored children until very recently have had no available private schools, and even the school they now attend is a temporary expedient. Apart from this expedient, the result is that Prince Edward County school children, if they go to school in their own county, must go to racially segregated schools which, although designated as private, are beneficiaries of county and state support.

A State, of course, has a wide discretion in deciding whether laws shall operate statewide or shall operate only in certain counties, the legislature "having in mind the needs and desires of each." A State may wish to suggest, as Maryland did in Salsburg, that there are reasons why one county ought not to be treated like another. But the record in the present case could not be clearer that Prince Edward's public schools were closed and private schools operated in their place with state and county assistance, for one reason, and one reason only: to ensure, through measures taken by the county and the State, that white and colored children in Prince Edward County would not, under any circumstances, go to the same school. Whatever nonracial grounds might support a State's allowing a county to abandon public schools, the object must be a constitutional one, and grounds of race and opposition to desegregation do not qualify as constitutional.

The time for mere "deliberate speed" has run out, and that phrase can no longer justify denying these Prince Edward County school children their constitutional rights to an education equal to that afforded by the public schools in the other parts of Virginia.

# The Civil Rights Bill of 1964
*1964*[67]

SEC. 403. The Commissioner is authorized, upon the application of any school board, State, municipality, school district, or other governmental unit legally responsible for operating a public school or schools, to render technical assistance to such applicant in the preparation, adoption, and implementation of plans for the desegregation of public schools. Such technical assistance may, among other activities, include making available to such agencies information regarding effective methods of coping with special educational problems occasioned by desegregation, and making

---

[67] 78 U. S. Statutes, 241, July 2, 1964.

available to such agencies personnel of the Office of Education or other persons specially equipped to advise and assist them in coping with such problems.

SEC. 404.   The Commissioner is authorized to arrange, through grants or contracts, with institutions of higher education for the operation of short-term or regular session institutes for special training designed to improve the ability of teachers, supervisors, counselors, and other elementary or secondary school personnel to deal effectively with special educational problems occasioned by desegregation. Individuals who attend such an institute on a full-time basis may be paid stipends for the period of their attendance at such institute in amounts specified by the Commissioner in regulations, including allowances for travel to attend such institute.

SEC. 405.   (a) The Commissioner is authorized, upon application of a school board, to make grants to such board to pay, in whole or in part, the cost of —

(1)   giving to teachers and other school personnel inservice training in dealing with problems incident to desegregation, and

(2)   employing specialists to advise in problems incident to desegregation. . . .

SEC. 407.   (a) Whenever the Attorney General receives a complaint in writing — . . . and . . . believes the complaint is meritorious . . . the Attorney General is authorized, after giving notice of such complaint to the appropriate school board or college authority and after certifying that he is satisfied that such board or authority has had a reasonable time to adjust the conditions alleged in such complaint, to institute for or in the name of the United States a civil action in any appropriate district court of the United States against such parties and for such relief as may be appropriate, and such court shall have and shall exercise jurisdiction of proceedings instituted pursuant to this section, provided that nothing herein shall empower any official or court of the United States to issue any order seeking to achieve a racial balance in any school by requiring the transportation of pupils or students from one school to another or one school district to another in order to achieve such racial balance, or otherwise enlarge the existing power of the court to insure compliance with constitutional standards.

SEC. 601.   No person in the United States shall, on the ground of race, color, or national origin, be excluded from participation in, be denied the benefits of, or be subjected to discrimination under any program or activity receiving Federal financial assistance. . . . Sec. 602. Each Federal department and agency which is empowered to extend Federal financial assistance to any program or activity . . . is authorized and directed to effectuate the provisions of section 601 with respect to such program or activity by issuing rules, regulations, or orders . . . Compliance with any requirement adopted pursuant to this section may be effected (1) by the termination of or refusal to grant or to continue assistance under such program or activity to any recipient as to whom there has been an express finding on the record, after opportunity for a hearing, of a failure to comply with such requirement . . . , or (2) by any other means authorized by law: *Provided, however,* That no such action shall be taken until the department or agency concerned has advised the appropriate person or persons of the failure to comply with the requirement and has determined that compliance cannot be secured by voluntary means.

## Segregation and Educational Quality
### *1964*[68]

It has been clear to me that the concern about the quality of education provided for Negro children has been crucial to the present civil rights movement. One need only be generally familiar with the facts of life to know that the education provided for Negro children in segregated schools — whether these schools were segregated by law or by fact — has been consistently inferior. So pervasive has been the inferiority of education, the inefficiency in the schools which Negro children were compelled to attend, that one could almost consider the system of segregated education as a very effective device for maintaining the inferior caste status of the American Negro people, a device for blocking him out of the mainstream of American life, and reducing his chances and possibilities of competing effectively for jobs and the rewards of a middle-class society. . . . A systematic study of the consequences of schools segregated by law, finds that there are no significant differences. In fact, the similarities dominate. . . . The deterioration of education provided for Negro youngsters in northern urban centers seems to be developing at a more accelerated pace than that of those Negro youngsters coming out of an historically segregated setup. This is a major development of the last two or three decades. . . . I repeat that this problem is at the very heart of the Negro's civil rights thrust today. . . . There must be a massive upgrading of educa-

---

[68]Kenneth B. Clark, "Social and Economic Implications of Integration in the Public Schools," in U. S. Department of Labor, *Seminar on Manpower, Policy, and Program* (Washington: Government Printing Office, 1964), pp. 9-11.

tion for underclass children in America. . . . Before manpower programs, training programs, and equal employment opportunity programs can be effective there must be a total, massive reorganization of our educational system towards increasing its efficiency, as far as these youngsters are concerned.

## Democracy Demands Inclusive Schools
*1964*[69]

Sometimes it is said that those responsible for schools should take no account of the racial, social, or national backgrounds of their students—that, on the contrary, fair and equal treatment is possible only when teachers are colorblind and beneficently neutral toward all the antecedent differences of students. On its face, this argument is plausible and appealing, for at first glance it seems the epitome of non-discrimination and democracy. The trouble with it is that it can be and is used to justify ghetto schools and to rationalize teaching that overlooks massive obstacles to learning. . . .

To ignore in the school the peculiar handicaps the American Negro pupils suffers because of his history and status in this country, or to fail to teach so as to compensate for those handicaps, is to be irresponsible and unrealistic. When schools are as deeply imbedded in the life of the nation as ours are, when so many hopes rise and fall on the outcome of a family's efforts to educate its children, when education is the key to so many other opportunities, no public school that ignores the special conditions affecting its Negro pupils can be either faithful to its duties or effective in discharging them. . . .

The record of success of many American schools in providing such opportunities for disadvantaged children is by no means impressive. Some schools have failed because they have never had a chance to succeed. A community or a state that will not support decent schools for its children can hardly expect those children to become well-educated men and women.

In other places, where the schools are better, those responsible for them often pay more attention to the fortunate than to the unfortunate among their pupils. Too many of us who teach are ready to accept credit for what we get rather than for what we give. . . .

---

[69]John H. Fischer, "The Inclusive School," *Teachers College Record*, LXVI, 1 (October, 1964), 1-6.

Other schools fail to meet the needs of children from depressed minorities because of a restricted conception of what opportunity means. Even schools which open their doors freely to all comers often overlook the crucial truth that no situation is an opportunity except for those who can see its possibilities. . . .

Where, for geographic or other good reasons, separate schools may for a time be unavoidable, we have no choice but to do the best we can within them. In virtually all such schools, the opportunities for improvement are impressively visible. But we must constantly emphasize the essential importance of bringing children of all races into school together. Action to accomplish this must be taken deliberately, systematically, and rapidly wherever it can be taken without clear damage to the educational opportunities of the children involved. . . .

The most compelling argument for integrating schools is that all our children of whatever race must learn to live in a world in which no race can any longer choose to live apart. . . .

If our schools are to prepare our children as they should, as in all reality they must, the schools themselves must become more, and more deliberately, inclusive. They must move in this direction not to offer grudging charity to those who have been excluded, but for the clear educational benefit of *all* pupils. It is one of the paradoxes of our time that the figure of the shrinking earth describes only relationships of space and time. With respect to human relations, the world each of us personally inhabits grows steadily and rapidly larger. No man today has any choice but to be part of a greater and more diverse community. To forego the opportunity to educate our children faithfully and imaginatively for this larger world will be to fail them tragically and inexcusably. . . .

## School Boards May Draw Attendance Lines
## to Achieve Racial Balance
### *1964*[70]

The question for decision: Will the courts hold invalid the adoption by a board of education of a "zoning plan" for a new public school because the board in addition to other relevant matters took into account, in delimiting the zone, the factor of racial balance in the new school? Stating the issue in another form: Does an otherwise lawful and reasonable districting plan for a newly instituted school become unlawful because it is

---

[70]Balaban v. Rubin, 250 New York Supplement 2d 281 (May 7, 1964).

intended to, and does, result in an enrollment which is one-third negro, one-third Puerto Rican and one-third non-Puerto Rican white? . . .

There can be no doubt . . . that *de jure* segregation is unconstitutional. The question, however, as to whether there is an affirmative constitutional obligation to take action to reduce *de facto* segregation is simply not in this case. The issue, we repeat, is: May (not must) the schools correct racial imbalance? The simple fact as to the plan adopted and here under attack is that it excludes no one from any school and has no tendency to foster or produce racial segregation.

Furthermore, we hold, section 3201 of the Education Law is in no way violated by this plan, nor was there any other legal impediment to its adoption.

## California Requires Black History
### *1965*[71]

The study of the role and contributions of American Negroes and other ethnic groups in the history of this country and this state shall be an integral part of the required courses in the history of the United States and California. . . .

When adopting the textbook and teachers' manuals for use in elementary schools for the teaching of courses in civics and the history of the United States and California, the State Board of Education shall include only such textbooks which conform with the required courses and correctly portray the role and contribution of the American Negro and members of other ethnic groups in the total development of the United States and of the State of California. . . .

## Elijah Muhammad on Education
### *1965*[72]

My people should get an education which will benefit their own people and not an education adding to the "storehouse" of the teacher. We need

---

[71]California Assembly Bill No. 580, Sec. 1 and 3, July 6, 1965.
[72]Elijah Muhammad, *Message To the Blackman in America* (Chicago: Muhammad Mosque of Islam No. 2, 1965), pp. 39-41.

education, but an education which removes us from the shackles of slavery and servitude. Get an education, but not an education which leaves us in an inferior position and without a future.

Education for my people should be where our children are off to themselves for the first 15 or 16 years in classes separated by sex. Then they could and should seek higher education without the danger of losing respect for self or seeking to lose their identity. . . .

I want an education for my people that will let them exercise the right of freedom. We are 100 years up from slavery. We are constantly told that we are free. Why can't we take advantage of that freedom? I want an education for my people that will elevate them. . . . Do not get an education just to set it up as some useless symbolic monument to the black man in the Western Hemisphere. We need an education that eliminates division among us. Acquire an education that creates unity and makes us desire to be with our own.

The acquiring of knowledge for our children and ourselves must not be limited to the three R's — 'reading, 'riting and 'rithmetic [sic]. It should instead include the history of the black nation, the knowledge of civilization of man and the universe and all the sciences. It will make us a greater people of tomorrow.

We must instill within our people the desire to learn and then use that learning for self. We must be obessed [sic] with getting the type of education we may use toward the elevation and benefit of our people — when we have such people among us, we must make it possible for them to acquire this wealth which will be beneficial and useful to us.

# The Coleman Report
## 1966[73]

The great majority of American children attend schools that are largely segregated — that is, where almost all of their fellow students are of the same racial background as they are. Among minority groups, Negroes are by far the most segregated. Taking all groups, however, white children are most segregated. . . . For Negro pupils, segregation is more

---

[73]James S. Coleman, *Equality of Educational Opportunity* (Washington: U.S. Government Printing Office, 1966), pp. 3, 22. Provision for this national survey of equality of educationl opportunity was made in the 1964 Civil Rights Act.

nearly complete in the South (as it is for whites also), but it is extensive also in all the other regions where the Negro population is concentrated: the urban North, Midwest, and West. . . . The same pattern of segregation holds, though not quite so strongly, for the teachers of Negro and white students. For the Nation as a whole, the average Negro elementary pupil attends a school in which 65 per cent of the teachers are Negro; the average white elementary pupil attends a school in which 97 per cent of the teachers are white. . . . In its desegregation decision of 1954, the Supreme Court held that separate schools for Negro and white children are inherently unequal. This survey finds that, when measured by that yardstick, American public education remains largely unequal in most regions of the country, including all those where Negroes form any significant proportion of the population. . . .

The average white student's achievement seems to be less affected by the strength or weakness of his school's facilities, curriculums, and teachers than is the average minority pupil's. To put it another way, the achievement of minority pupils depends more on the schools they attend than does the achievement of majority pupils. Thus, 20 percent of the achievement of Negroes in the South is associated with the particular schools they go to, whereas only 10 percent of the achievement of whites in the South is. Except for Oriental Americans, this general result is found for all minorities.

The inference might then be made that improving the school of a minority pupil may increase his achievement more than would improving the school of a white child increase his. Similarly, the average minority pupil's achievement may suffer more in a school of low quality than might the average white pupil's. . . . This indicates that it is for the most disadvantaged children that improvements in school quality will make the most difference in achievement. . . .

It appears that variations in the facilities and curriculums of the schools account for relatively little variation in pupil achievement insofar as this is measured by standard tests. . . . The quality of teachers shows a stronger relationship to pupil achievement. Furthermore it is progressively greater at higher grades, indicating a cumulative impact of the qualities of teachers in a school on the pupil's achievements. Again, teacher quality seems more important to minority achievement than to that of the majority. . . . Finally, it appears that a pupil's achievement is strongly related to the educational backgrounds and aspirations of the other students in the school. . . . Analysis indicates, however, that children from a given family background, when put in schools of different social composition, will achieve at quite different levels. This effect is again less for white pupils than for any minority group other than Orientals. . . . This general result, taken together with the earlier examinations of school differences, has important implications for equality of educational opportunity. For the earlier tables show that the principal way in which the school environments of Negroes and whites differ is the composition of their student bodies, and it turns out that the composition of student bodies has a strong relationship to the achievement of Negro and other minority pupils.

## Black Parents Demand Changes in Urban Schools
### *1967*[74]

We believe that if Afro-American children are to be given motivation and are to be helped develop a desirable self-image, the inner city schools must realistically seek to compensate for all the disadvantages which are foisted upon inner city residents by a white society and which tend to make inner city children feel that they are inferior. To this end, we propose that inner city schools be given a different educational orientation from outlying schools. Inner city schools must become creative centers capable of giving Afro-American children and young people a knowledge of their history, their culture and their destiny. To do this, the schools and their teachers must have flexibility in the selection of textbooks and in the utilization of creative teaching techniques. Standard textbooks which ignore or demean the contributions of Africa and Afro-Americans certainly must be supplanted by books which teach our children their worth and value. More classes must be problem-centered in terms of the discussion and understanding of the everyday urban problems which must eventually be solved under the leadership of Afro-Americans. The creative abilities of Afro-American children in the arts, dance, and creative writing must be developed but not at the expense of academic studies. In all these respects an effective school curriculum for inner city schools would differ markedly from the curriculum of the outlying schools. This must not be interpreted to mean than inner city schools will not be required to meet the same grade level of achievement as outlying schools. Rather, it means that this is the only method by which inner city children will be able to meet the objective achievement standards which we have proposed be set by the State Board of Education.

---

[74]Inner City Parents Council, "Detroit Schools—A Blueprint for Change," *Liberator*, VII, 9 (September, 1967), 11.

This new orientation for inner city schools not only requires Afro-American administrators and teachers in inner city schools but also the transfer out of these schools of white personel who are unable or unready to teach within this educational framework. There are too many white teachers in inner city schools who cannot possibly give Afro-American children a sense of pride and belief in their own destiny because, consciously or unconsciously, they believe in the inferiority of all non-whites.

After 400 years of the white man's enforced separation, Black people are rejecting the dream of integration as the goal for their struggle and are instead finding pride in their own history, culture and power, seeking to develop their own independent leadership, organizations and programs, and determined that the separation which the white man has forced upon them shall now be used for their advancement rather than for their exploitation. After 400 years of self-defeating 'individualism' born of oppressions and the psychological need of the oppressed to identify with the oppressor through the search for status, special privileges and crumbs from the master's table, Black people are coming to realize that the Black man's freedom from oppression and exploitation is not an individual thing to be fought for and won person by person — but a group accomplishment to be secured only through the power of a united Black people.

We feel strongly that no city can long endure if it refuses to face realistically the problem created by its continuing failure to educate more than 50% of its population. We are confident that our proposals are realistic and constructive and can halt the steady disintegration of this urban community.

## Opportunities Industrialization Center
### 1967[75]

OIC was born two and a half years ago in an old jail house. It began as a training program that invited all men and women, regardless of race, color or creed, or previous condition of servitude, or lack of the most elemental preparation, to come through its doors for training. . . . Al-

---

[75]Leon H. Sullivan, "Conquering Poverty Through Self-Help," in *Christian Economics*, (September 30, 1969), pp. 1, 3. *Christian Economics*, 7960 Crescent Avenue, Buena Park, California 90620. Sullivan was pastor of Zion Baptist Church in Philadelphia, and founder of Opportunities Industrialization Centers of America.

though the average educational attainment of the OIC trainee is less than the 9th grade and the median age is over 27, 80 per cent of the OIC trainees have been placed in industrial jobs immediately after completion of their training. . . .

Among the most significant features of OIC is a prevocational, preparational, and attitudinal training center known as the Feeder School. To our knowledge, this is the first prevocational school of its kind in the history of the world. Here students by the thousands are taking, or have taken, confidence courses, and are learning basic lessons in various interpretation skills.

Here trainees are taught the basic elements of Reading, Writing and Arithmetic. People are not anxious for others to know that they want to learn to read and write and do arithmetic, and so we call it "communications skills" and "computation arts" and people by the thousands flock into the classrooms.

Here in the Feeder School, we teach a man how to groom himself, how to know the value of a dollar, how to tell a fresh loaf of bread from a stale loaf of bread by the markings on the wrappers. We teach him how to walk. We teach him how to talk. But most of all, we teach him how to put his head up, and his shoulders back, for we have found that the most important aspect of motivation is self-respect. For if a man does not respect himself, he has no desire to go anywhere, but if a man respects himself, he will get up and make life better for himself and for his family.

From the Feeder School our trainees are then fed into OIC Training Centers, where with the support and the assistance of private industry, we are able to provide them with skills, while at the same time maintaining the attitudinal training. . . .

This is purely an American program in the tradition of the American dream. Beginning in the heart of a poverty community in an old jail house, frustration was turned into aspiration and despair into productivity.

# The Meaning of Education
## *1968*[76]

What we understand by education is the application of all one's knowledge for the benefit of the collective which in turn will benefit each indi-

---

[76]Donald Freeman, Rollie Kimbrough, and Brother Zolili, "The Meaning of Education," *Journal of Negro Education*, XXXVII (Fall, 1968), pp. 432-34.

vidual within the collective. To this end what must constitute a basic part of one's education is the understanding of people rather than things. We realize that once people understand themselves, their knowledge of things is facilitated, that the exclusive knowledge of things does not guarantee knowledge of people and in fact contributes to the erosion, disintegration, and destruction of the creativity of man.

Therefore, education must (1) teach Black People who they are, (2) teach Black People what they are fighting for, (3) teach Black People who they must identify with, (4) teach Black People where their loyalty must lie, (5) teach Black People what must be done to obtain what we are fighting for, (6) teach Black People how to do it, and (7) teach Black People that the destinies of all black people are inseparably linked whether we are in North, Central, or South America, the West Indies, Europe, Asia, or Africa.

These things education must teach black people and assure us of our unification. . . . The first step is *inspiration by emotion*. In the field of education we realize that it is the youth who are inspired by their emotions to learn and try new ways and methods of thinking and doing things. We realize that feeling or intuition or emotion is also a valid form of knowledge that has been misunderstood, neglected and undervalued by the West and that it must be replaced into its righteous position toward understanding man and the universe. The second step, is *enlightenment by reason*. Once one has apprehended the world through one's senses he must be able to systematize his perceptions into ideas and concepts or comprehend the world by one's reason. It is usually older Black people who have varied and wider experiences and have enlightenment by reason and who must teach this part to younger Black people. When both aspects are combined we have *sustenance by knowledge*, the unity of practice and theory, of apprehension and comprehension, of perception and understanding. It is this step that will guarantee that the life-forces of our ancestors will be transmitted through us to our children and *sustain* the existence of all Black people. . . .

Now, there must be a complete unity of all aspects of one's life and in particular education must be indelibly linked with one's life processes for the benefit of each Black man and woman and all Black people. Those who have knowledge primarily from books must be linked with those who have knowledge from the streets and plantations, and vice versa, to confront and solve all the problems of Black people. Education must assure that all of what one learns can be and will be applied to concrete practical problems and their solutions. . . . Mathematics, physics, electronics, sociology, religion and other sciences must not be viewed as abstractions, but comprehended as the concentrated experiences of man's interrelationships with man, nature, and the universe to mold and control his own destiny.

The best way to accomplish these objectives is to create *independent* Black educational institutions like the New School of Afro-American Thought. . . .

## Education and Revolution
### *1969*[77]

Historically the struggle in the educational arena, in terms of black people, has been waged from, on the one hand the slavemaster not even wanting black people to learn how to read and write, to black people wanting to learn how to read and write on the other. The struggle then transposed itself over into what black people were allowed to read and write, until today black people have reached a point where they want to control totally what they read and write.

This has been a steady struggle against the opposition of the slavemaster, it has been defeat after defeat for the slavemaster, until now we have burst into consciousness, until now we have realized the necessity of taking control of our education. When we see this long line of progression from the struggle to become literate to the struggle today to control totally the education, we can see the true nature of the opposition that we face now and faced then. All of these racists and liberals who are opposing our moves today to gain control of our education, are nothing but the descendants of the outright racist slavemasters who opposed us in our attempts to learn how to read and write on the plantations during the days of slavery. . . .

One of the great dangers that our revolutionary struggle faces, perhaps the greatest danger, is that we historically have tended to compartmentalize our struggle; that is, we get hung up on one aspect of the struggle, without having an overall revolutionary perspective and without realizing that the struggle we wage is against the total social organism. We focus all of our attention and all of our energy on the educational system, and we don't realize — or our tactics and our strategy would seem to indicate that we don't realize — that this is only one aspect of our

---

[77]Eldridge Cleaver, "Education and Revolution," *The Black Scholar*, I, 1 (November, 1969), 48, 49, 51.

struggle and that the same people who control the educational facilities, control the rest of the social structure. Everything, the economy, the judiciary, the political parties, the political instruments, every aspect of society is in the same hands. We need a broader strategy, a revolutionary strategy that aims at overthrowing the rule of this class as a whole, so we will not just be going through changes on the college campuses. . . .

In the final analysis, the struggle that is now going on on the college campuses cannot be settled on the college campuses. It has to be settled in the community, because those that sit on the boards of administration of the colleges do not derive their power from the fact that they are sitting on the board, but rather they sit on the board because they have power in the community. . . .

We have to destroy their power in the community, and we're not reformists, we're not in the movement to reform the curriculum of a given university or a given college or to have a Black Students Union recognized at a given high school. We are revolutionaries, and as revolutionaries, our goal is the transformation of the American social order.

## Educational Relevance and the Black Militant
### *1969*[78]

And now it must be said, that as far as the demands for a Black Com- muniversity or a black studies program are concerned, neither should be used as cop-outs or excuses for students not taking care of business vis-a-vis the books. I'm saying that the "militant" student should be the best student on campus, if he has the capability. Of course much of what you learn will not be relevant to your black thing. Learn it anyhow. Learn everything. Regurgitate that which is not relevant or useful to you later on. It should be clear to all of us, that in order to beat Charlie's game you've got to know his system.

So that, while we work for and emphasize black studies, we, simul- taneously, learn everything we can about this game the man has been running on us for centuries. Otherwise, we would be working in an unreal situation, and most black people and black students would have better sense than to follow us and would be justified. What I am saying, brothers

---

[78]John O. Killens, "The Artist and the Black University," *The Black Scholar*, I, 1 (November, 1969), 63, 64.

and sisters, is that some of us are shucking and jiving and hiding behind the cover of "militance and relevance". The Liberation Movement needs doctors, teachers, lawyers, engineers committed to the movement, and some of you are coping out because "it ain't relevant." There is a great danger of a whole crop of "militant" students, wonderful people, becoming *irrelevant* to the movement. Dig it.

The Black University and the cultural revolution is not separate and apart from the Liberation Movement. It is at the core of the movement; the brain of the movement, that builds the engine, that puts the movement into motion. There should be no contradiction between the Cultural Revolution and the Black Liberation. Picture a brother down-South in Mississippi or up-South in New York City. He is a committed revolutionary, right? And Chuck's police is chasing him and he runs onto the airstrip to make his getaway on a waiting plane. You are the pilot. Right? There you stand in a beautiful dashiki underneath an Afro so way out the sun can't get to you. You are turning white for lack of sunlight. But there you stand pumping your arm up and down and shouting "Black Power!" The only problem is: you forgot to learn how to fly the plane because it wasn't relevant. Can you dig it?

## Black Students, Black Studies
### *1970*[79]

The duty on the part of the Black student is to work to educate the masses, to be one-in-one with the masses and not to just isolate themselves on the campuses. . . . What I have just finished saying is, in essence, the direction that Black Students' Unions and Black studies programs on college campuses throughout the country should take. David Hilliard, Black Panther Chief of Staff, puts it in very correct form: "Black Students, BSU's and Black Studies Programs must understand that the only way to get a clear understanding of what the ideology of the revolutionary movement is today is to understand the history of the Black Panther Party, the BSU, the history of Black people, all historical experience; all of this, the history of the Party, the history of the struggle, the movement, presently, in terms of the Black Panther Party, of the historical events of Black people being

---

[79]Bobby Seale, "Revolutionary Action on Campus and Community," *The Black Panther*, Vol. IV, No. 6, pp. 10, 11.

translated by way of Marxist-Leninism. . . . This same philosophy must be used as a means to translate our everall historical experience here in the exploitative decadent system of America. Black studies must be seen in this fashion, but not limited to non-participation and non-action. . . . It's not enough for students to just sit down and be able to articulate an idea or a principle. The thing is to be able to implement it into a program and try to make it for real for the people, and in turn defend it, even when it is unjustly attacked, as many times it will be.

## Letter to Jim Crow
### *1970*[80]

Dear Jim:

Well, I see you're back in the schools again. You're really persistent, with more lives than a cat.

We thought we got rid of you back in 1954, when the Supreme Court said you were unconstitutional. Of course, you hung on. We knew you would. But when the Court said a few months ago that Jim Crow schools had to be ended instantly, I really thought we'd seen the last of you. . . .

Part of the reason why you came back in the schools is the phony smokescreen raised about integration. Code words like "busing" were much nicer to use than the "Keep the schools white," your supporters once used.

Of course, there is more bussing going on now to keep schools segregated than there ever would be to integrate them, but most people don't want to hear about that. . . .

When we sent you scurrying back into the woodwork during the civil rights revolution of the 'sixties, we thought we'd seen the last of you. We didn't expect that there would be a massive failure of leadership in this nation, a situation where many leaders don't lead, but rather follow those elements in the society that are least representative of its ideals and commitments.

So we're back where we started — fighting Jim Crow. We won once; we'll win again.

Yours in battle, WHITNEY M. YOUNG, JR.

---

[80]Whitney M. Young, Jr., "An Open Letter To Jim Crow," *Chicago Daily Defender* (April 18-April 24, 1970), Vol. LXV, No. 50.